ILLUSION AND REALITY

PRINTS BY JIŘÍ ANDERLE

THE ANNE AND JACQUES BARUCH COLLECTION

ILLUSION AND REALITY
PRINTS BY JIŘÍ ANDERLE
THE ANNE AND JACQUES BARUCH COLLECTION

KRISTIN L. SPANGENBERG   CINCINNATI ART MUSEUM   2008

ILLUSION AND REALITY
PRINTS BY JIŘÍ ANDERLE

is published on the occasion of the exhibition *Illusion and Reality: Prints by Jiří Anderle* held at the Cincinnati Art Museum, September 27, 2008 through January 4, 2009.

Cincinnati Art Museum, 953 Eden Park Drive, Cincinnati OH 45202

Author: Kristin L. Spangenberg

Manuscript editor: Anita Buck

Photography: Scott Hisey

Typography and design: Paul Neff

Printer: The Merten Company

Photo credits: The Cincinnati Art Museum would like to thank the institutions as cited in the figure captions for permission to publish comparative photographs of the works in their collections and archives.

Cover Image: *Carpe diem, carpe noctem I* (detail, plate 84) 1984, WV 281 (2005.175)

The Cincinnati Art Museum gratefully acknowledges the generous exhibition support from Duke Energy and operating support provided by the Fine Arts Fund, the Ohio Arts Council, the City of Cincinnati, Carol Ann and Ralph V. Haile, Jr./U.S. Bank Foundation, and our members. The printing of this publication was underwritten in part with support from Skip Merten and The Merten Company.

LIBRARY OF CONGRESS CATALOGING-IN-PUBLICATION DATA

Spangenberg, Kristin L.
Illusion and reality : prints by Jiří Anderle : the Anne and Jacques Baruch collection / Kristin L. Spangenberg.
p. cm.
Catalog of an exhibition at the Cincinnati Art Museum, Sept. 27, 2008-Jan. 4, 2009.
Includes bibliographical references.
ISBN 0-931537-34-7 (softcover : alk. paper)
1. Anderle, Jiří, 1936---Exhibitions. I. Baruch, Anne. II. Baruch, Jacques, 1922- III. Cincinnati Art Museum. IV. Title.

NE2225.A5A4 2008
769.92--dc22

2008034706

Figure 1

(Previous page)
Jiří Anderle in his studio holding the plate for *Belle Époque?* (plate 55), Prague, April 2007.
© 2007 Kristin L. Spangenberg.

1943. IT IS WAR. I AM IN MY SIXTH YEAR AND DAD IS DYING OF TUBERCULOSIS OF THE LUNG. AFTER THE WAR I AND MY MOTHER GO REGULARLY FOR X-RAYS. ONCE I CANNOT RESIST AND I LOOK INTO THE DIM ROOM. THE VISUAL PERCEPTION OF THE GLOWING BLUE-GREEN SQUARE IN WHICH MOTHER'S HEART BEATS IS UNFORGETTABLE FOR ME. PERHAPS THIS IMAGE FROM MY YOUTH ALSO AFFECTS MY WORK. I ALWAYS WANT TO PENETRATE INTO THE INVISIBLE WORLD INSIDE A PERSON. IN THIS UNIQUE WORLD I CAN REGROUP SHAPES IN LINE WITH WHAT I AM LIVING THROUGH AND WHAT I WANT TO SAY. IT IS EXCITING TO MOVE IN AN AREA OF IMAGINATION AND MULTIPLE MEANINGS.

Jiří Anderle, from *Jiří Anderle: Drawings, Prints, Paintings, Objects 1954 / 1995*

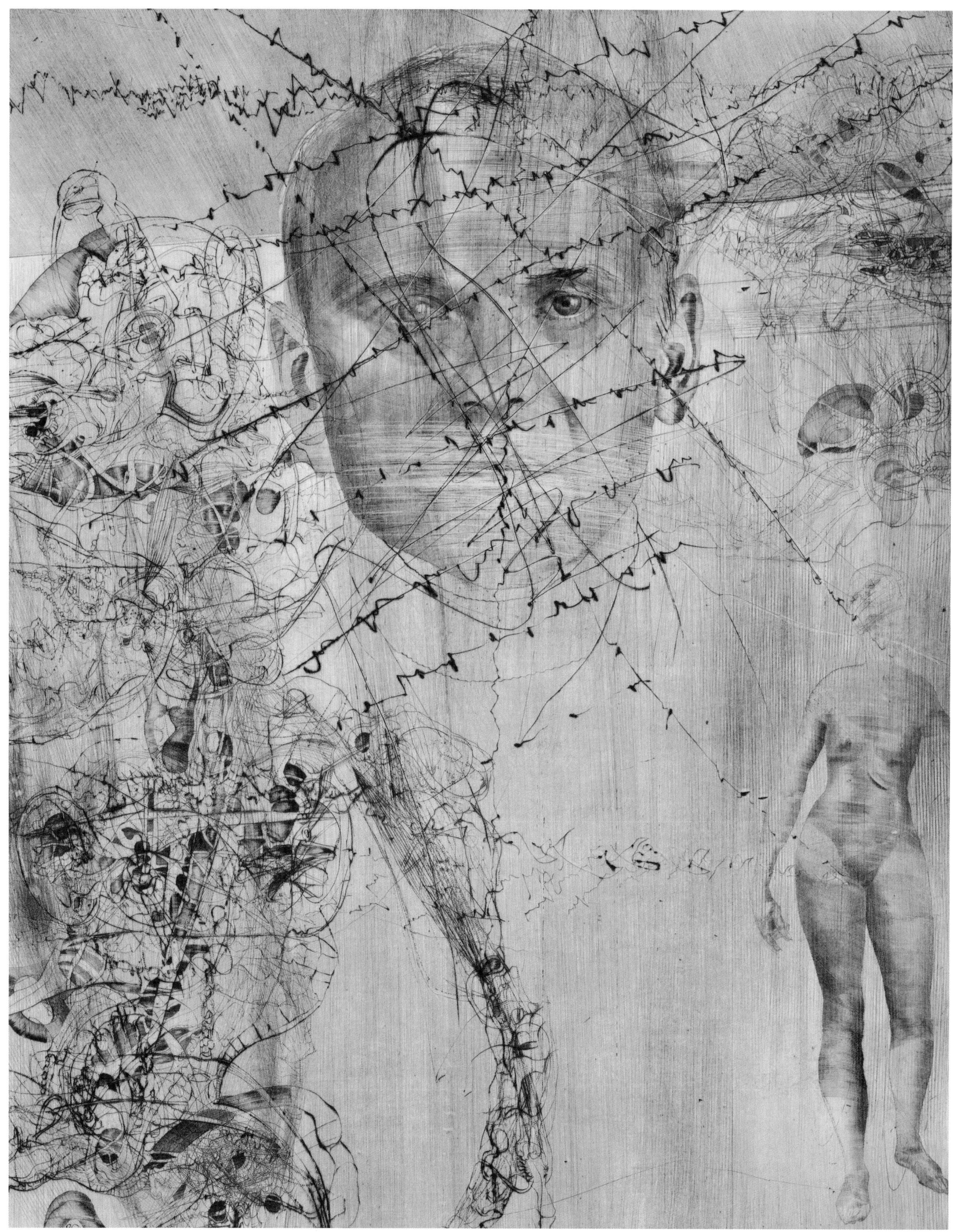

CONTENTS

Closed Door, Jiří (detail, plate 50)
1979, WV 157 third state (2005.577)

FOREWORD

From the founding of the Jacques Baruch Gallery in 1967, Anne and Jacques Baruch dedicated themselves to pioneering the contemporary art of Central and Eastern Europe in the United States. In 1975 curator Kristin L. Spangenberg organized *Eastern European Printmakers* for the Cincinnati Art Museum in cooperation with the Jacques Baruch Gallery, Chicago, and began a long-term relationship that brought contemporary Eastern European printmakers into the permanent collection, culminating in 2005 with the significant gift of contemporary Czech printmakers, making the Museum a major repository for the study of Czech printmaking in the second half of the twentieth century. Recognizing the Museum's commitment to exhibit contemporary printmakers and to inspire current and future generations, the Anne and Jacques Baruch Collection graciously donated 501 prints by twenty Czech printmakers to the Museum. The gift was immediately celebrated in a survey exhibition, *Strength and Will: Czech Prints from Behind the Iron Curtain, a Gift of the Anne and Jacques Baruch Collection.* The gift made the Museum the largest repository of the prints of Jiří Anderle in the United States and plans were made for a retrospective of the artist's prints.

The Cincinnati Art Museum's commitment to exhibit contemporary art is fundamental to our mission to exhibit, interpret, and collect the art of all periods. The print collection—the largest holdings in the Museum—represents over fifty nationalities in the second half of the twentieth century. The Museum's commitment to exhibit a world-wide range of international prints springs from the exhibitions of and acquisitions from five *International Biennials of Contemporary Color Lithography* (1950–58) and two *International Biennials of Color Prints* (1960–62). Since that time exhibitions have continued to bring printmakers from around the world to Museum visitors. Over the years international prints from Czechoslovakia (1922), Hungary (1926), Poland (1957), Brazil (1958), and Yugoslavia (1958) have been featured. The special interest of Howard and Caroline Porter in twentieth-century Japanese prints led the Museum to feature their extensive collection in five exhibitions: *Japanese Prints of the Twentieth Century* (1967); *Ay-Ō, Hatsuyama Shigeru, Kōsaka Gajin* (1969); *Three Generations: Woodcuts by Hiratsuka Un'ichi, Munakata Shikō and Matsubara Naoko* (1971); *Ikeda Masuo, Arakawa Shusaka, Noda Tetsuya* (1976); and *Innovation and Tradition: Twentieth-Century Japanese Prints from the Howard and Caroline Porter Collection* (1990).

Likewise the Museum has showcased in solo exhibitions contemporary prints by living American and international artists over the last half century, including Zao Wou Ki (1955), Johnny Friedlaender (1956), Jozsef Domjan (1958), Pablo Picasso (1959 and 1961), Antonio Frasconi (1965), Victor Vasarely (1968), June Wayne (1969), Rolf Nesch (1970), Julian Stanczak (1972), Mark Tobey (1972), Maurits Cornelis Escher (1973), Louise Nevelson (1974), Jim Dine (1979), John Cage 1993, Tōkō Shinoda (1994–95), R. B. Kitaj (1995), Munakata Shikō (1995–96), Vladimír Gažavič (2001), Jacob Kainen (2005), Shōichi Ida (2007), and Robert Rauschenberg (2008). *Illusion and Reality: Prints by Jiří Anderle*, drawn from the gift of the Anne and Jacques Baruch Collection, ensures that this commitment to showcase the talent of internationally recognized printmakers continues today. As Director of the Cincinnati Art Museum, I am grateful for Anne Baruch's foresight in making the Museum a partner in Anne and Jacques's commitment to bringing the work of Eastern Europe to American audiences now and in the future. We are pleased to have had Anne's assistance in the early stages of preparing the exhibition and publication; her death in October 2007 was a tremendous loss to the art world and to all who knew her.

The Cincinnati Art Museum gratefully acknowledges the generous exhibition support of Duke Energy. We would also like to thank the Fine Arts Fund, the Ohio Arts Council, the City of Cincinnati, Carol Ann and Ralph V. Haile, Jr./U.S. Bank Foundation, and our members for operating support. The printing of this publication was underwritten in part with support from Skip Merten and The Merten Company.

This exhibition would not have been possible without the enthusiastic cooperation of the artist and his generous gift of recent prints to round out the Museum's holdings. We would like to thank Richard Drury, Curator of the Czech Museum of Fine Arts, Prague, for his assistance with the manuscript.

Lastly I would like to thank Kristin L. Spangenberg, the Art Museum's Curator of Prints, who conceived this exhibition, wrote this publication, and brought this exhibition to fruition.

Aaron Betsky
Director

ACKNOWLEDGMENTS

First and foremost, I wish I could thank Dr. Anne Baruch for the generous gift from the Anne and Jacques Baruch Collection in 2005, and for her unflagging support for this exhibition and publication on Jiří Anderle's prints. Anne passed away in October 2007, knowing this project would come to fruition in the fall of 2008. We last got together in March 2007 when Anne, assisted by Barbara Kalwajtys, provided access to the gallery's thirty years of records of and resources on Anderle's works and exhibitions. Since that time Barbara Kalwajtys has continued to serve as a liaison with the Anne and Jacques Baruch Collection records.

This exhibition and publication would not have been possible without the patient support of the artist. Although I am a long-time admirer of his prints, we first met only in 1997, when he traveled to Chicago for the thirtieth anniversary of the Jacques Baruch Gallery. We met again in April 2007 in Prague, where I had the opportunity to interview him over the period of a week and to visit Galerie Anderle in Villa Pelle. Anderle supplied me with biographical information and exhibition records. He also gifted the Museum four prints from his archive, including an *épreuve d'artiste* of *The Smile*, two prints from the *Commedia dell'arte* cycle, and *Banquet* from *Appassionata Humana*, rounding out the Museum's collection of his works. Anderle also introduced me to Richard Drury, Curator at the Czech Museum of Fine Arts, Prague, who has served as a liaison and editor of the biographical and exhibition information.

This exhibition also includes a small selection of the prints given in 1986 as a centennial gift by Granvil I. and Marcia G. Specks. In addition, Dr. Paula S. Biren, M.D., has generously shared for this exhibition her final state of *The Smile* so that it could be compared with the early proof given by Anderle. On behalf of the Museum, I thank Mr. and Mrs. Specks and Dr. Biren.

Leonie Stachelscheid of Baukunst Galerie, Cologne, answered my queries regarding the *Jiří Anderle, Prag: Vollstandiges Werkverzeichnis der Graphik mit allen Zuständen*, and Ilse Götz of Galerie + Edition Götz, Stuttgart, assisted with its sequel. Dr. Kathryn Gutzwiller, Department of Classics, University of Cincinnati, fielded my questions about classical literature. Nadine Orenstein, Curator, the Department of Drawings and Prints, The Metropolitan Museum of Art, helped locate the elusive prints by Jan Saenredam after Hendrick Goltzius.

Roberta Waddell of the New York Public Library; staff at the Mary R. Schiff Library, Cincinnati Art Museum; The Museum of Modern Art Library; Christine Hopper, Museum Manager, Cartwright Hall Art Gallery, Bradford, UK; Dr. Silvio Fuso, Galleria Internazionale d'Arte Moderna di Ca' Pesaro, Venice; and the University of Cincinnati Art Library provided various resources and helped me locate biennial catalogues. I would like to thank my colleagues and the professional staff of the following institutions for confirming their holdings of the artist's work: Achenbach Foundation for Graphic Arts, Fine Arts Museums of San Francisco; Amarillo Museum of Art; The Art Institute of Chicago; Berkeley Art Museum and Pacific Film Archive; Mary and Leigh Block Museum of Art; California College of Arts and Crafts; Chazen Museum of Art; The Cleveland Museum of Art; Des Moines Art Center; The Detroit Institute of Arts; Faulconer Gallery; Fisher Gallery; Grand Rapids Art Museum; Grinnell College Art Collection; Grunwald Center for the Graphic Arts, Hammer Museum; Harvard University Art Museums; The Jewish Museum; Jundt Art Museum; Kresge Art Museum; Library of Congress; The Metropolitan Museum of Art; The Museum of Modern Art; National Gallery of Art; Nevada Museum of Art; The New York Public Library; Portland Art Museum; Samuel P. Harn Museum of Art; Smart Museum of Art; Sterling and Francine Clark Art Institute; Tampa Museum of Art; University of Iowa Museum of Art; West Virginia University College of Creative Arts; and Western Illinois University Art Gallery.

No exhibition is possible without the support of professional staff at the Cincinnati Art Museum, which is so smoothly efficient it often goes unnoticed. Emily Holtrop, Curator of Education, facilitated the interpretive program with her staff. Scott Hisey, Head of Photographic Services, and his staff photographed all the prints and provided the digital files for the publication and the Museum's collection program. Rebecca Montfort, Chief Registrar, facilitated the loan. Cecile Mear, Conservator of Works on Paper, oversaw the needed conservation. Everage King skillfully matted and framed the works for the exhibition. Christopher P. Williams and crew displayed the prints to stunning effect. Jade Sams, Curatorial Administrative Assistant, efficiently secured the rights and images for comparative illustrations. The publication would not have been realized without the editorial skills of Anita Buck and the elegant design of Paul Neff. Lastly I would like to thank my husband, John E. Gilmore, for processing my digital files for the catalogue and for his all-around support.

Kristin L. Spangenberg
Curator of Prints

DEDICATED TO ANNE BARUCH (1925–2007) AND JACQUES BARUCH (1922–1986)

Figure 2

Anne and Jacques Baruch, Rochester, New York, 1978. Unidentified photographer. Courtesy of the Anne and Jacques Baruch Collection.

THE RADIANCE, THE HOPE THAT JACQUES AND ANNE — AND THEN, AFTER JACQUES' PASSING, ANNE ALONE — BROUGHT INTO MY LIFE LIVED BEHIND THE IRON CURTAIN, IS INDESCRIBABLE. TO GIVE ME COURAGE, SHE SENT ME ADMIRING LETTERS FROM MY COLLECTORS AND REGULARLY PHONED ME. ANNE REMAINS AN INTEGRAL PART OF MY LIFE TO THIS DAY. SHE WROTE A STORY IN MY LIFE THAT ONLY TAKES PLACE IN FAIRY TALES.

Jiří Anderle, Prague, April 7, 2008

dedicated to jacques BARUCH
CRUEL GAME
FOR A MAN

THE ANNE AND JACQUES BARUCH COLLECTION

The creation of the Anne and Jacques Baruch Collection of Eastern European art was set into motion in September 1967 with the opening of the Jacques Baruch Gallery in Chicago specializing in Eastern and Central European artists. At the time the mainstream art world was focused on Op Art and Pop Art. The Baruchs' goals and motivation arose from their ancestral ties and from Jacques Baruch's knowledge of and attachment to his rich cultural heritage.

Jacques Baruch was born to an aristocratic Jewish family in Warsaw. He was raised in the intellectual and creative milieu between World Wars I and II. He had been trained as an artist and architect at the Warsaw Academy of Fine Arts. During World War II he saw his parents gunned down by the Nazis, was a prisoner of war, a resistance fighter, a labor camp inmate, and a survivor. After his release from the prisoner of war camp, Jacques served as a translator for the British and American armies. In 1946, Morris Handman, an American soldier from Chicago, befriended him and sponsored his immigration to the United States.

Lillye Anne Stern's parents fled to the United States to escape the pogroms in Russia and Romania, arriving in Chicago in 1920, leaving behind families who were lost. Anne Stern was born in Chicago and married Jacques in 1951.

In 1967 Anne and Jacques decided to open a gallery. They undertook their search for artists in Soviet bloc countries during the Cold War, amid the difficult climate of unfriendly East-West relations. They began with Poland so that Jacques could discover the fate of family members and friends. This was their introduction to the hardships and restraints of life under communism. The country lacked life's bare necessities and there was little available in the way of supplies or material with which artists could work.

In July 1968, the Baruchs expanded their search for new artists to Czechoslovakia. They arrived in Prague during the period of reforms of the Dubček era known as the "Prague Spring." Anne and Jacques were charmed by the city and captivated by the art and artists they found there. While isolated from the mainstream of art and living under the harsh and restrictive systems, first of Nazi Germany and then Soviet-style communism, artists had been creating provocative, compelling, and highly personal work little known in western Europe and the United States. The Baruchs made a commitment to bring these accomplished artists the recognition they deserved and see that they were accorded their place in the history of contemporary art.

Cruel Game for a Man (detail, plate 28)
1975, WV 122 (1976.332)

In conjunction with the artists and Art Centrum, the Czechoslovak government art agency, Anne and Jacques purchased a number of works and planned an extensive exhibition program. They were notified that they would have to leave a day early. Upon their departure many of the artists joined them at the airport, to celebrate the future presence of Czech art in the United States. Their excitement was short-lived, because the following day, August 21, 1968, the media carried the shocking news that Soviet tanks had occupied Prague. The Prague Spring had turned to winter, and reforms came to a stunning end. It was only with great difficulty that the Baruchs were finally able to receive the work they had purchased in Prague. They opened their first Czech exhibition in the summer of 1969.

Returning to Prague the following autumn, Anne and Jacques found a city shrouded in sadness, with few tourists, no exhibitions of note, and the intimidating presence of the police and military everywhere. The mission of Art Centrum had been revised to encourage displays and sales of work by officially sanctioned artists registered with the Artists Union. Almost none of the artists the Baruchs were interested in were registered artists. At the same time, Jacques Baruch developed serious health problems and could no longer travel the Iron Curtain route.

The Baruchs strongly believed in their mission and in the artists whose work had touched them so deeply. To continue to support the artists they focused their attention on works on paper, which was less complicated to hand-carry to Chicago. Anne Baruch began making annual trips to Czechoslovakia, bearing heavy suitcases filled with art supplies and other necessities of life, and enduring delays, inspections, and interrogation by customs officers. She acquired art directly from the artists and encouraged them and offered them hope. Together the Baruchs worked tirelessly to promote the work of their artists, many of whom now have international reputations, throughout the United States.

I first met the Baruchs while visiting Dr. Harold Joachim, Curator of Prints and Drawings at the Art Institute of Chicago, in September 1973. Dr. Joachim told me he had some people he would like me to meet, and took me to the Jacques Baruch Gallery at 900 North Michigan Avenue. There Joachim introduced me to the work of a number of Eastern European artists and purchased for the Cincinnati Art Museum a print. Under Gustave von Groschwitz, Curator of Prints, the Cincinnati Art Museum had held international biennials of color lithography from 1950 to 1958, and international biennials of color prints in 1960 and 1962, from which a small selection of prints had been purchased from Eastern Bloc artists in Czechoslovakia, Yugoslavia, and Poland. Fascinated with this work by a generation of printmakers that had been previously little known in the West, I organized for the Museum one of the early exhibitions in the United States of sixteen of these artists: *Eastern European Printmakers*, held from April 10 through June 8, 1975. By that time I had already acquired for the Museum *Four Masks* (plate 1) by Jiří Anderle. Over the subsequent decades I have taken great pleasure in following the careers of a number of the printmakers represented in the exhibition and by the gallery.

The Jacques Baruch Gallery was a mix between a museum and a gallery. It became the most important place in the United States to study art from behind the Iron Curtain. The Baruchs represented artists in a variety of media, including paintings, prints, drawings, sculpture, photography, fiber, and glass. In 1972 they gave Jiří Anderle his first solo exhibition in the United States and gave him eight solo shows through 1997. Other Eastern European artists the gallery represented included Magdalena Abakanowica, Jiří Balcar, Albín Brunovský, Vladimír Gažovič, Jiří John, Jan Krejčí, Oldrich Kulhánek, Jan Saudek, Josef Sudek, and Adriena Šimotavá. In addition to the gallery's exhibition activities, Anne Baruch crisscrossed the United States carrying portfolios of Eastern European prints, drawings, and photographs. She introduced museums, universities, and other cultural institutions and organizations to the gallery's work, generously lending to exhibitions and fostering educational activities. The Baruchs developed an enthusiastic audience for the work of their artists. With the death of Jacques Baruch in 1986, Anne Baruch kept the gallery open. In 1993 the gallery's name was formally changed to the Anne and Jacques Baruch Collection, under which title it continued to pursue the gallery goals.

The tireless efforts of the Baruchs received national attention in 1987 when Anne Baruch was awarded the honorary degree of Doctor of Letters by Gonzaga University, Spokane, Washington. That same year the People's Republic of Poland awarded Dr. Anne Baruch the Medal of the Order of Cultural Merit. In June 1988 Dr. Anne Baruch received the Silver Medal of Merit from the Ministry of Foreign Affairs, Czechoslovak Society for International Relations, for the Baruchs' support of Czech artists.

In 2005 Dr. Anne Baruch selected the Cincinnati Art Museum to receive 501 prints and drawings by twenty artists from the Anne and Jacques Baruch Collection. This gift expanded the existing holdings of the permanent collection and made Cincinnati a major venue for the study of Czechoslovakian printmakers. The gift of the Anne and Jacques Baruch Collection to the Museum continues for future generations their love story with Eastern European art.

ATELIER
PRAGUE

"THE DISTINCTION BETWEEN PAST, PRESENT AND FUTURE IS ONLY AN ILLUSION, HOWEVER PERSISTENT."

—ALBERT EINSTEIN-LETTER TO MICHELANGELO BESSO, MARCH 21, 1955

JIŘÍ ANDERLE PRINTS: A HUMANISTIC VISION

In 2006 Jiři Anderle received a gold medal from the President of the Czech Republic for his contributions to Czechoslovakian culture.[1] A master draftsman in the age of photography, Anderle was solidly trained in the tradition of the old masters. During his career spanning five decades he has pushed the boundaries of his art to further his humanistic vision. He looks to the past and the present as a source of wisdom in asserting, without cultural distinction, the continuity of human life, and offering new possibilities for the future. His exploration of fundamental issues facing mankind determines the content and graphic character of the cycles. He uses the human body as a means to visualize the soul. Created in a variety of media, including printmaking, painting, drawing, and sculpture, his works serve as metaphors and allegories for his *Theatrum Mundi*. Anderle uses the term "spiral" to describe the evolution of his ever-transforming interconnected cycles. He starts and ends a theme at different points along the continuum, but they all spring from his deeply rooted concern for man and his condition. Throughout Anderle's work there are references to his multifaceted background, incorporating his passion for music, literature, theater, and art, thereby reaffirming his personal and national identity through the celebration of Western art.

A virtuoso with the drypoint needle, Anderle pursued printmaking with strength and will as a means of survival, both mental and physical, under the hard-line communist regime that controlled his homeland for most of his life. To have touched on current politics would have incurred censorship and could have precipitated imprisonment. While Anderle could not safely deal with the politics of the day, his inclination to focus on issues facing mankind transcended everyday political reality. He explored human experience and survival, past and present.

The Czechoslovak Republic came into being in 1918 with the breakup of the Austro-Hungarian Empire in the aftermath of World War I.[2] Prague, the capital of this new Republic, was at the crossroads between East and West: it had experienced external domination, subjugation, and suppression by nearly every European army over the past five hundred years. During the Republic the artistic community openly exchanged with western European artists such as the Surrealists, who had a significant impact on the artistic environment. With the Nazi occupation beginning in 1939, modern art was branded *entartete Kunst* (degenerate art) and was suppressed. A brief restoration of republican government in 1945 again gave the artistic community

Soldier (detail, plate 59)
1980, WV 183 (1983.251)

the opportunity to interact with contemporary stylistic and technical movements in western Europe. After the Communist Party overthrew the Republic in 1948, official art was restricted to Social Realism in the service of government propaganda. Artists were cut off from official patronage, watched by government censors, and were generally unable to earn a living from their work.

During the late 1960s, the liberalizing forces in opposition to political and artistic repression culminated in the short-lived "Prague Spring" of 1968. From January 5 to August 21, artists were able to renew contacts outside the country and exhibit publicly. Important periodicals such as *Výtvarné umění (Graphic Art)* and *Výtvarná práce (Graphic Work)* available to the artist during this period of gradual liberalization focused on contemporary Czech and international art.[3] This outside contact was brutally terminated by the invasion of Warsaw Pact troops in August 1968. Under the new political policy of "Socialism with a Human Face" the Czechs were subjected to repression and censorship that continued until November 17, 1989, when student protests in Prague initiated the bloodless "Velvet Revolution" that terminated communist control. Except for the brief period of the Prague Spring, during the decades of the 1960s, 1970s and 1980s Czechoslovakian artists lived in isolation from the public and critics. Non-conformist art was banned and large public gatherings were prohibited. Artists' knowledge of developments in the West was incomplete because books and periodicals on contemporary developments were unavailable and travel was banned.

Jiří Anderle was born into a generation that experienced the trauma of World War II and lived under the subsequent hard-line communist regime. Anderle was born September 14, 1936, in Pavlíkov, near Rakovník, in the western part of Czechoslovakia near the Bavarian border.[4] His mother Marie worked for the Otta manufacturer family in Rakovník. His father, Adam, had been a locksmith before going to work in the Otta soap factory.[5] He died of tuberculosis when Anderle was six.

Anderle's natural talent for drawing was evident at an early age. By the time he was ready to choose his life's direction, however, the short life of the Third Republic was over and the country was under the thumb of the Czechoslovak Communist Party. During the following decades Stalinism took an iron grip on all aspects of the country's social, economic, political, and cultural life, making it an unfavorable time for artists who did not follow the official party line.

Yet in 1951, at the age of 15, Anderle was encouraged by his stepfather, Miroslaw Král, to become a painter. He followed the advice of his drawing teacher, Jan Mostecký, and applied to the Secondary School of Applied Art in Prague. Anderle's future career might have taken a different path if Mr. Kopecký, the leader of the local branch of the National Committee and the Czechoslovak Communist Party, had not given Anderle permission to go to Prague to pursue his artistic training.[6] After the School of Applied Art, Anderle continued his studies in 1955 at the Academy of Fine Arts, Prague. He studied painting with Antonín Pelc, printmaking with Vladimír Silovský, and art history with Jiří Kotalík (who would later become deputy director of the National Gallery in Prague and promoted Anderle's work internationally).

During his student years in Prague, Anderle played the drums at weekend dances in the Rakovník and Beroun districts near his home town. Sitting behind the drums, he had the opportunity to observe the general populace as it unwound and people lost their inhibitions to the music and the rhythmic power of dance. At the time of Anderle's graduation from the Academy in 1961 he had a solid foundation as a draftsman and had begun his first mature thematic print cycle, *Village Dances*.

Anderle saw dance as an ancient ritual transcendent of human spirit and senses. In 1962, while in Prague, he executed five prints of the *Village Dances* cycle. *Four Masks* (plate 1) exaggerates the extremes between young and old, beauty and grotesquerie, with the grimaces of masquerades. *Large Dance* (plate 2) captures the explosive vitality of expression and interaction of frenzied dancers. For this group of prints Anderle used the unconventional mixed media printmaking approach of collagraph, building up the printing surface with various materials and then vigorously scratching through the surface with a drypoint needle before printing.

After completing his studies at the Academy of Fine Arts, Anderle set aside his pursuit of a career as a painter and joined the Black Theatre of Prague, a black light theatre organized by the director, artist, and composer Jiří Srnec. This association lasted eight years, and provided Anderle the extraordinary opportunity to travel across Europe and to the continents of Asia, Australia, Africa, and America. Initially a stagehand, Anderle shortly became a mime performer. His years as an actor would teach him the importance of gesture and expression, insight that would come to play an important role in his future work.

The opportunity to travel with the company outside Czechoslovakia, a privilege rarely granted by the government, introduced Anderle to different cultures. Also, he saw twentieth-century art to which Czechs now had no access. In 1962, while performing at the Edinburgh Art Festival, Anderle discovered the work of Paul Klee, Jean Dubuffet, and Francis Bacon. A stop in London gave him the opportunity to study the old masters at the National Gallery. The following year, while on a tour of Germany, Anderle saw a retrospective exhibition of the work of Max Ernst in Cologne. The impact of this experience can be seen in a dramatic change in his imagery. In *Head with Violin* (plate 3), Anderle abandons the textured collagraph technique for simple drypoint outlines suggesting a head, and arms playing the violin, an instrument he himself played as a youth.

During a Black Theatre tour of Australia in 1964, Anderle married fellow actor Milada Daňhelová, also a former student from the Academy of Fine Arts, Prague, at the Czechoslovakian consulate in Sydney. While in Australia, Anderle was inspired by his encounter with the symbolic language of aboriginal art. In August of that year he performed at the theatre festival in Venice in connection with the Biennale di Venezia. The work Anderle saw at the Biennale, his meeting in Paris with the Czech expatriate painter and illustrator Josef Šimá (1891–1971), and his discovering the "Art Informal" of German artist Wols [Alfred Otto Wolfgang Schulze (1913–1951)], combined with his enthusiasm for aboriginal art, precipitated a new direction that autumn in the *Heads* cycle (1964–65) of thirteen prints.

Around 1965 the regime's official prejudice that so stifled creativity began to relax, and there was an explosion of new theatre, cinema, literature, and visual arts in Czechoslovakia. During the Black Theatre's tour that year Anderle carried zinc plates in his trunk. He worked on them during his spare time as the troupe toured Düsseldorf, East Germany, Cuba, Italy, Yugoslavia, and the Soviet Union. The plates for *Instigator* (plate 4) and *Nude* (plate 5) from the *Heads* cycle were executed while performing in East Germany and printed upon his return to Prague. The *Heads* cycle strips away the outer shell of figures to explore the pulse of the inner psyche. Anderle chose to work with drypoint for reasons of economy and convenience while traveling. He pushed the advantage of the autographic quality of the drypoint line with its velvety burr, spinning an intricate spidery web of hair-like lines into figures that coalesce and dissolve.

The *Skinless* cycle (1965–67) of thirteen prints overlaps with the *Heads* cycle. Anderle's strong sense of composition is evident in his images from the *Skinless* cycle, including *The Harried One, the Strong One Attack the Weak One Who Is Caught in His Own Net* (plate 6), *Conversation* (plate 7), and *Beasts of Prey* (plate 8). The phantasmagorical figures and schematic bodies reflect situations rather than actual events and mirror the subjective feelings of humanity—love and hate, envy and treachery, and power and abuse. These skinless figures with multiple appendages and fragmentary anatomical detail appear enigmatic as they emerge and retreat into the writhing organic whole, as if springing from the subconscious. For his *Skinless* cycle Anderle began to explore subtle color variations. For aesthetic effect as well as economy he began his lifelong practice of adding color *à la poupée* (multiple colors are placed on the plate, which is printed on one pass through the press). Thus there is a variation of color from one impression to another.

In 1966 Anderle executed *Variation on Dürer's* The Great Fortune *(Nemesis)* (plate 9), which pays tribute to the draftsmanship of the German master engraver Albrecht Dürer (fig. 3). Anderle interprets the goddess as a vengeful figure with a powerful, muscular body in an aggressive stance, rather than seeking the classical proportions Dürer was studying at the time of his engraving.[7] The bridle symbolizes the restraining of those who do evil and the goblet suggests the dangers of drink and the incitement of lust. This drypoint is one of the few instances in which Anderle portrays a background landscape, yet he does not copy Dürer's view of the Tyrolian town.

Figure 3

Albrecht Dürer (German, 1471–1528). *Nemesis (The Great Fortune)*, ca. 1501–02, engraving, 13 x 9 in. (33 x 22.9 cm). Cincinnati Art Museum, Bequest of Herbert Greer French, 1943.188.

In 1966 Anderle benefited from the newly relaxed political atmosphere when he received his first one-man exhibition of the *Heads* and *Skinless* cycles in Liberec and Prague. More importantly, his work received international exposure in *Current Trends in Czech Art*, an exhibition featuring younger artists that coincided with the AICA Congress of International Art Critics in Prague. The following year prints from the *Skinless* cycle were included in the international print biennale in Ljubljana. For Anderle it was encouraging that the prints he made in his spare time on tour and in short return trips to Prague received positive response and recognition both at home and abroad.

Smile of Happiness (plate 10), executed in Paris in 1967, points to a new direction in Anderle's printmaking. In this transitional print, Anderle for the first time explores the creative possibilities of mezzotint. Traditionally, mezzotint was used in the eighteenth century to replicate paintings, but Anderle takes his use of mezzotint far beyond its reproductive role. Not only does he use a variety of mezzotint rockers to create tonal transitions between light and dark, but also to create fantastic volumetric shapes that move in and out of space, as in *Eye of the Tortoise* (plate 11). This is particularly true in the *Comedy* cycle (1967–69) of nearly thirty plates created during the time leading up to and during the Prague Spring, and the turmoil of its harsh aftermath.

The *Comedy* cycle was an important turning for Anderle for another reason. In 1967, Anderle began his association with the print workshop of the Dřímal brothers,[8] Pavel and Milan, who would print his subsequent editions (fig. 4). With *Dawn* (plate 12), the first print in the *Comedy* cycle, the plates were steel-faced before editioning to preserve the delicate burr of the wiry drypoint lines for large editions.

Figure 4

Dřímal Workshop, Dittrichova Street, Prague. Left to right: Milan Dřímal and his son, Jiří Anderle, Pavel Dřímal, April 2007. © Kristin L. Spangenberg.

In *Variation on Dürer's* Knight, Death, and the Devil (plate 13), Anderle returns to meditate on Dürer's master engravings *Knight, Death, and the Devil* (fig. 5) and *Melancholia*, which he transforms as he once did Dürer's *Nemesis (The Great Fortune)*. Albrecht Dürer, the first international artist and the spiritual forefather of European printmaking, brought Renaissance scientific rationalism north. (In 1971 Anderle's prints were included in the international exhibition in Nuremberg celebrating the 500th anniversary of Dürer's birth.)[9]

On August 21, 1968, the Prague spring abruptly ended with the arrival of Soviet troops, and the life of the entire country was dramatically altered. Two weeks later, Anderle left with the Black Theatre for Dublin. While in the city of James Joyce, he executed *And There Is No Hope* (plate 14), using Dante's inscription *Lasciate ogni speranza* over the entrance to the gates of hell in *The Inferno*. The following year this print won a major award at the biennale in Ljubljana. Unlike the world to the west, whose citizens lived with the freedom to pursue prosperity, behind the Iron Curtain "normalization" stifled artistic freedom and time in effect stood still. From this time forward Anderle's cycles focused on the condition of man and the meaning of human existence.

Working in isolation with all the time in the world in his studio at Loretánská 5,[10] a former workshop for Prague Castle, Anderle devoted his time to his print cycles, laboriously working the large plates in multiple states and exploring color variants. The individual plates for *Comedy No. 13* were first editioned individually as *Monkey* (plate 17) and *Girl* (plate 18), then the plates were combined for two variants of *Monkey and Girl* (plate 19) with different-colored backgrounds. The print references indirectly the macaque Bonny, who made a multi-day series of Earth revolutions in 1969, and queries the fate of man in the ongoing space race between the United States and the Soviet Union. The *Comedy* cycle prints won the "ex aequo" prize at the Second Biennale of Graphics in Cracow.

The *Comedy* cycle alternates with the *Perspectives* cycle (1969–73). This new print cycle reveals for the first time the artist's reflection on the old masters and personal interpretation of great paintings of the past. Stimulated by a treatise on perspective, Anderle pays homage to the courtly *fêtes galantes* of Antoine Watteau (1684–1721). In *Homage to Watteau* (plate 20) Anderle synthesizes references to several of the artist's paintings.[11] Perspective space becomes a conscious dimension in the lower portion of the composi-

Figure 5

Albrecht Dürer (German, 1471–1528). *Knight, Death and the Devil*, 1513, engraving, 9 ¹¹⁄₁₆ x 7 ⁷⁄₁₆ in. (24.6 x 18.9 cm). Cincinnati Art Museum, Bequest of Herbert Greer French, 1943.199.

tion, although it had been ignored previously in his work. Recognizable human figures are juxtaposed with organic entities in a two-tiered theatrical space. This contrasts with *Cogito ergo sum (I Think Therefore I Am)* (plate 21), in which the brain cells are exposed and viewed above and explode with a myriad of emotions below. The artist's own self-portrait projects the dynamics of his creative energy in *Self Image* (plate 23) as it freely flows beyond his body. The prints from these *Comedy* and *Perspectives* cycles were the featured works in a solo exhibition at the Ninth International Biennial Exhibition of Graphics in Ljubljana in 1971—an honor for being the award winner in the 1969 biennial.

In 1969 Anderle concluded his *Comedy* cycle. He also resigned from the Black Theatre troupe and accepted a position as assistant lecturer (1969–73) in the illustration and printmaking studio at the Prague School of Fine Arts under Jiří Trnka and subsequently under Zděnek Skelnář. Between 1969 and 1972 several important relationships developed outside Czechoslovakia and had a lasting impact on the international promotion of Anderle's work. Jacques Ludovicy, a citizen of Luxembourg passionately interested in Czechoslovak culture, introduced Anderle's work to Irene Gerling and Gerd Köhrmann at the Baukunst Galerie in Cologne, beginning Anderle's twenty-two-year association with the gallery, which first presented his work in 1969. With Dr. Köhrmann's encouragement Anderle began to keep a systematic log of all the work he produced. Jacques Ludovicy went on to publish the portfolio *Adventures of the Mind: New Trends in Czechoslovak Graphic Art* in 1970 and *Ricercari* in 1972, including Anderle's prints along with those of his contemporaries Jiří Balcar, Vladimír Gažovič, Albín Brunovský, Oldřick Kulhánek, and Jan Krejčí.

Beginning in 1969 Anderle was represented in the United States by Anne and Jacques Baruch of the Jacques Baruch Gallery in Chicago. The Baruchs' goal was to introduce the rich talent of Eastern European artists to audiences in the United States (a goal that continues with the work of the Anne and Jacques Baruch Collection). The Jacques Baruch Gallery presented the first comprehensive exhibition of Anderle's prints in the United States during the summer of 1972 and continued to promote his work over the ensuing three decades.

Anderle was fortunate that in 1972 an ongoing arrangement was made between the Baukunst Galerie and Art Centrum (the state cultural art agency) in Prague to publish his prints and arrange exhibitions in western Europe. Twice a year Anderle was allowed to travel to Cologne to consult or to open a new exhibition of his work at the gallery. The regime permitted no flexibility on dates, which needed to be requested three months in advance.[12] Only occasionally was Anderle's wife, Milada, whose sister resided in Germany, allowed to travel with him. The artist would drive his car to the border, which was patrolled by soldiers with dogs and automatic weapons. He would be taken to a shack between the barbed-wire fences of no man's land where he was interrogated and, on occasion, stripped in spite of having official permission to leave the country. For a few days Anderle would participate in the high life of the Baukunst Galerie exhibition opening and rub shoulders with the rich and famous, knowing that he would have to return to isolation in Czechoslovakia, with its inverted values and fears.

Art Centrum took a percentage of sales of the print editions published by Baukunst Galerie. Anderle was paid in Tuzex crowns, which could be spent in special hard-currency shops where Western goods otherwise not available to the general populace could be purchased.[13] Printmaking supplies were in short supply in Czechoslovakia. Only one fine art paper, which was of poor quality, was manufactured in the country, and printmaking inks were made in a limited number of colors. Other than these, art supplies had to be imported from Vienna or Brussels. When Anderle drove to Germany he would load up his car with supplies and the jazz records he loved on his return trip.

The *Kamasutra,* the ancient Sanskrit text on love, inspired the *Kamasutra* cycle of three prints. Sexuality, as in *El Motadani* (plate 25), was a subject that could be treated openly and did not raise red flags with government censors. Direct political commentary however would have drawn attention. The *Games* cycle (1975–77) reflects the games that people play in the larger sense and indirectly draws metaphors to contemporary events that reflect the upheaval and anxiety of the time. *Game for 122 Persons* (plates 26 and 27), with its tumult and writhing humanity, recalls countless depictions of conflict from Raphael to Signorelli. In the final state of the print the artist adds a head and extended arm in the upper portion of the composition, suggesting the need for stopping the destruction and bringing order to human chaos.

In 1975 Anne Baruch commissioned *Cruel Game for a Man* (plate 28) in honor of her husband Jacques Baruch, a Holocaust survivor. This print from the *Games* cycle, with its strong anti-war cry and depth of anger, commemorates the thirtieth anniversary of the end of World War II.[14] The chronicle of events on Earth as seen from space appears as a series of film stills, beginning with marching German soldiers destroying cities and human lives, and ending with the victorious Russians hanging their flag in Berlin. In the lower left, victims of the concentration camps obliterate Hitler's head. To the right, the head of a child, who does not yet know fear, is juxtaposed with the fearful face of her mother. The lineup of monsters throughout history ends with a German soldier. The mesmerizing power of the print with its rich velvety surface attracts, and then the gut-wrenching subject repels attention. Anderle's skillful reference to the Nazi past served as an indirect reference to the communist present.

The artist takes this theme further using the classical world as metaphor, suggesting the cataclysmic end of the world in his print *Appassionata* (plate 29). Classical architecture crumbles and rational society disintegrates. This print suggests the devastating impact of suppression of freedom on the lives of the Czechoslovakian people under communism: ethical and cultural values were

Figure 6

Alesso Baldovinetti (Italian, 1426–1499). *Portrait of a Lady in Yellow,* ca. 1465, egg tempera and oil on panel, 24 ¾ x 16 in. (62.9 x 40.6 cm).
© The National Gallery, London.

annihilated while the government presented a mask of normality. In his cycle *Relations – Interpersonal Relationships* the following year Anderle focuses on the individual. The skinless figures in *Confrontation* (plate 30) turn aggressive in pretend conversation, insinuating the manipulative quality of relationships. *Dialogue with Myself* (plate 31) probes deeper into the psychological machinations of the ego in isolation.

The cycle *Portraits in the Passage of Time* (1978–79) sees the past and the present as inseparable. Through portraits of friends and family that reverberate with a range of emotions, the psychological characterizations of familiar paintings by European masters are transposed into a creative reexamination of the human condition. These portraits go beyond the Cubist portraits of Pablo Picasso and Georges Braque. Anderle's deep understanding of facial expression as a mirror of the human psyche is communicated in the faceted countenance of his portraits. The range of sensation and emotions runs from pleasure to pain, and from joy to grief. Anderle takes his first step in single portraits beginning with *The Smile* (*El Sorriso*) (plates 32 and 33), after Alesso Baldovinetti's *Portrait of a Lady in Yellow* (fig. 6), and *Saskia* (plate 34), after Rembrandt's *Saskia Van Uylenburgh in a Red Hat* (fig. 7).

Anderle goes on to explore in *Portraits in the Passage of Time* the multitude of personalities of each of the women in his life: his wife, mother, and grandmother. *My Wife* (plate 35) brings to life the many facets of his wife, Milada, the woman whom he knew as an actress in the Black Theatre and knows yet as partner in life. Anderle increases the intensity and complexity exponentially by flipping the plate one hundred and eighty degrees for the second state. Random marks vibrate across the composition, providing a rhythmic counterpoint to the portrait and its myriad expressions. (Anderle's rhythmic sense of line springs at least in part from his passion for classical and jazz music, which he listened to daily over Radio Free Europe.) Most poignant is his drypoint *The Last Spring of My Grandmother* (plate 36), created with reverence for his beloved grandmother, who died at the age of ninety-six. This print, with its universal appeal, garnered international recognition in 1980 at *World Print III* in San Francisco.

In addition to the women in his family, the *Portraits in the Passage of Time* cycle celebrates many of Anderle's contemporaries, particularly among the Czech intelligentsia. Under the Czechoslovak communist regime, everyone was solicited to spy on one another. Having trustworthy friendships outside the family was important in combating isolation. Anderle pays tribute to persons whose confidence and friendship he valued in a series of prints as part of the cycle. The portrait of the artist and poet Jiří Kolář (1914–2002) in *Girl and*

Rembrandt Harmensz van Rijn (Dutch, 1606–1669). *Saskia Van Uylenburgh in a Red Hat*, ca. 1633–44, oil on canvas, 63 ¼ x 51 ¼ in. (160.7 x 130.2 cm). Museumslandschaft Hessen Kassel.

Figure 7

Man with Spectacles B (plate 37) is juxtaposed with the fifteenth-century *Portrait of a Young Lady* by Petrus Christus.[15] *Portrait of My Friend* (plate 38) commemorates the encouragement and support of the art historian Jiří Mašín (d. 1991), who Anderle met in 1966. Mašín wrote the first essay on the artist's work in 1968 and later became Deputy Director of the National Gallery in Prague. *Quiet Monologue of Bohumil Hrabal* (plate 39) pays tribute to the Czech writer who contributed an essay to the first monograph on the artist. *Vibrations of Jan Smetana* (plate 40) recognizes the painter Jan Smetana (1918–1998). Most stunning of the prints is the *Portrait of Anne B* (plate 41), commissioned by the Jacques Baruch Gallery. The frontal bust-length portrait of Anne Baruch conveys the serious determination and conviction of the sitter; the presence of a heart at the right of the composition affirms that she is also a person of compassion.

Perhaps the most compelling aspect of the cycle *Portraits in the Passage of Time* is Anderle's reinterpretation of the portrait of Giovanni Arnolfini and Giovanna Cenami (fig. 8) after the Flemish painter Jan van Eyck (plates 42 and 43). It is the first print in which the artist innovatively violates the image space. He worked on the plate strictly in drypoint in 1978–79 and then returned to the subject in 1981, perforating and radically cutting away portions of the printing plate, creating two separate editions. He further explores this radical departure in a second version of the theme, *Girl Reading Letter III* (plate 44), after the painting *Girl Reading a Letter at an Open Window* (fig. 9) by the Dutch painter Jan Vermeer. In the final state Anderle brings the letter into sharper focus by cutting away the plate following the outline of the letter. Even *Woman in Fur* (plate 46), after the famous painting by Peter Paul Rubens,[16] changes the focus to emphasize the vulnerability of and violence to Hélène Fourment by sequentially stripping the figure and at the same time overlaying the work with myriad static lines.

In 1979, simultaneously with the *Portraits in the Passage of Time* cycle, Anderle executed the autobiographical cycle *Rooms*. He expresses individual alienation in *Open Door, Milada* and *Closed Door, Jiří* (plates 49 and 50), and finishes up the cycle with a tribute to Franz Kafka in *Ceiling: After Kafka's Metamorphosis* (plate 51). Kafka's novels, including *The Trial* (1925) and *The Castle* (1926), concern troubled individuals in a nightmarishly bureaucratic and impersonal world. Kafka's family home lies in the shadow of the Prague Castle, where Anderle had his studio.

Figure 8

Jan van Eyck (Flemish, ca. 1390–1441). *Portrait of Giovanni (?) Arnolfini and His Wife*, 1434, oil on wood, 32 5/16 x 23 5/8 in. (82 x 60 cm). The National Gallery, London.
Photo Credit: Erich Lessing / Art Resource, NY.

In 1979 Anderle also began the striking cycle *Fragments* (1979–81). Old and new are brought together in jarring juxtaposition as the artist contemplates larger issues facing mankind. The impact of these images is strengthened by the physical alteration of the plates by drilling and cutting, as if they were riddled with bullets and drastically damaged by the elements of time. Anderle's reference to the historic past was safe, unlike a specific reference to the political present. In *Vox Humana* (plate 52), youth and beauty are ravaged by age, just as mankind's voice across the millennia has been ignored. *Free Floating Anxiety* (plate 53) reverberates with the anguished scream of a person in internal agony. Even though humankind has evolved since his primate ancestors began walking upright, *Belle Époque?* (plate 55) raises the question whether there will ever be a time when humans can live together in peace and prosperity. The face of the past in the portrait of Emperor Franz Josef, the cryptic notations "1900, 1914, 1939, ?!, 2000" to the left of his head, and the presence below of the innocent young girl suggest the destiny of future generations threatened by a nuclear mushroom cloud. Even more devastating is the *Homage to Victims of Terrorism* (plate 56). The innocent female figure, adapted from *Portrait of a Lady* by Rogier van der Weyden,[17] is transmuted by Anderle into a woman in prayer brutally violated by the wedge-shaped gouge into the plate, while the whole is overlaid with a trail of perforations like bullet holes forming a cross. The dissonance between the two figures emphasizes the fear of violence and the annihilation of the individual.

In the fall of 1979, while on one of his officially sanctioned trips to Cologne, Anderle traveled to Paris, where he saw two major retrospectives that captured his attention: a Picasso exhibition at the Grand Palais,[18] and the photographs of Diane Arbus. Anderle reinvents the legacy of Picasso in *Salomé* from the *Saltimbanques* (fig. 10). In Anderle's drypoint the power of dance is given greater emphasis and he transforms the accidental horizontal scratches on Picasso's plate into a pulsing band of lines reiterating the rhythmic energy of the dance (plate 58). The terrifying realism of the Diane Arbus photographs brought new ideas to Anderle's painting, and photography was to function as an important stimulus for his next series of paintings and prints.

Jan Vermeer (Dutch, 1632–1675). *Girl Reading a Letter at an Open Window*, ca. 1657, oil on canvas, 32 ¾ x 25 ⅜ in. (83 x 64.5 cm). Gemäldegalerie Alte Meister, Staatliche Kunstsammlungen, Dresden.

Figure 9

Anderle's cycle *Illusion and Reality* (1980–82) denounces war and senseless conflict and confronts dreams and reality, past and present. The chance find of a photograph of a World War I Austro-Hungarian soldier in a Prague bookshop led to a scathing cycle of prints and paintings. The artist capitalizes upon the expressive tension between the collaged photograph and the translated image to delve into questions of victimization and abuse. This cycle pits the contemporary illusion of the album photograph of the soldier in dress uniform against the absurd fate of everyday reality. Ordinary soldiers are victims stripped to grotesque blood-splattered nudes with expressions of agony, reflecting lives and families shattered by the false dreams of destiny. This cycle is one instance in which the painting came first. Anderle dedicates *Soldier* (plate 59), the first print in the series, to Jacques Baruch. The print portion of the cycle, including *Soldier and Bride* (plate 60); *Soldier, Son, and Wife; Soldier, Girl, and Parents;* and *Soldier and Three Women*, culminates with

Figure 10

Pablo Picasso (Spanish, 1881–1973). *Salomé*, drypoint, 15 ¾ x 13 ¹¹⁄₁₆ in. (40 x 34.7 cm). Cincinnati Art Museum, Mr. and Mrs. Ross W. Sloniker Collection of Twentieth Century Biblical and Religious Prints, 1954.98.

with specific reference to the protagonists of war in *Elite (Kaiser and Crown Prince)* (plate 61). Playing up the detail of their medals and faces, the artist identifies, from left to right, a short, stocky Kaiser Wilhelm II, shriveled left arm on his sword; the Crown Prince, a skull and bones on his helmet; and a confused and immobilized Prince Oskar. *Elite* is a stinging commentary about the lives of the many controlled by a deadly agenda of the few. To the artist, the historic reference served as a veiled resistance and means of survival in his own situation, while providing a more generalized warning to humanity against future conflicts. The print cycle struck a responsive chord and was awarded the prestigious Grand Prix when exhibited at the Fourteenth International Biennial Exhibition of Graphics in Ljubljana in 1981. Five of the cycle's paintings received international recognition the following year in the exhibition *Arte come Arte: Persistenza dell'Opera* in the Central Pavilion at the Fortieth Venice Biennale in 1982.

The cycle *Illusion and Reality* was too close to the immediate historical present, and Anderle began to distance himself by alternating with a new cycle, *Antiquity* (1981). Although his first exposure to classical antiquity—in 1965 while touring with the Black Theatre—did not have an immediate impact on his work, a 1979 trip to Rome and a lecture on Ovid's *Metamorphoses* turned his attention to the fates of the Greek gods and lessons from antiquity for inspiration. Unlike the photographs of soldiers, only fragments of classical sculpture remain, so Anderle's images spring from his poetic imagination. The idealized figures and radically cut plates suggest that the mythology of the past survives, yet only as fragments, like ancient wall frescoes. Obliquely, the fates of the Greek heroes are transmuted to suggest the transitory nature of those who hold and abuse power.

The drypoint *Pan, Syrinx, and Old Woman* (plate 62) references the story of the god Pan's amorous pursuit of the chaste nymph Syrinx. Desperate to escape his embraces, Syrinx was turned into a reed, from which Pan fashioned his pan pipes, called a syrinx. The two prints *Perseus and the Graeae* and *Andromeda and Medusa* (plates 63 and 64) allude to feats of the hero Perseus, who forced the Graeae, the aged sisters of the Gorgons, to aid him in his quest to behead the Gorgon Medusa. Perseus later claimed the princess Andromeda in marriage, after first rescuing her from the sea monster to which she was to be sacrificed in punishment for her mother's arrogance. *Oedipus and Antigone* (plate 65) captures the compelling anguish of Oedipus, king of Thebes, who, in unwitting fulfillment of a prophecy, kills his father, marries his mother, and sires two sons and a daughter, Antigone, through incest. Oedipus blinds himself in horror when he realizes what he has done; disaster falls on his city as well as his family.

Throughout his career Anderle has paid homage to master painters. In the cycle *Dialogues with the Great Masters* (1982–83) he internalizes the work of the artists he most admires, studying their legacy, paraphrasing their motifs, and using their works as a vehicle to translate his concerns and experiences with contemporary reality into his own prints and paintings addressing fundamental universal issues facing humankind in the context of the twentieth century. At the same time that he pays homage to these artists, he measures himself against their talent and seeks his own place in the continuum of the great masters.

Anderle's evocation of Dürer's woodcuts from the *Large Passion* and *The Apocalypse* for two versions of *Ecce Homo* and *The Four Horsemen* (plates 66 and 67, fig. 11) validate Dürer's humanity and his own. He returns to the subject of Nemesis, the Great Fortune (fig. 3) in *Fortuna* (plate 68). While the figure of Fortuna closely quotes Dürer, Anderle replaces the master's innocent landscape with a representation of mankind's bestiality. In the *Dialogues* cycle, in addition to Dürer, Anderle explores the legacy of Leonardo da Vinci, Piero di Cosimo, Giuseppe Arcimboldo, Hieronymous Bosch, François Clouet, Rembrandt, Caravaggio, Ingres, and the artists of the School of Fontainebleau.

Taste, Touch, and *Sight* (plates 72–74) belong to a series of engravings devoted to the five senses by Jan Saenredam after Hendrick Goltzius (fig 12).[19] Allegorical series of prints were popular in the sixteenth and early seventeenth centuries. Anderle's original drawing for *Sight* (plate 75) reveals his working method for this series. With bold pencil lines he draws his subject on a tissue-thin sheet of paper, transferring the design into the soft ground layer protecting the copper plate. The residue of the ground remains on the verso of the paper. The lines exposed in the soft ground layer are then etched and the printed image prints left to right. This is one of the few instances in which the artist did not work directly onto the plate.

As Anderle reached middle age time took on new urgency as he contemplated the transitory nature of beauty, youth, and life itself. *Bacchus* (plate 76) after Caravaggio (fig. 13) meditates on how excess in drink will take its toll on youthful elegance, insinuated by the presence of overripe fruit. Anderle continued these meditations in his *Vanitas* cycle (1983–84). He does not use traditional symbols associated with *Vanitas*, such as skulls, snuffed candles, and timepieces, to warn of the passage of time. Instead he portrays lush arrangements of flowers, fruit, and insects in the tradition of northern European seventeenth-century still life painting. The underlying implication is that the fruit and flowers depicted in their prime will decay with the passage of time, reiterating the knowledge of the brevity of life. Youth and beauty are graphically transformed in *Vanitas VI* (plate 78) by progressive aging, from the serene flawless face of youth to the anguished disfigurement of old age in the shadow of encroaching death. The symbolic warning of the *Vanitas* cycle is elemental, the message universal, providing the viewer with a reminder of the fleeting passage of life.

Figure 11

Albrecht Dürer (German, 1471–1528). *The Four Horsemen* from *The Apocalypse*, ca. 1497–98, woodcut, 15 7/16 x 11 1/8 in. (39.2 x 28.3 cm). Cincinnati Art Museum, Bequest of Herbert Greer French, 1943.212.

Classical literature, particularly the work of the Roman poet and satirist Horace (65–8 BC), who considered himself heir to the Greek poets, helped shape Anderle's humanism. The cycle of prints and paintings *Horace: Beware of Asking What Tomorrow May Bring (Quid sit futurum cras, fuge quaerere)* (1983–84) alludes to the first book of *Odes* by Horace and to classical literature overall.[20] Anderle uses this cycle to address the larger question of man's survival in the post-nuclear era. *Beware of Asking What Tomorrow May Bring I* (plate 79) brings together a kaleidoscope of seemingly incongruent images. As a youth the artist walked under a solitary pear tree in an abandoned garden on the outskirts of his home village. As an adult he ruminates on what the tree would say if it could tell the story of the past, of three generations of Anderle's family: grandmother, mother, and Anderle himself. The print carries the inscription "Pictures from Autumn" in the lower center. The image speaks to passing generations and asks the question of what time will bring to future generations, and in broader terms, to the country itself. Will innocents be gobbled up by the fantastic creature? The question is answered in later prints in the cycle. *Bestia Triumfans III* (plate 81) brings the terror of the unknown future to the fore. A menacing beast devours humans without remorse, much as the communist government has stripped freedom and individuality from its citizens.

In titling *And Now Only Tears II – Emperor* (plate 82), Anderle paraphrases Virgil: *Sunt lacrimae rerum* ("Human circumstances bring tears"). Aeneas speaks these words when he surveys a series of wall paintings depicting the fall of his native city, Troy.[21] Anderle alludes in this print to the reality that all humankind, even emperors, are not immune to tragedy.

The *Carpe diem, carpe noctem* cycle begun in 1984 continues the artist's translation of classical literature to contemporary messages. He takes the phrase *Carpe diem* ("Seize the day") from Horace, *Odes I*, and adds the clever supplement *Carpe noctem* ("Seize the night"), thereby adding the more provocative activities of night to the overall theme.[22] In *Carpe diem, carpe noctem I* (plate 84) the man tempts the woman to share the present, reiterated by the woman reaching for the fruit and the intimate interaction of the couples in the background. The presence of death reinforces the taking the pleasure of the moment in the shadow of inevitable mortality. Other prints in the cycle revisit the old masters—Caravaggio in *Sick Bacchus* (plate 86) and Rembrandt in *Rembrandt and Saskia* (plate 87)—transposing these old master works into contemporary warnings against overindulgence and dissipation. In *Sick Bacchus* Anderle plays with the extremes

Jan Saenredam (Dutch, 1565–1607). *Sight* from *The Senses* after Hendrick Goltzius, engraving, 6 3/16 x 4 3/4 in. (15.7 x 12.1 cm). © The Trustees of the British Museum.

Figure 12

of pleasure and pain implied by overindulgence in the youthful Bacchus clasping a handful of grapes while a frenzied group of fantastic beings fornicate below. The raucous interpretation *Rembrandt and Saskia,* created in honor of fellow Czech artist Albín Brunovský's fiftieth birthday, uses Rembrandt's painting *Self-Portrait and Saskia in the Parable of the Prodigal Son* (fig. 14) as springboard for a broader theme. Rembrandt made self-portraits throughout his career, chronicling his life from youth to old age.[23] Anderle quotes various self-portraits by Rembrandt for the progressive aging of man across the image with the implied admonition to enjoy life without youthful wastrelcy. It was with the close of this cycle in 1984 that Edition Götz, Stuttgart, began arranging European exhibitions and continued publishing the print descriptions of the artist's editions through 1991.

In 1985 Anderle returned to the theatre for inspiration. His *Commedia dell'arte* cycle of prints and paintings (1985–1990) uses the symbols and conventions of theatre to explore the manipulation of power through fear and repression. For this cycle he also introduces a crayon resist, drawing directly on the bare plate with a lithographic crayon, which serves as a resist when the plate is bitten by the acid, producing white lines in the final print. In *The King and Jester with Beautiful Mask* (plate 94), the artist created his own *Commedia dell'arte* plot satirizing the relationship between a megalomaniacal king and a hapless jester. The king toys with the jester; their relationship progresses from toleration to execution in *The King Kicks the Jester* and *The King Kills the Jesters* (plates 95 and 96). The cycle serves as a metaphor prophesying the unraveling power of the communist regime as it nears implosion.

The fall of the Berlin Wall on November 10, 1989, was shortly followed by the fall of the Communist Party in Czechoslovakia. On November 17, 1989, an officially approved demonstration commemorating the Nazi destruction of Czech universities sparked protests and demonstrations that led to the rapid toppling of the communists—the Velvet Revolution. With the advent of democracy in Czechoslovakia following the long period of oppression, Anderle abandoned the themes of warning he had portrayed throughout numerous cycles.

In the midst of the joy and dynamic change precipitated by the Velvet Revolution, the death of Irene Gerling, an early champion of Anderle's work, struck a sad note and brought to a close Anderle's long association with the Baukunst Galerie.

Figure 13

Michelangelo Merisi da Caravaggio (Italian, 1573–1610). *Young Bacchus,* 1589, oil on canvas, 37 ⅜ x 33 7/16 in. (95 x 85 cm). Uffizi, Florence.
Photo Credit: Scala / Art Resource, NY.

In his subsequent cycle, *Appassionata Humana* (1990–93), Anderle brings to life fantastic beings that embody the virtues and evils of mankind while questioning the burdens and fate of the individual, society, and mankind in the twenty-first century. *The Festival Eater* and *Banquet* (plates 99 and 100) demonstrate the basest sin of gluttony. This cycle amplifies the earlier cycle *Carpe diem, carpe noctem* by further exaggerating the theme of excess with vile beastly figures.

In the 1990s, under the new democratic freedoms enjoyed since the Velvet Revolution, Anderle has turned from the strenuous activity of printmaking to focus on his career as a painter. He continues to scrutinize the fate of the individual in the modern world. In 1995 the National Gallery of Prague, located at the Kinský Palace, organized a major retrospective exhibition of the artist's prints and drawings. The following year he received a major retrospective of his paintings at the Imperial Stables of Prague Castle. Now free to travel abroad, in 1997 Anderle made his first visit to Chicago, for the thirtieth anniversary celebration of the Anne and Jacques Baruch Gallery. A stop at The Metropolitan Museum of Art in New York, and visits to the Náprstek Museum in Prague, kindled a passion for collecting ethnic art from Africa and inspired Anderle's *Primordial* cycle.

In his sixth decade, Anderle undertook cycles of paintings: *At the Close of the Century* and *At the Close of the Millennium* (both 1998). His color palette turned brash and brilliant. Organic forms, free fantasy and historic milestones of the twentieth century—World War II, the Iron Curtain, the Velvet Revolution—are interwoven with new themes on globalization and the disparity of hunger versus materialism.

Galerie Anderle opened in the Pellé Villa, District 6, Prague, in 2003, featuring a retrospective of the artist's prints, paintings, drawings, and sculpture, as well as his personal collection of African tribal sculpture. In 2004 Anderle received the Vladimír Boudník prize for his contribution to Czech graphic art. In 2006 he received a gold medal from the president of the Czech Republic for his contribution to Czech culture. The artist continues to work and live in Prague.[24]

Rembrandt Harmensz van Rijn (and workshop?) (Dutch, 1606–1669). *Self-Portrait and Saskia in the Parable of the Prodigal Son*, 1635–39, oil on canvas, 63 ⅜ x 51 ⁹⁄₁₆ in. (161 x 131 cm). Gemäldegalerie Alte Meister, Staatliche Kunstsammlungen, Dresden. Photo Credit: Erich Lessing / Art Resource, New York.

Figure 14

NOTES

Epigraph. Albert Einstein, in a letter to Michelangelo Besso, March 21, 1955. www.oxfordreference.com/views/ENTRY.html?subview=Main&entry=t91.e825

1. Jiří Anderle, e-mail message through Richard Drury (translator) to author, April 7, 2008.
2. For a history of Czechoslovakia and the Czech Republic in the twentieth century see Hugh LeCaine Agnew, *The Czechs and the Land of the Bohemian Crown* (Stanford, CA: Hoover Institution Press, 2004), 167–331.
3. Jiří Anderle, e-mail message through Richard Drury (translator) to author, April 7, 2008.
4. Current biographical information supplied by the artist in personal interviews conducted April 23–27, 2007; also numerous e-mail and faxed messages. This is supplemented by the biographical chronologies in Bohumil Hrabal et. al., trans. Jan Čulik and Milan Mlačnik, *Jiří Anderle* (New York: Alpine Fine Arts Collection, Ltd., 1985), 233–241; Jiří Anderle, with intro. by Jiří Machalický, Anna Bryson, trans., *Anderle: Drawings, Prints, Paintings, Objects 1954 / 1995* (Prague: Slovart Publishing, Ltd., 1995), 318–319; and Richard Drury et al., trans. Anna Bryson, *Jiří Anderle—At the Close of the Millennium: Paintings, Prints, Drawings 1950–2000* (Prague: Slovart Publishing, Ltd., 2000), 259.
5. Jiří Anderle, pers. comm.
6. Anderle never joined the Communist Party. Victor Velek, "Light in a Time of Darkness," Prague *Post*, September 26, 2007, http://www.praguepost.com/articles/2007/09/26/light-in-a-time-of-darkness.php.
7. H. Diane Russell, *Eva/Ave: Woman in Renaissance and Baroque Prints* (Washington D.C.: National Gallery of Art / The Feminist Press at The City University of New York, 1990), 212–13.
8. Jiří Anderle, e-mail message through Richard Drury (translator) to author, April 21, 2008. The Dřímal workshop was formed in 1936 by Miro Pegrassi, the son of an Italian stonemason, in Vlesíčkyu Street, Prague 5, where it remained until 1975. Under the Czechoslovak communist regime immediately after the Second World War the family was allowed to stay on and work at the press that they had previously owned. Pegrassi's nephew, Pavel Dřímal, began printing with him in 1957. Pavel's brother Milan Dřímal joined the firm in 1966. The workshop relocated to Malostranské náměstí (Lesser Town Square), Prague 1, from 1975 to 1990. In 1990 it moved to Dittrichova Street, Prague 2, where it still operates today. With the end of communism the family had to buy back the workshop. They continue to print for fine art printmakers today.
9. Austellung der Albrecht Dürer Gellschaft im Germanisches Nationalmuseum Nürnberg—*Albrecht Dürer zu Ehren*, 1971.
10. The artist occupied his studio at Loretánské 5, Prague, from 1966 to 1990. Jiří Anderle, e-mail message through Richard Drury (translator) to author, April 21, 2008.
11. Jiří Anderle, e-mail message through Richard Drury (translator) to author, April 7, 2008.
12. Ibid.
13. Ibid.
14. Ibid.
15. Petrus Christus (Flemish, ca. 1410/1420–1475/1476). *Portrait of a Young Lady*, ca. 1470, oil on panel, 11 x 8 1/4 in. Gemäldegalerie, Staatliche Museen, Berlin.
16. Peter Paul Rubens (Flemish, 1577–1640). *The Fur (Helena Fourment)*, 1635/40, oil on panel, 69 x 38 in. Gemäldegalerie, Kunsthistorisches Museum, Vienna.
17. Rogier van der Weyden (Flemish, ca. 1400–1464). *Portrait of a Lady*, ca. 1460, oil on wood, 14 1/2 x 10 3/4 in. The National Gallery, Washington, D.C.
18. Grand Palais, 11 October 1979–January 1980, *Picasso: Oeuvres reçues en paiement des droits de succession*, Ministère de la Culture et de la Communication/ Editions de la Réunion des musées nationaux.
19. *The Five Senses* is a series of five engravings after Hendrick Goltzius. See K. G. Boon, *Hollstein's Dutch and Flemish Etchings, Engravings and Woodcuts ca. 1450–1700*, vol. 23 (Amsterdam: Van Gendt & Co., 1980), 76–78, H. 101–105. Illustrated in Walter L. Strauss and John Spike, eds., *The Illustrated Bartsch*, vol. 4 (Matham, Saenredam, Muller) (New York: Abaris Books, 1980), 411–415, TIB 95–99.
20. Horace, and Charles E. Bennett, trans., *Horace, the Odes and Epodes, with an English translation* (1927; repr., Cambridge, MA: Harvard University Press, 1968), 28–29.

    . . . quid sit futurum cras, fuge quaerere et
    quem Fors dierum cumque dabit, lucro
    appone nec dulces amores
    sperne puer neque tu choreas . . . .

    Cease to ask what the morrow will bring forth, and set down as gain each day that Fortune grants! Nor in thy youth neglect sweet love nor dances . . . .
21. Kathryn Gutzwiller, e-mail message to author, March 28, 2008.
22. Ibid.
23. The portraits quoted are: *Self-Portrait with Saskia (in the parable of the Prodigal Son)*, 1635–39, oil on canvas, Gemäldegalerie Alter Meister, Staatliche Kunstsammlungen, Dresden; *Self-Portrait as Zeuxix*, ca. 1663, oil on canvas, Wallraf-Richartz Museum-Foundation Corboud, Cologne; and *Self-Portrait (Self-Portrait in a Flat Cap)*, ca. 1633, overpainted 1642, oil on panel, The Royal Collection, London.
24. Richard Drury, e-mail message to author, April 8, 2008.

CHRONOLOGY OF CYCLES

1960–62
Village Dances, prints, paintings and drawings

1964
Australian Cycle, paintings

1964–65
Heads, prints

1965–67
Skinless, prints

1965–67
Comedy, prints

1970–73
Perspectives, prints

1973
Kamasutra, prints

1973–75
Games, prints

1975
Rivière Family Triptych, prints

1975–77
Relations – Interpersonal Relationships, prints, paintings and drawings

1978
Interiors, prints, paintings

Gluttons, paintings and drawings

Visual Scores – Instruments, paintings and objects

1978–79
Portraits in the Passage of Time, prints, paintings, and drawings

1979
Small Fragments, prints
Rooms, prints

1979–80
Fragments, prints
Portraits, paintings

1980
Variations on Given Themes, drawings

Homage to Diane Arbus, paintings, drawings

Elements, paintings

1980–82
Illusion and Reality, prints, paintings and drawings

Notebooks, paintings and drawings

1981
Antiquity, prints, paintings and drawings

Apocalyptic Antiquity, paintings

1982–83
Dialogue with the Great Masters, prints and drawings

Apocalyptic Genetics, prints, paintings, and drawings

1983
Vanitas, prints

Time and Space, paintings

1983–84
Horace: Beware of Asking What Tomorrow May Bring, prints and paintings

1984
Carpe diem, carpe noctem, prints

1985
Commedia dell'arte, prints, paintings

Notebooks, paintings
Livius, prints

1987–1993
Feasts, paintings

1987–1990
Drummers, paintings and drawings

1990–1993
Appassionata Humana, prints, paintings and drawings

1993
Variations on Leonardo's Fresco of the Last Supper, prints, paintings, drawings

1994–
Returns paintings and drawings

1995–98
Cities, prints, drawings, and paintings

1998
Masks, paintings, assemblages, mobile objects

Primordial, paintings

1998–2000
At the Close of the Century, prints

At the Close of the Millennium, paintings

Streets, paintings, prints, and drawings

2000
The Nostalgia of the End, paintings

2003
Memory of Landscape, paintings

2005
Tree of Life, paintings

2007
Dance Under Blue Sky, *Theatre of Time*, *Variations on Dürer's* The Great Fortune and *Melancholia*, paintings

2008
Work (in progress) on various-format paintings on the theme of *Theatrum Mundi* and the world in which we live

AN UNENDING DIALOGUE WITH HOW LIFE PROGRESSES, A DIALOGUE BETWEEN A SMILE AND SADNESS, REALITY AND DREAM, LIGHT AND DARK, OBJECTIVE REALISM AND IMAGINATION, OLD AGE AND YOUTH, CONCILIATORY SPIRIT AND AGGRESSION, WEAKNESS AND STRENGTH, A DIALOGUE BETWEEN A BASIC THEME AND VARIATIONS, SPEECH AND SILENCE, TRANQUILITY AND DISTURBANCE, A DIALOGUE BETWEEN WHAT WE CARRY INSIDE OURSELVES AND THE WORLD AROUND US, A SMALL GESTURE WITH INFINITY. . . .

Jiří Anderle, from *Jiří Anderle: View Back and Forward,* 2002

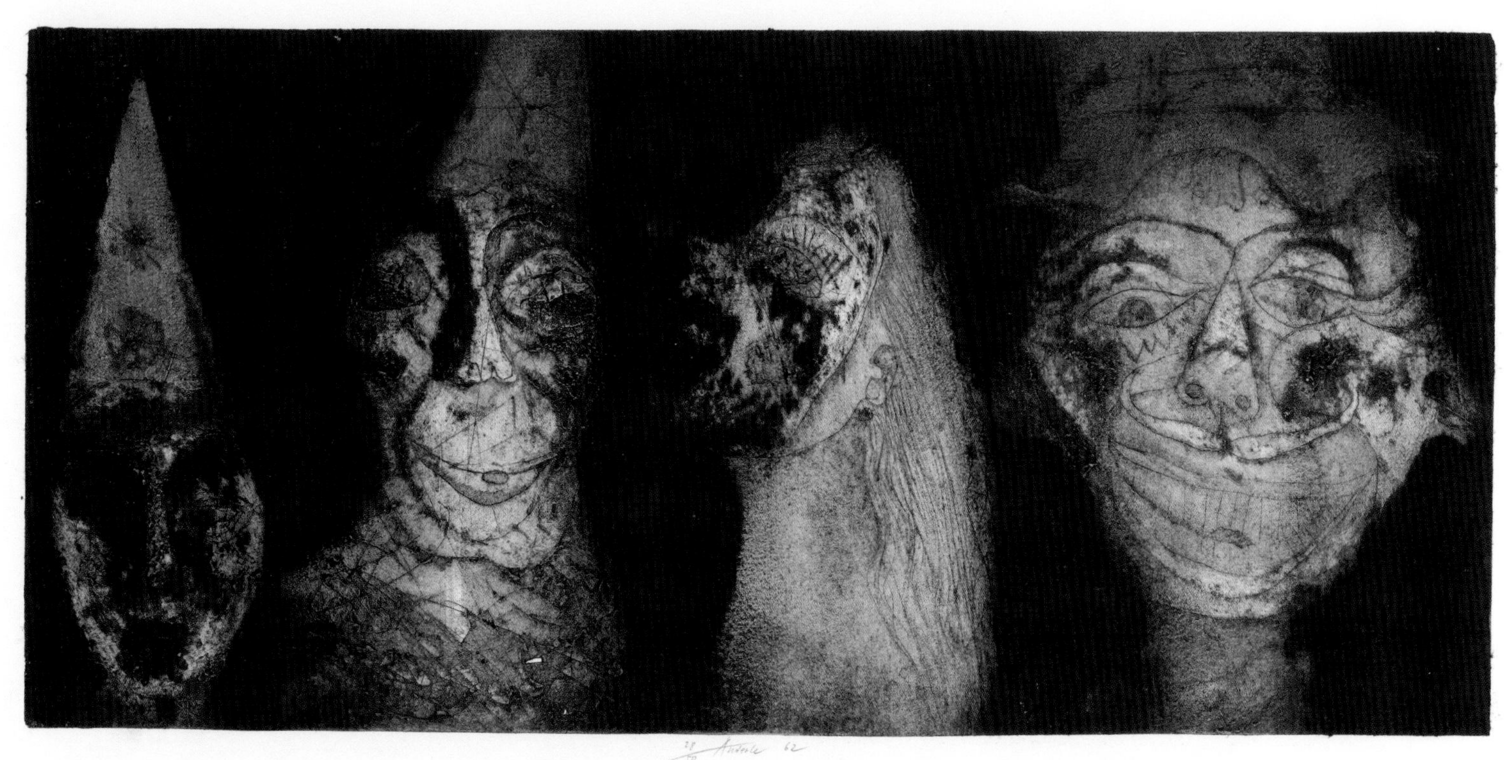

Four Masks
1962, WV 1 (1974.360)

1

2 *Large Dance*
1962, WV 3 (2005.505)

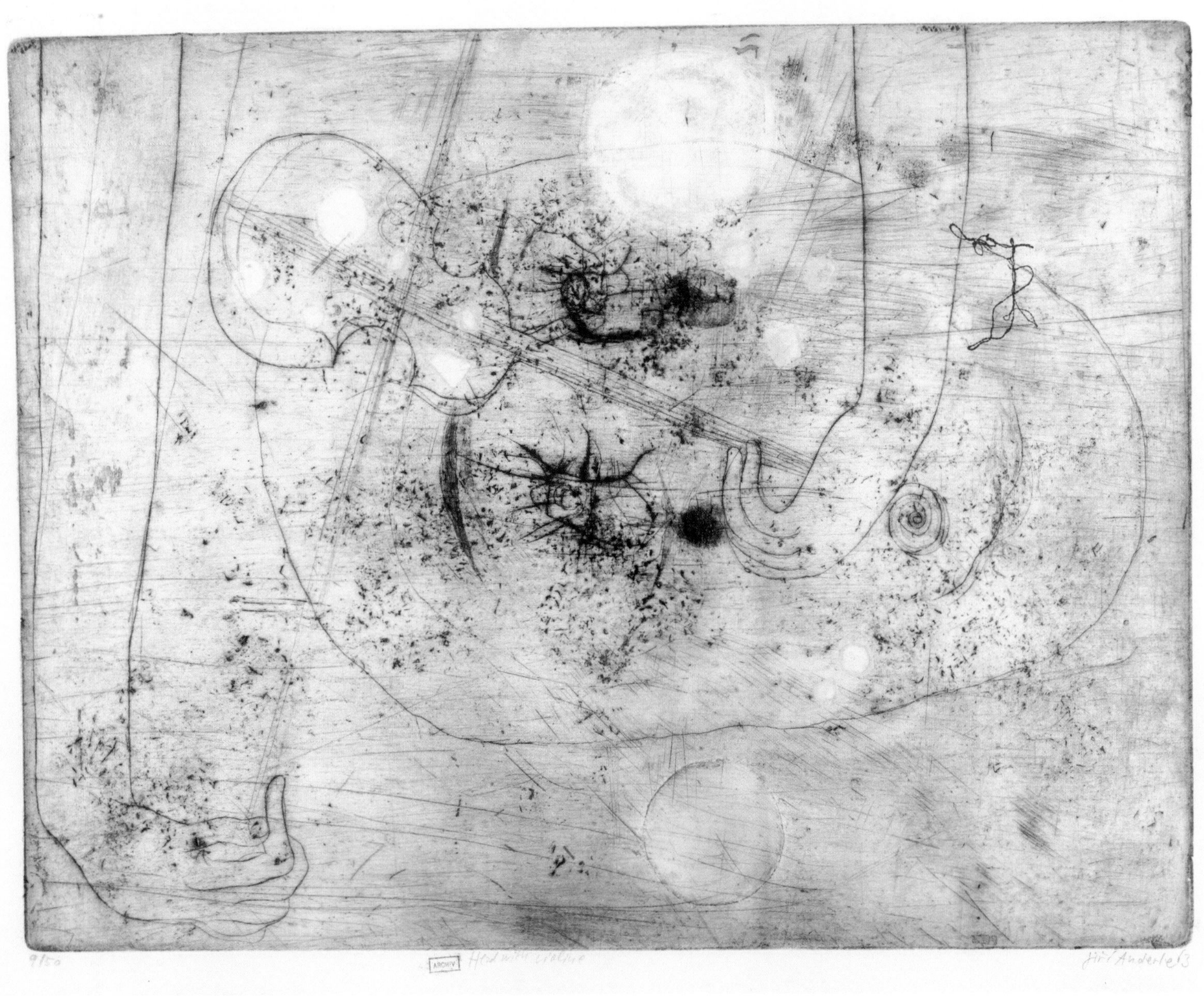

Head with Violin
1963, WV 6 (2005.507)

3

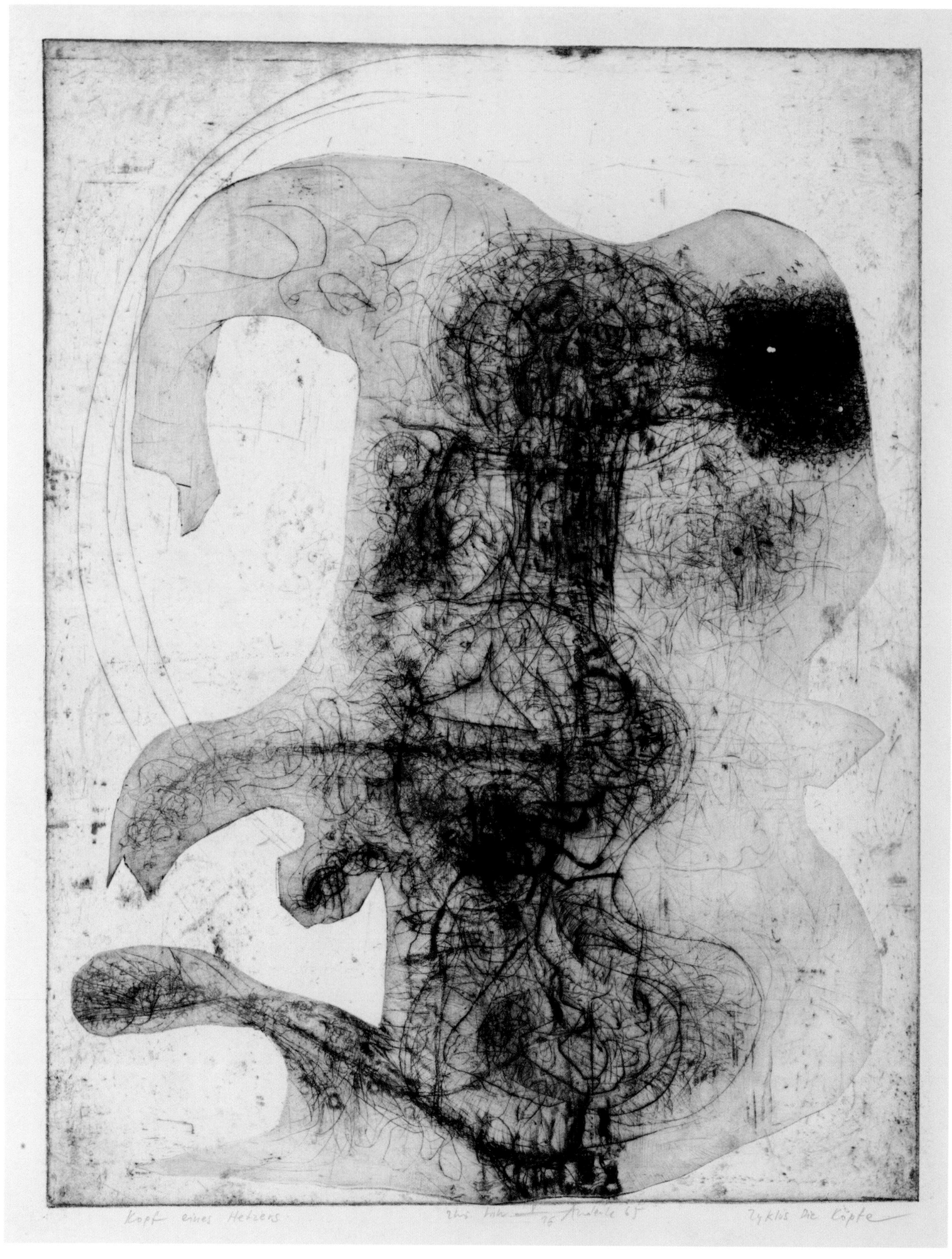

4 *Instigator*
1965, WV 10 (2005.508)

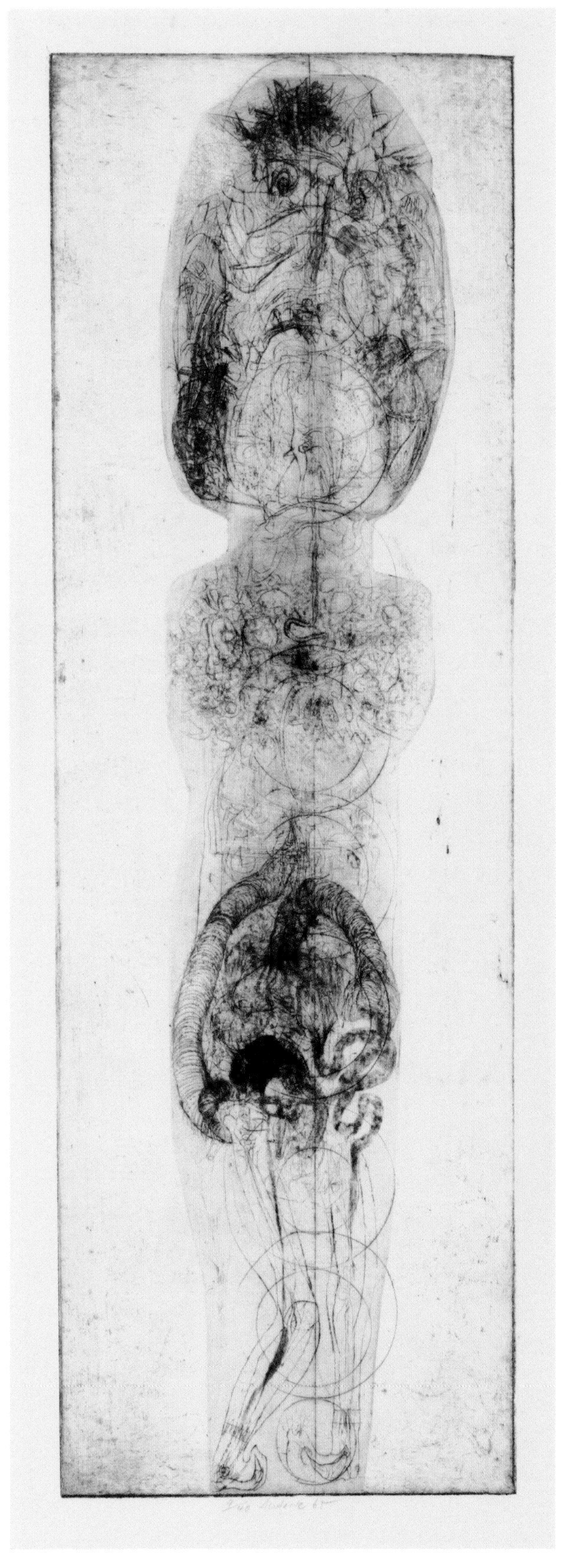

Nude
1965, WV 11 (2005.509)

5

6 *The Harried One, the Strong One Attack the Weak One Who Is Caught in His Own Net*
1965, WV 20 (2005.510)

Conversation
1966, WV 23 (2005.513)

7

8 | *Beasts of Prey*
1966, WV 28 (2005.517)

Variation on Dürer's The Great Fortune *(Nemesis)*
1966, WV 24 (2005.514)

9

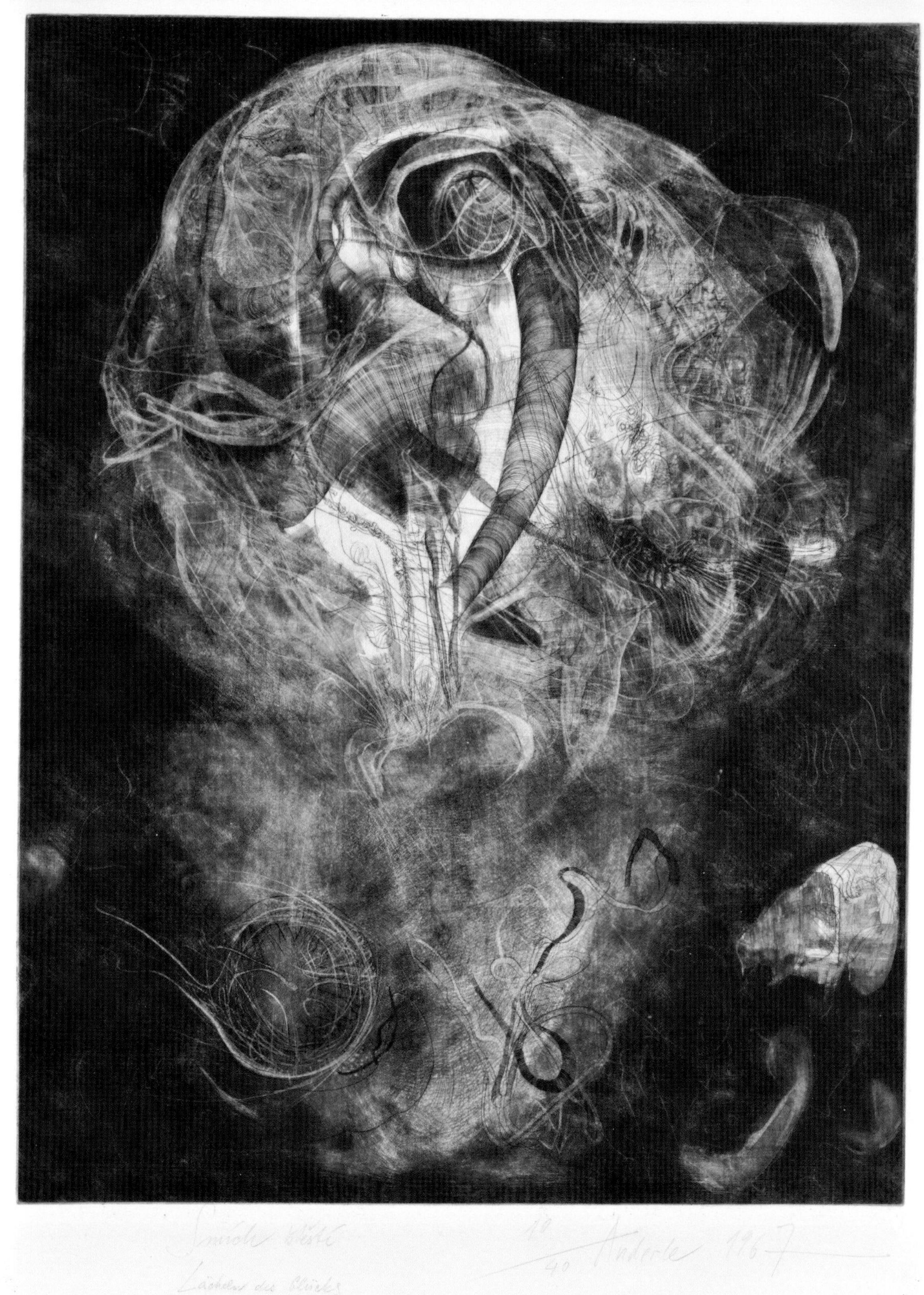

10 *Smile of Happiness*
1967, WV 33 (2005.521)

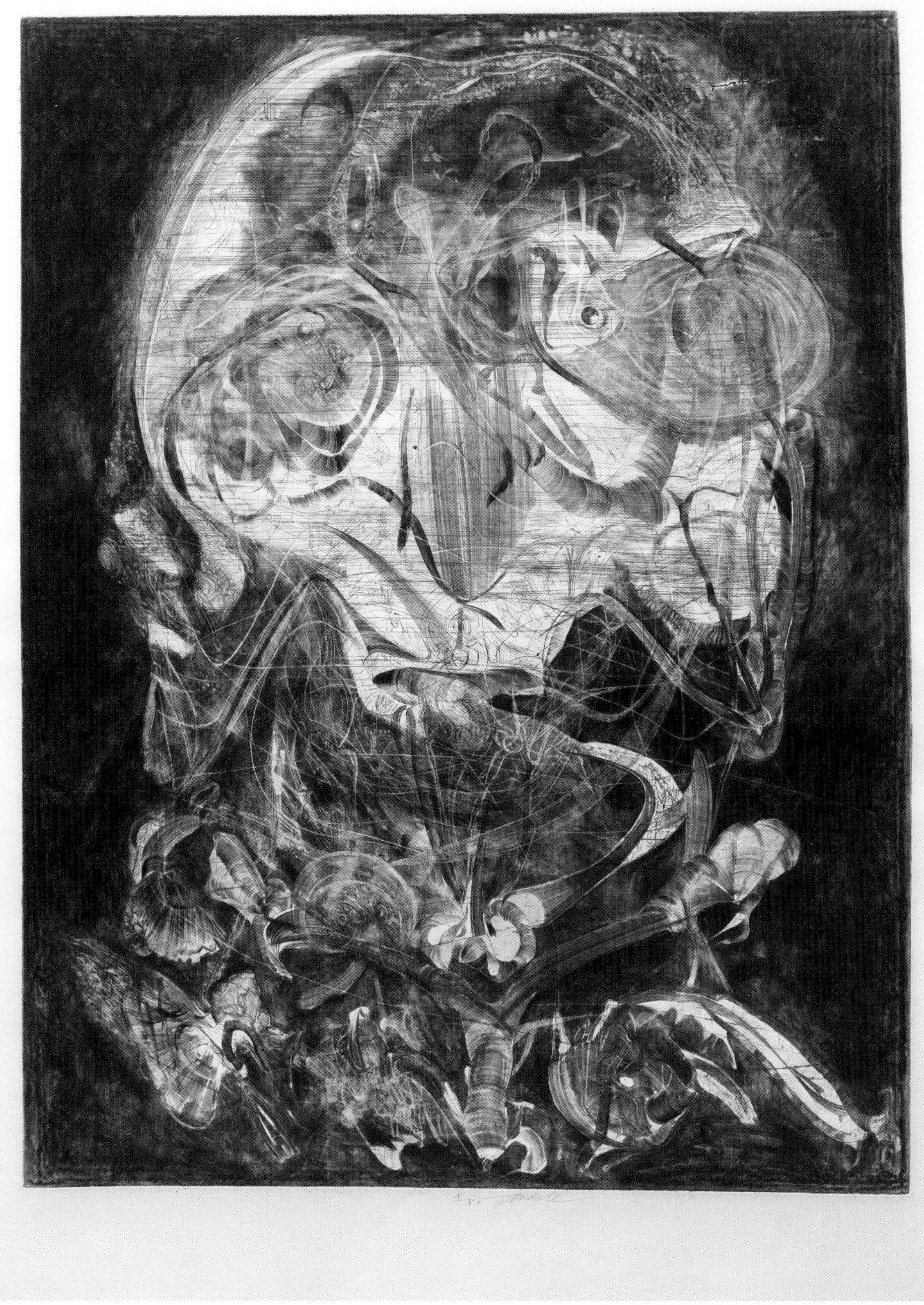

Eye of the Tortoise
1968, WV 39 fifth state (2005.524)

11

12 *Dawn*

1967, WV 34 third state (2005.522)

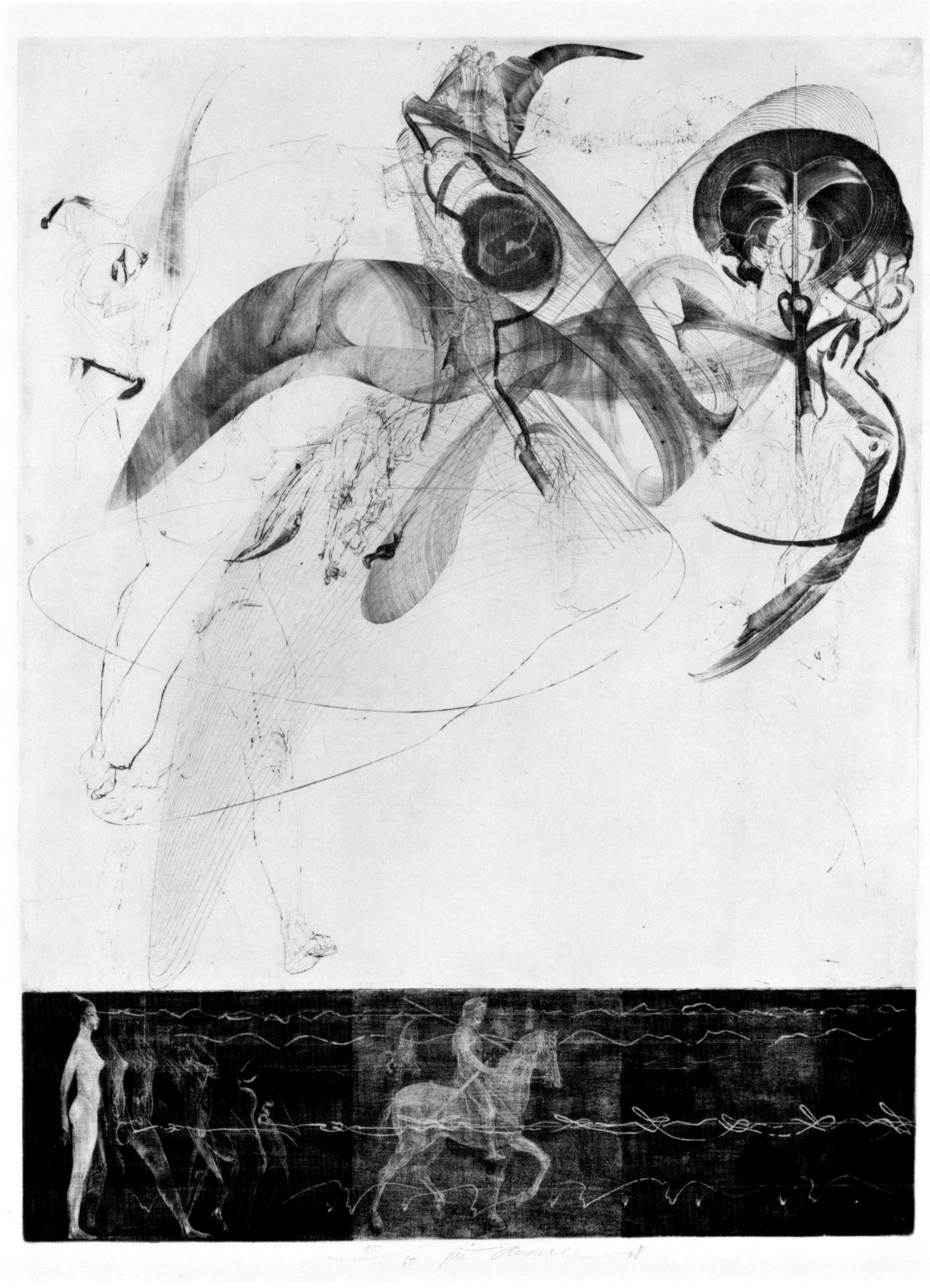

Variation on Dürer's Knight, Death, and the Devil
1968, WV 40 third state (2005.525)

13

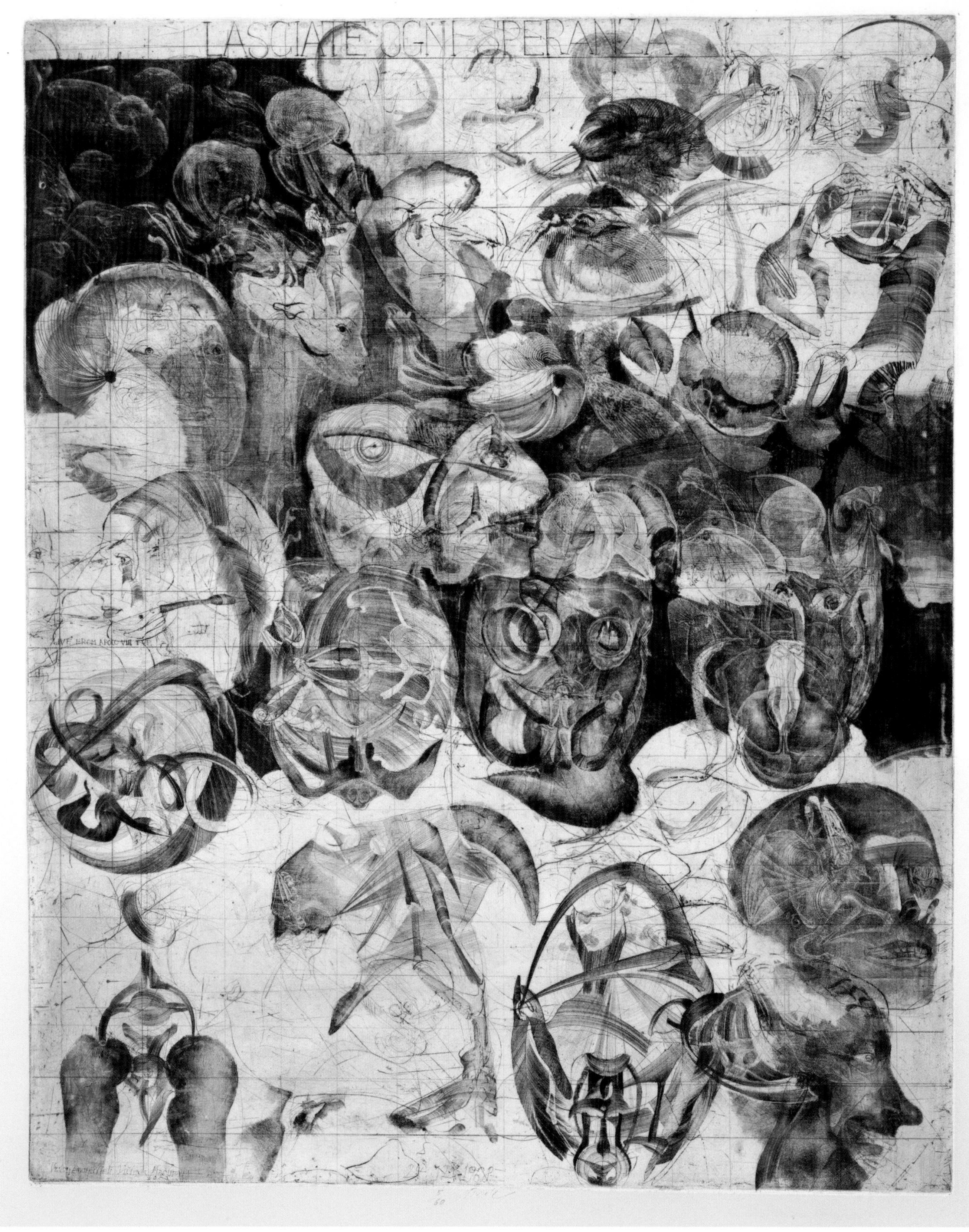

14 *And There Is No Hope*
1968, WV 42 (2005.526)

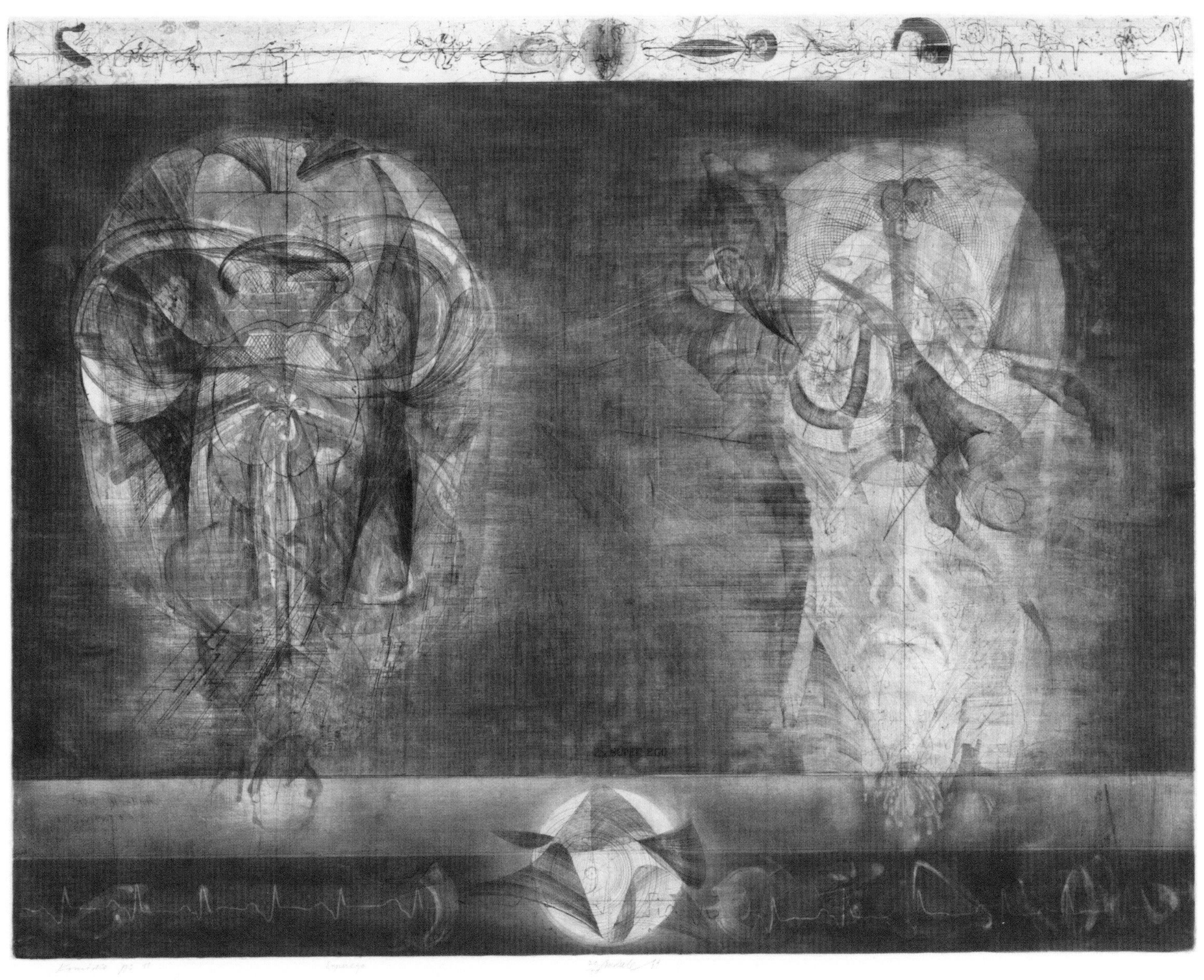

Superego – Man and Woman
1969, WV 74 (2005.531)

15

16 *As It Should Be – Meal*
1969, WV 76 (2005.533)

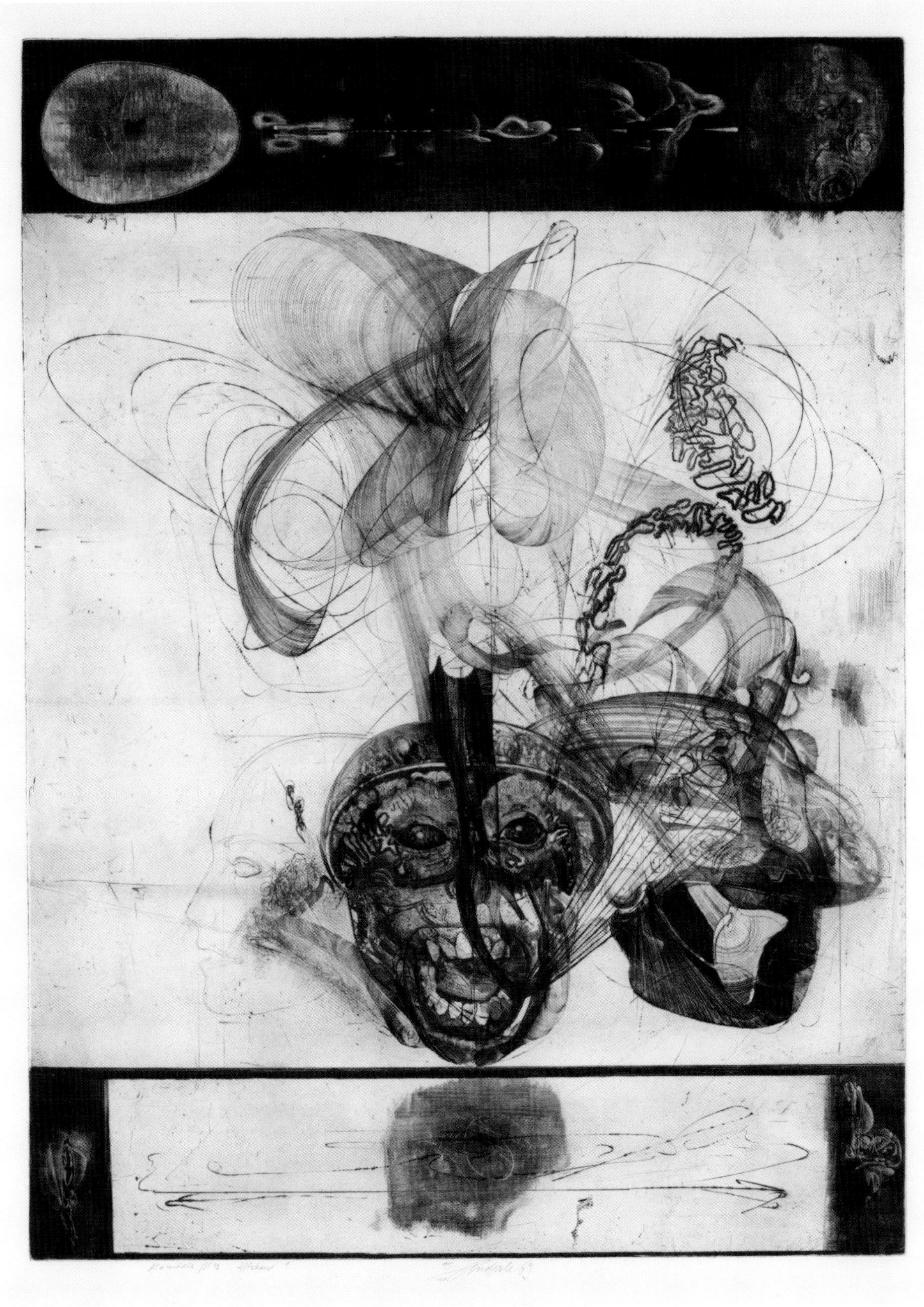

Monkey
1969, WV 79 (2005.534)

17

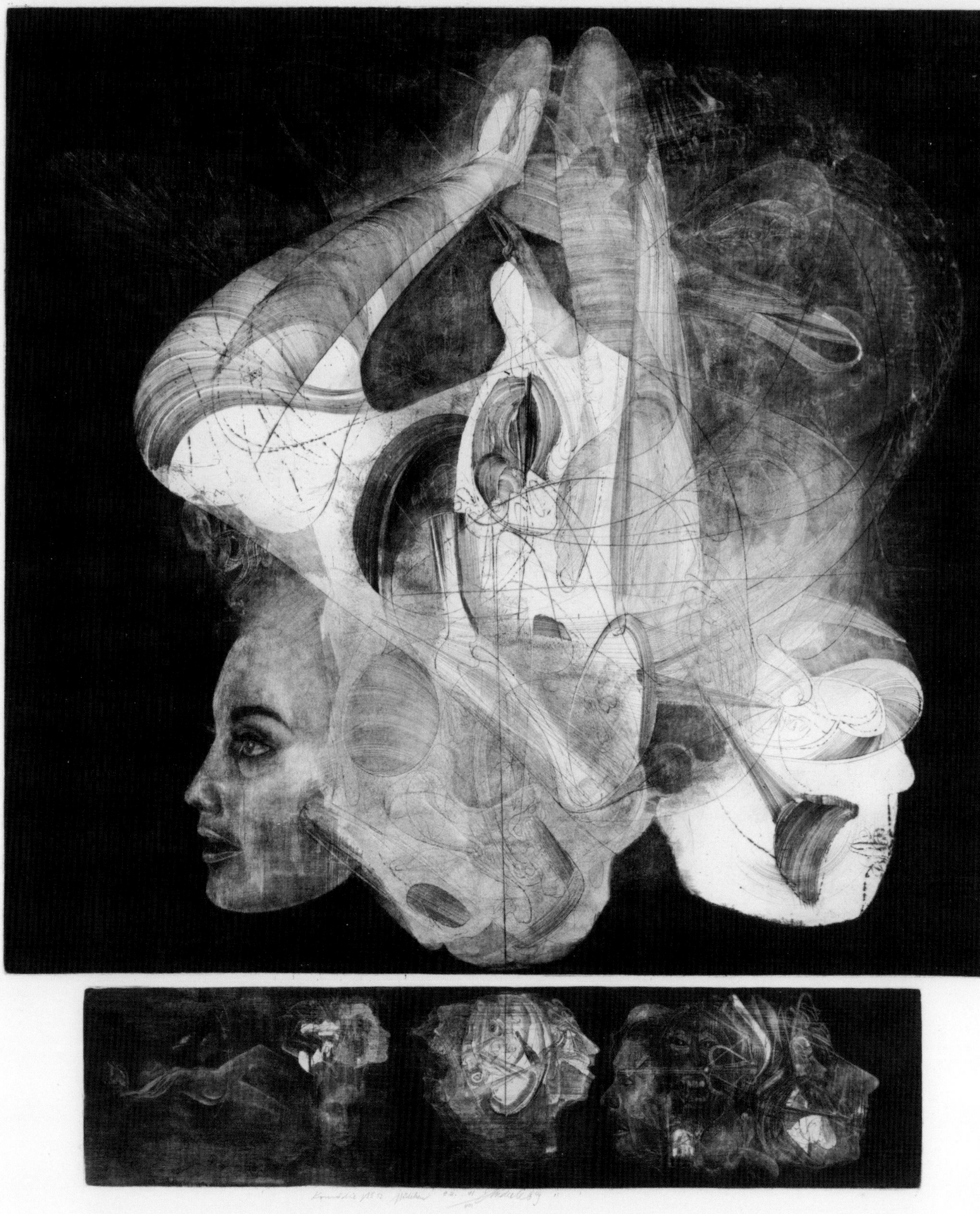

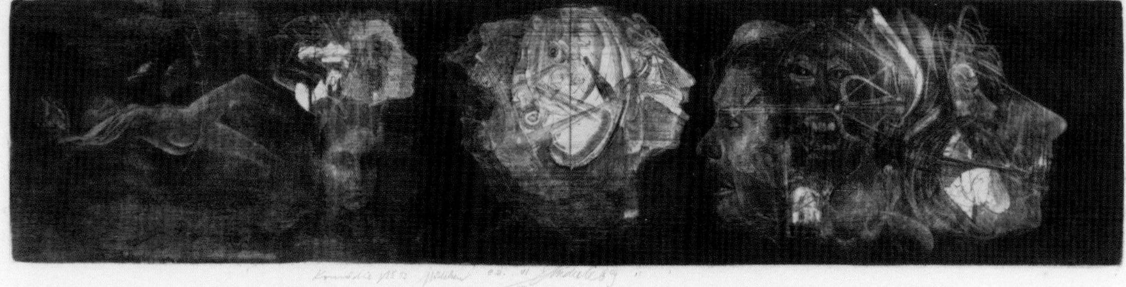

18 *Girl*

1969, WV 80 (2005.535)

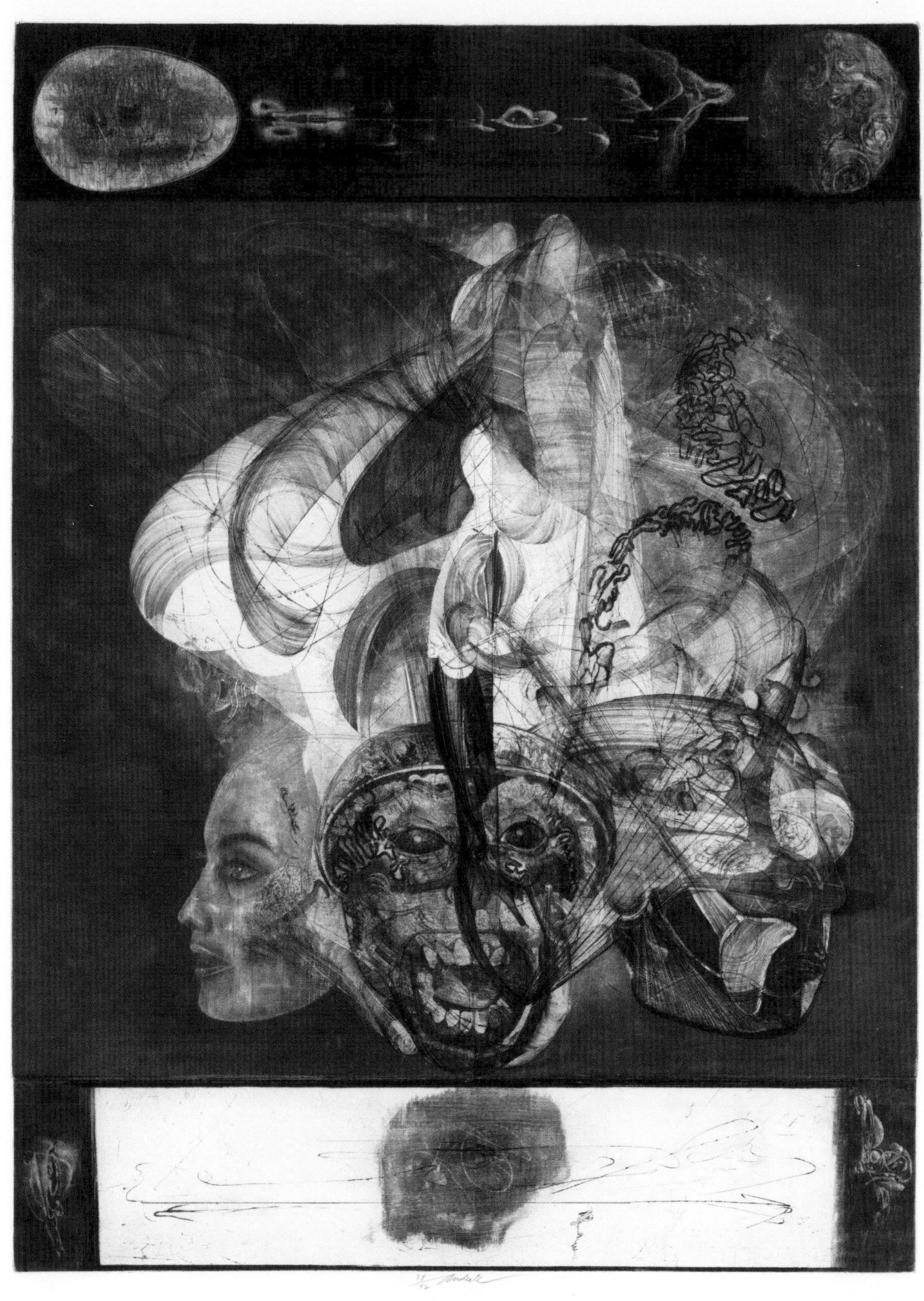

Monkey and Girl
1969, WV 81B variant (2005.536)

19

20 *Homage to Watteau*
1970, WV 83 unique proof (2005.538)

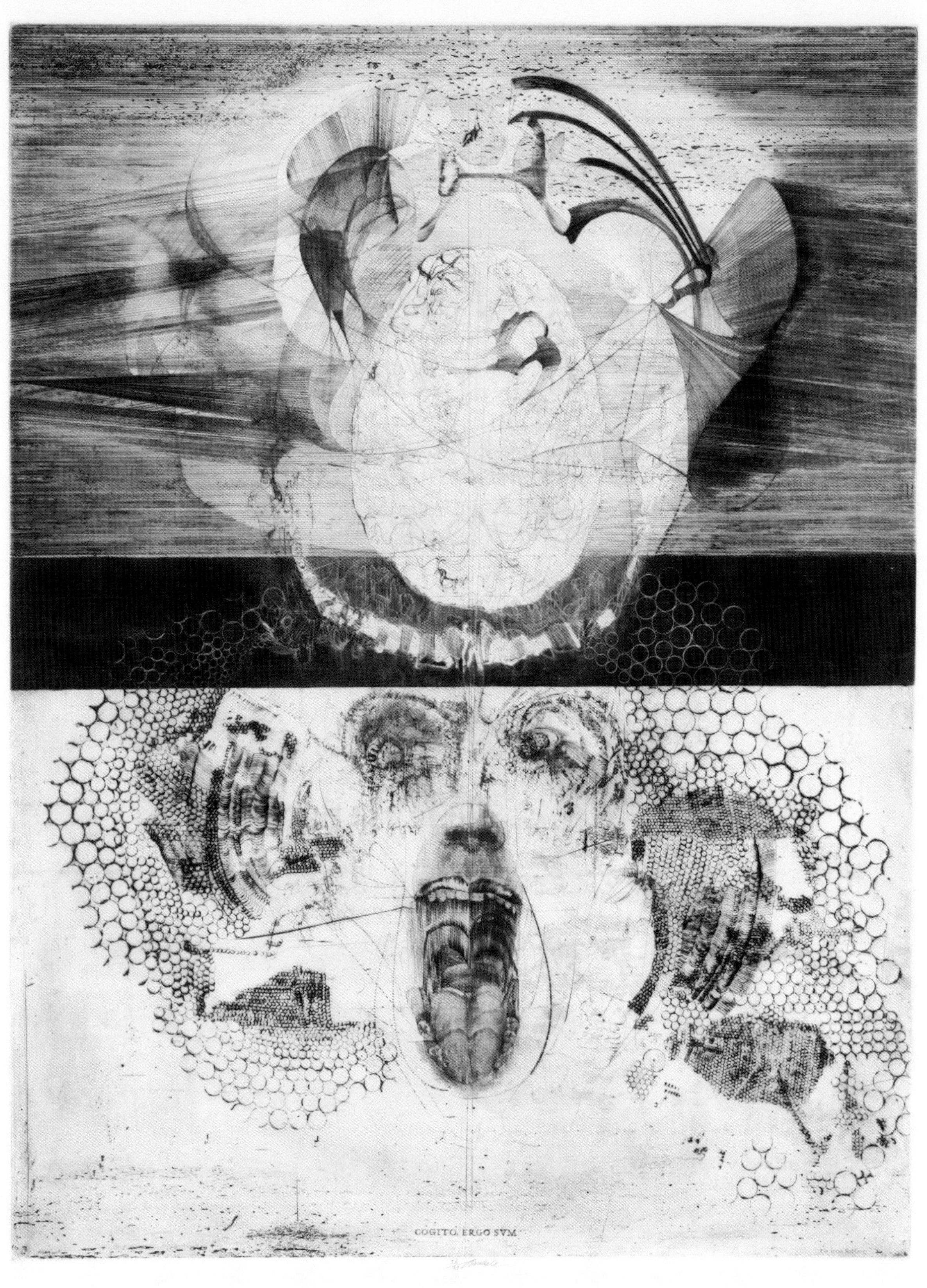

Cogito ergo sum (I Think Therefore I Am)
1971, WV 96 (2005.540)

21

22

Space for Two

1971, WV 98 third state (2005.541)

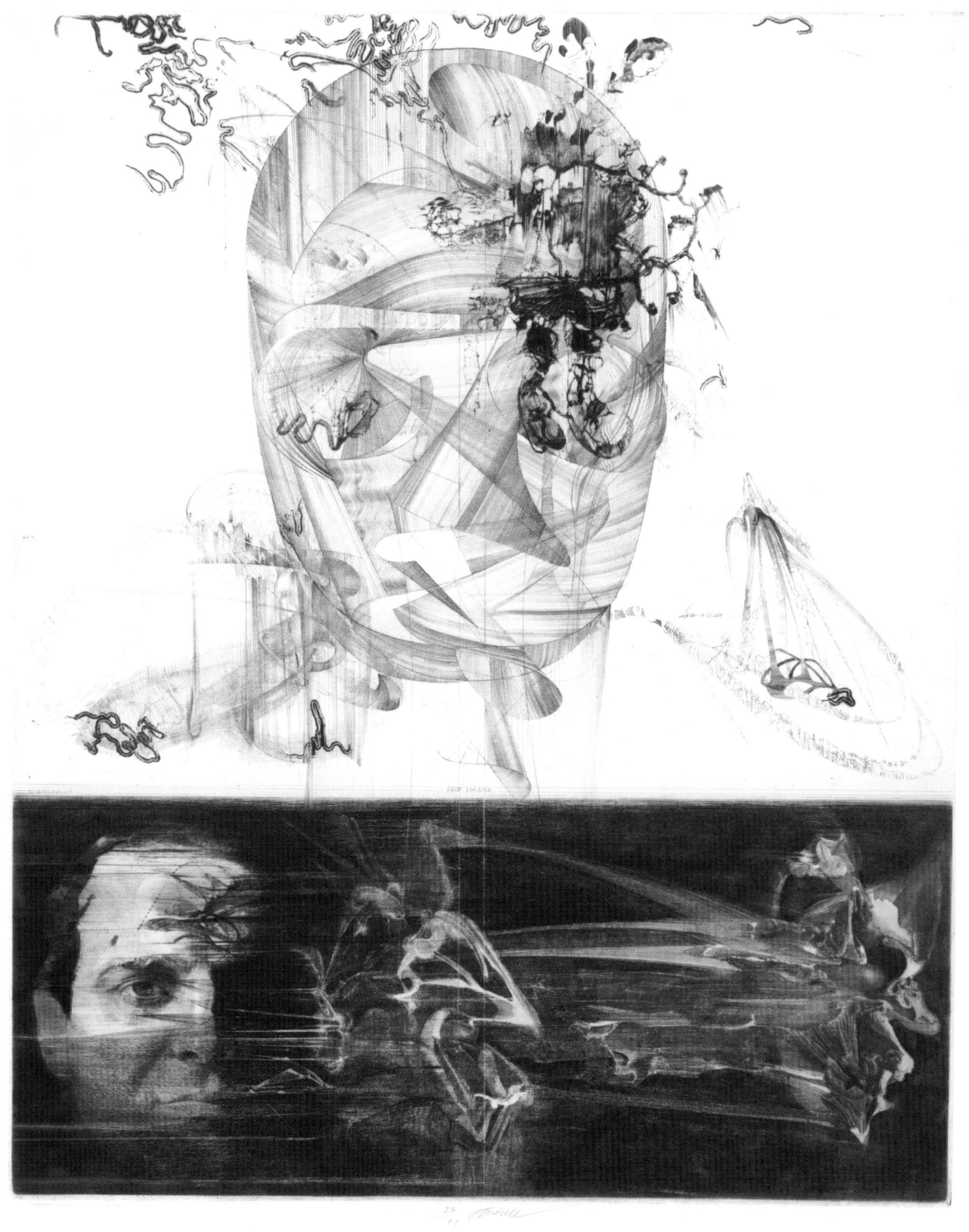

Self Image
1971, WV 99 third state (1986.317)

23

24

Gravitation

1972, WV 104 eighth state (2005.543)

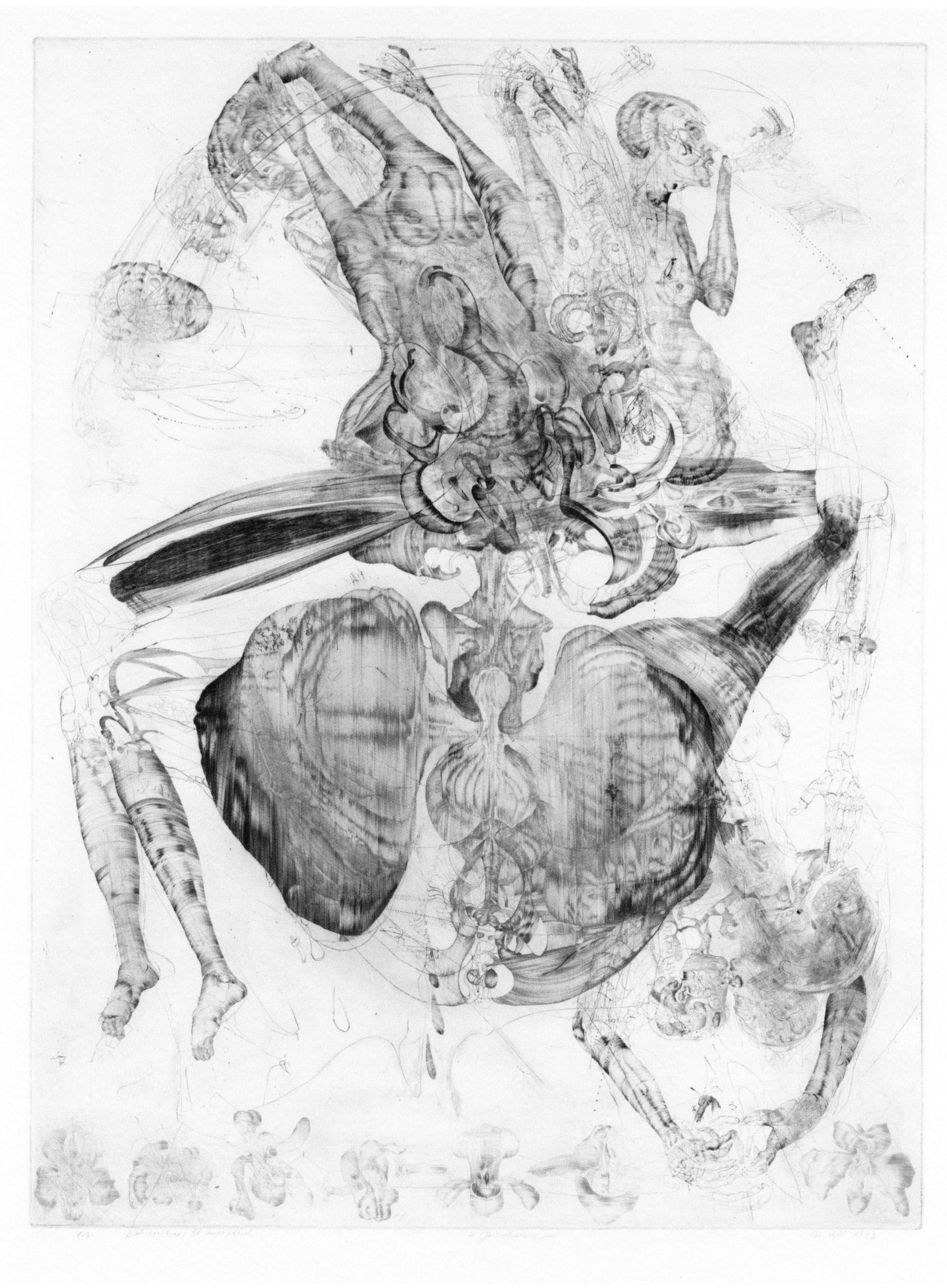

El Motadani
1973, WV 109 (2005.546)

25

26

Game for 122 Persons

1974, WV 112D fourth state (2005.549)

Game for 122 Persons
1974, WV 112 sixth state (2005.548)

27

28 *Cruel Game for a Man*
1975, WV 122 (1976.332)

Appassionata
1977, WV 133 fourth state (2005.560)

29

30 | *Confrontation*
1976, WV 132 (2005.559)

Dialogue with Myself
1975, WV 129 (2005.556)

31

32 | *The Smile*
1976–78, WV 142 proof (2008.18)

The Smile
1976–78, WV 142

33

34 Saskia

1978, WV 145A (2005.565)

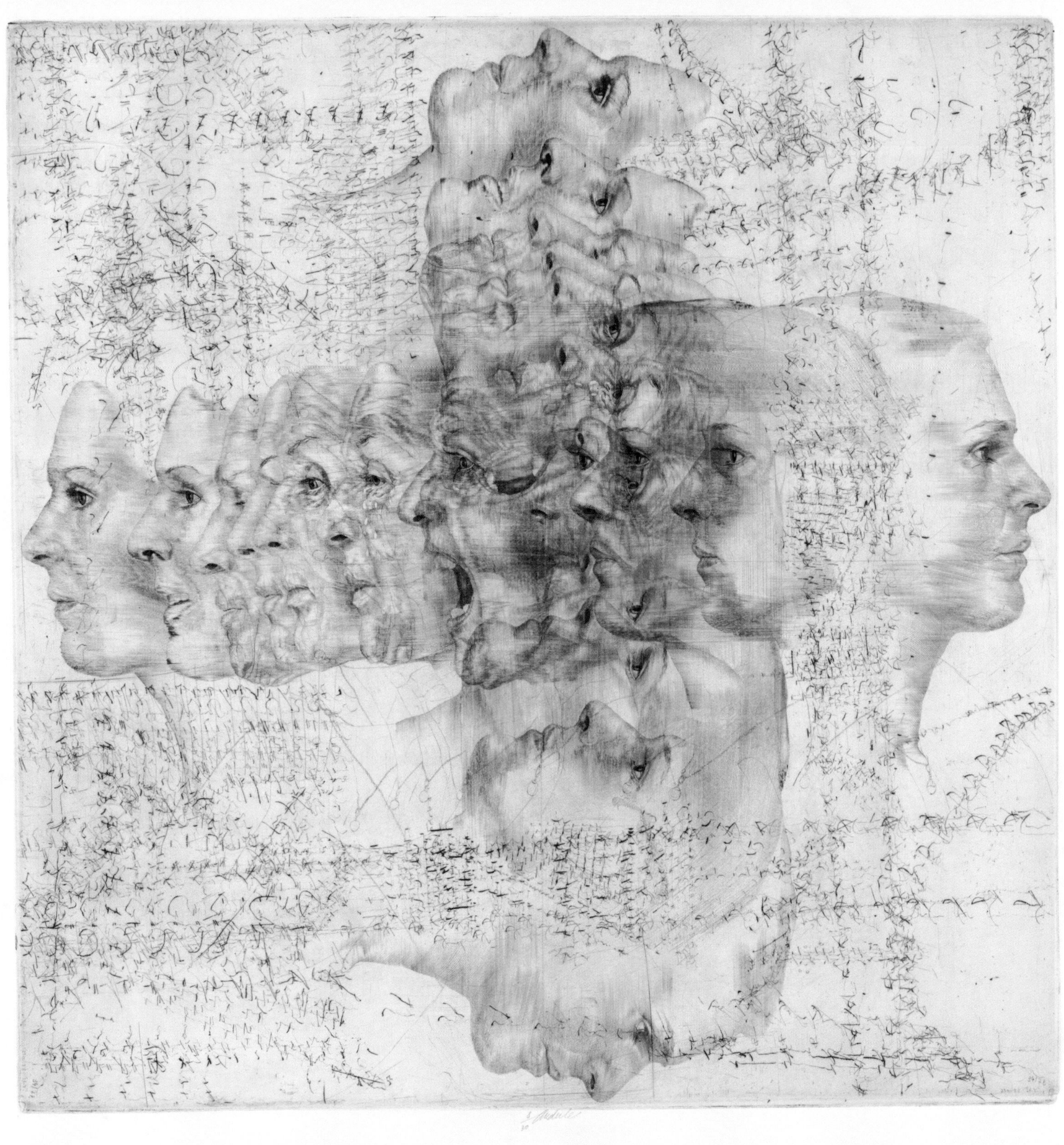

My Wife
1978, WV 148B third state (2005.569)

35

36 | *The Last Spring of My Grandmother*
1979, WV 170 proof (2005.589)

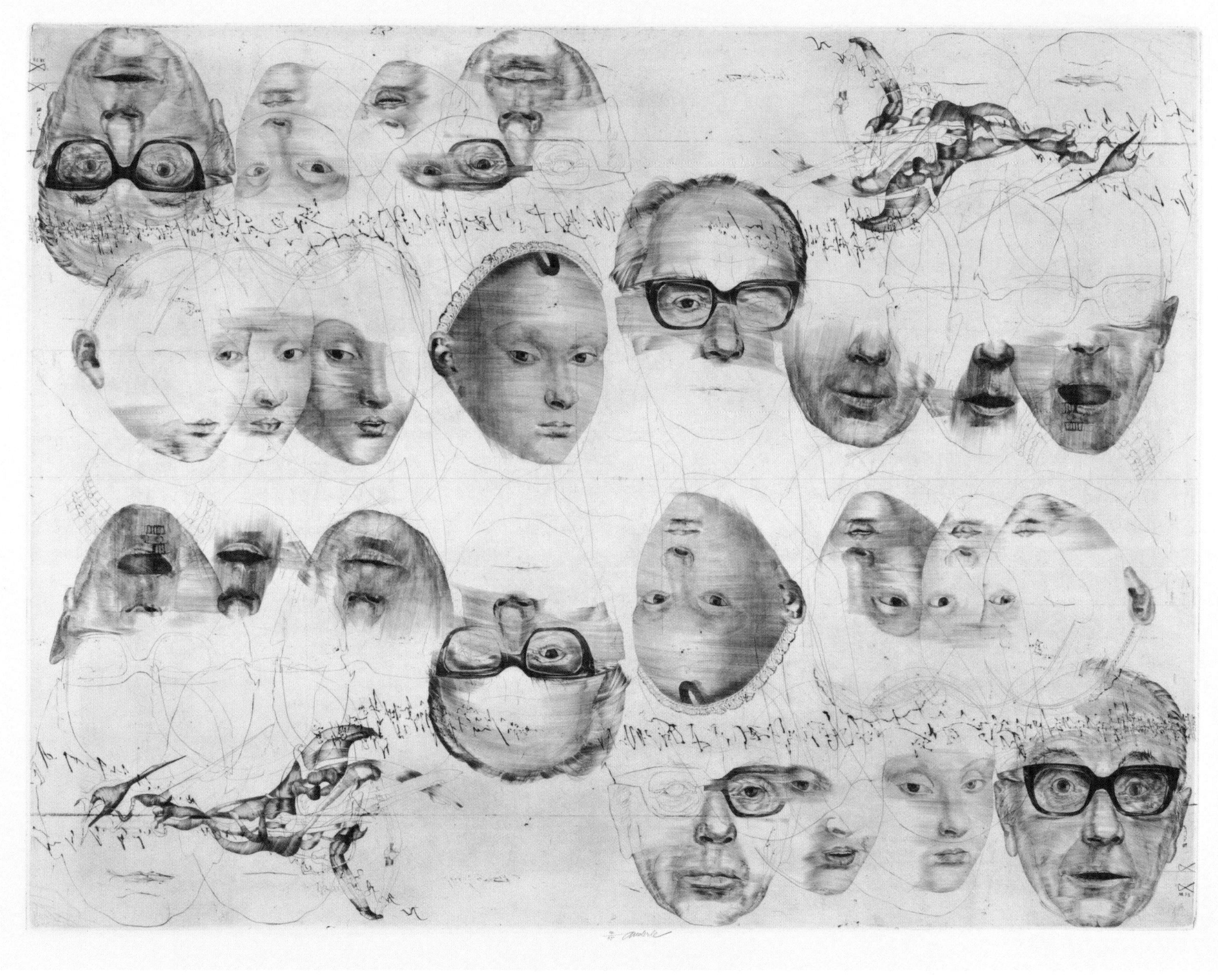

Girl and Man with Spectacles B
1978, WV 150B second state (2005.571)

37

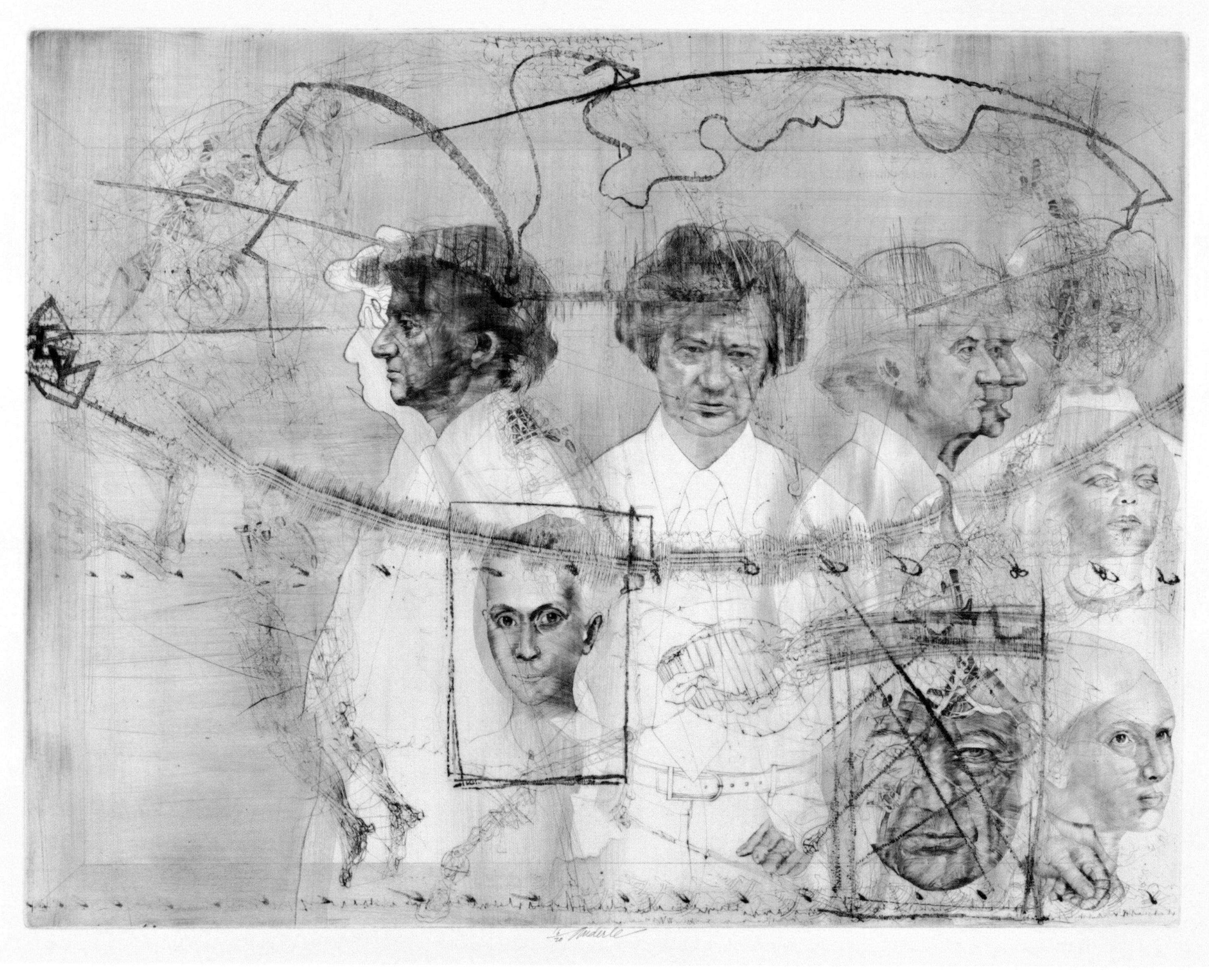

38 *Portrait of My Friend*
1979, WV 159 fifth state (2005.580)

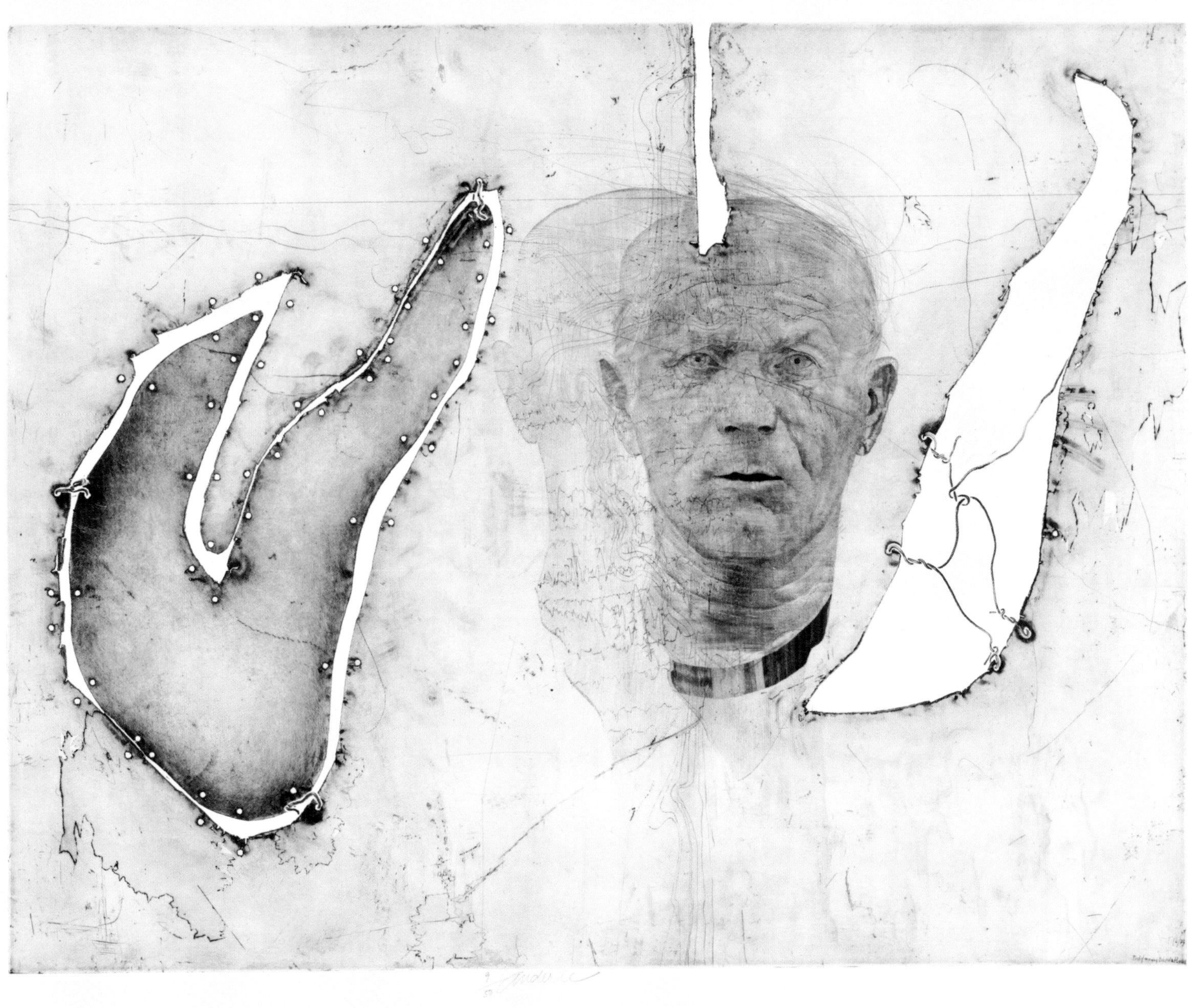

Quiet Monologue of Bohumil Hrabal
1979, WV 162 second state (2005.583)

39

40 *Vibrations of Jan Smetana*
1979, WV 163 (2005.584)

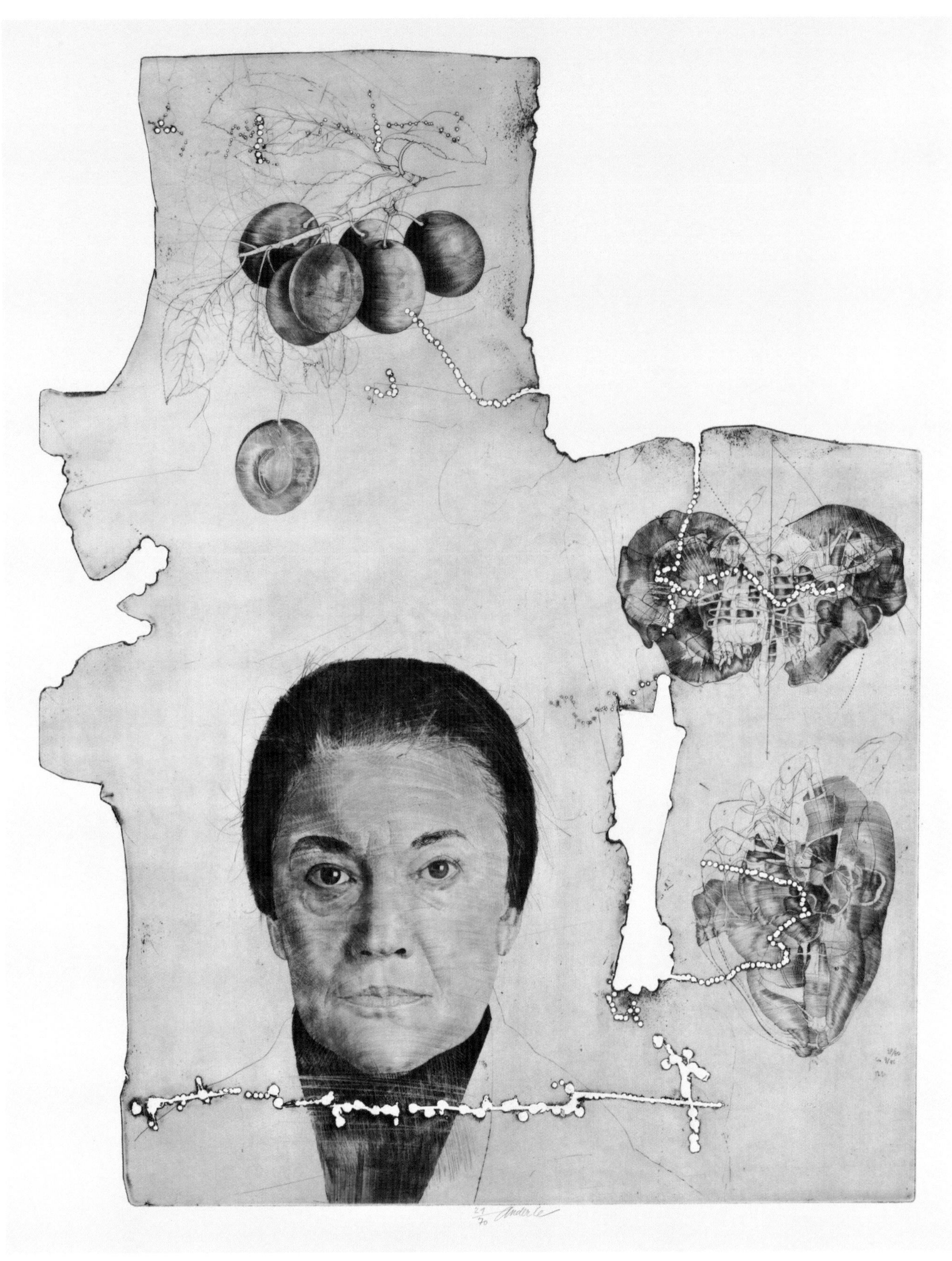

Portrait of Anne B
1980, WV 180 (2005.593)

41

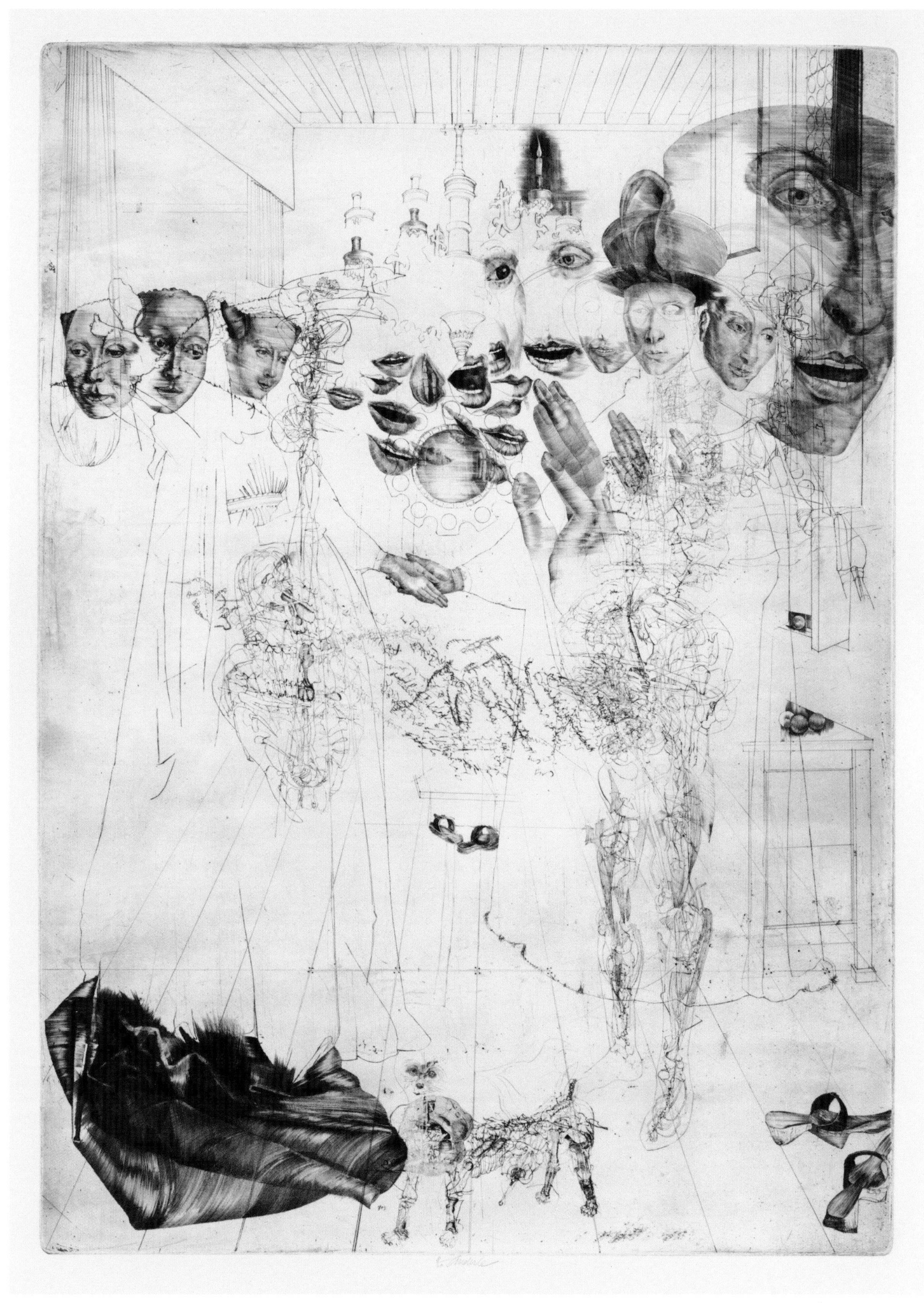

42 | *Arnolfini Portrait*
1978–79, WV 151 (2005.572)

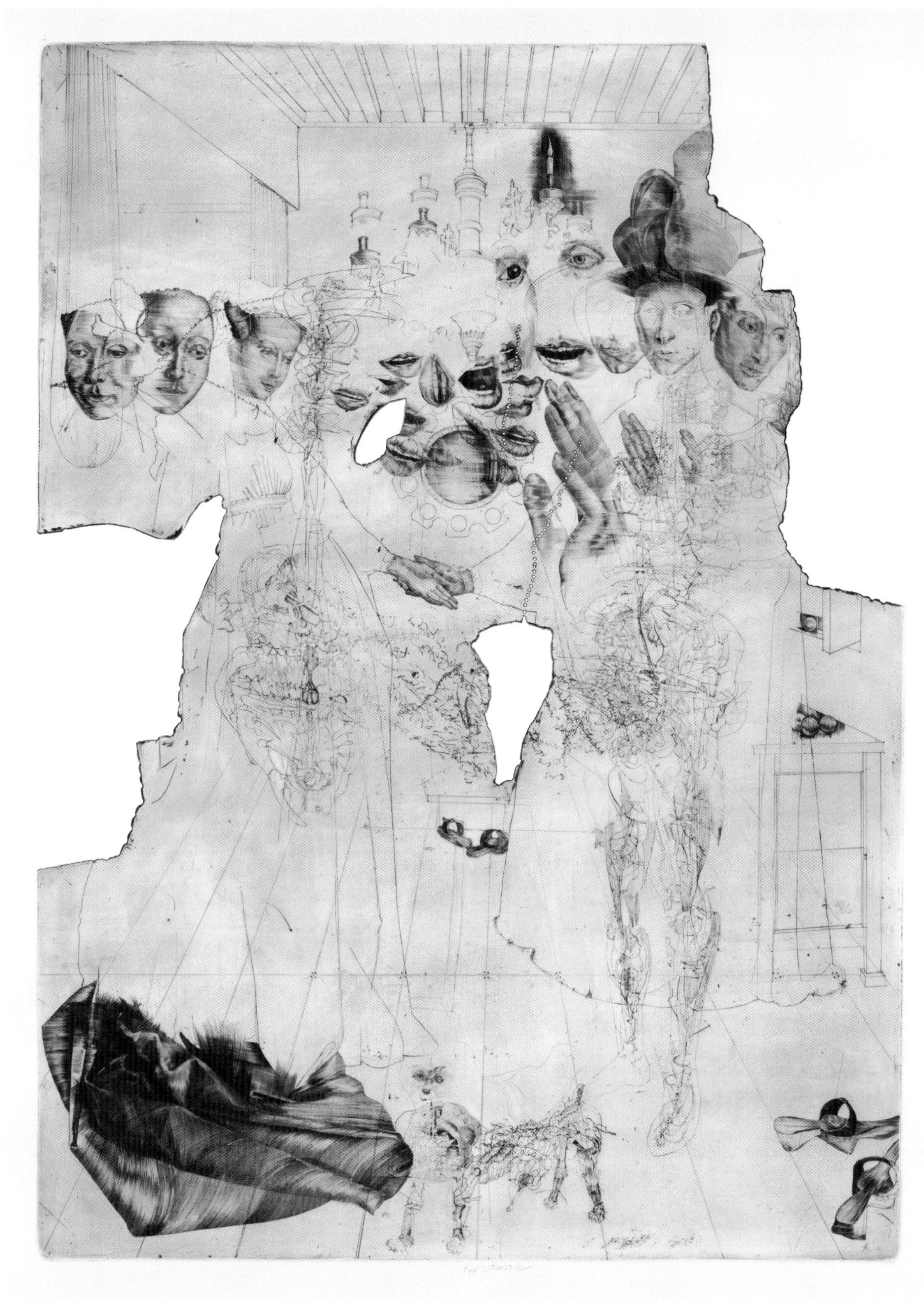

Arnolfini Portrait
1978/79–1981, WV 151 second state (2005.573)

43

44 | *Girl Reading Letter III*
1979, WV 165 third state (2005.585)

The Hazards of the Swing
1978, WV 140 (1986.322)

45

46 | *Woman in Fur*
1978, WV 147 (2005.567)

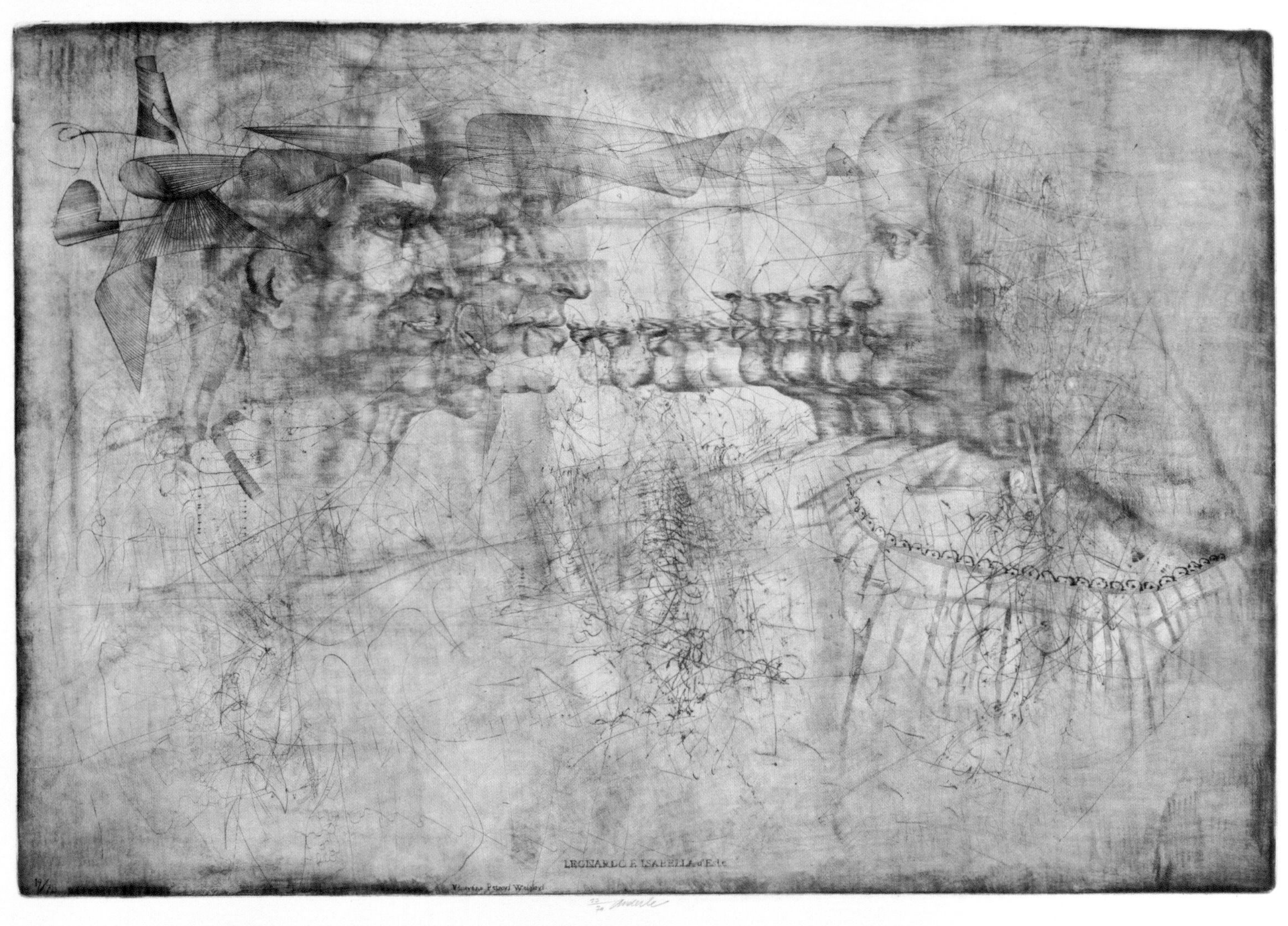

Leonardo and Isabella d'Este
1978, WV 143 (2005.564)

47

48 | *Madame Favart*
1980, WV 188 (2005.598)

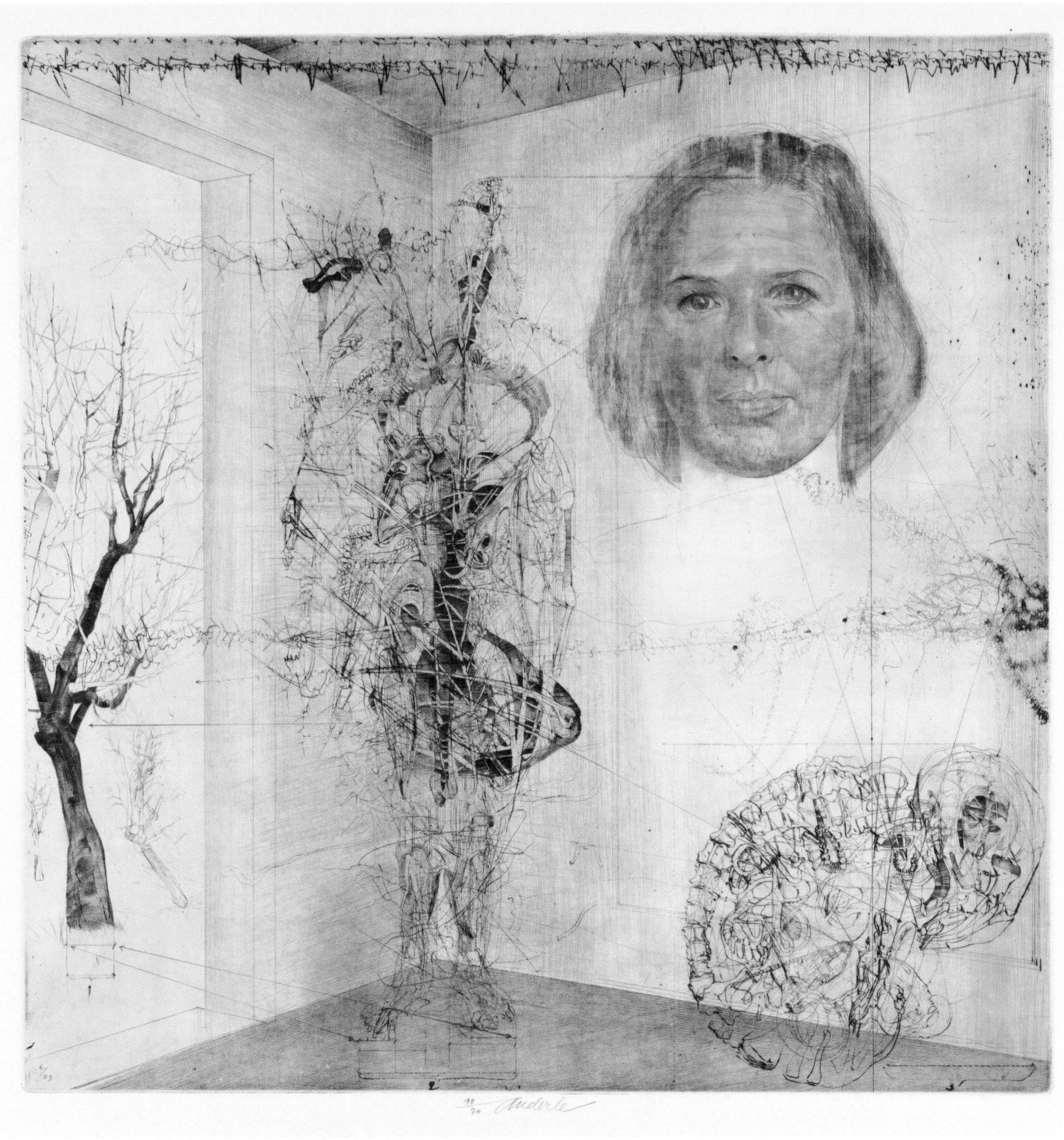

Open Door, Milada
1979, WV 156 (2005.576)

49

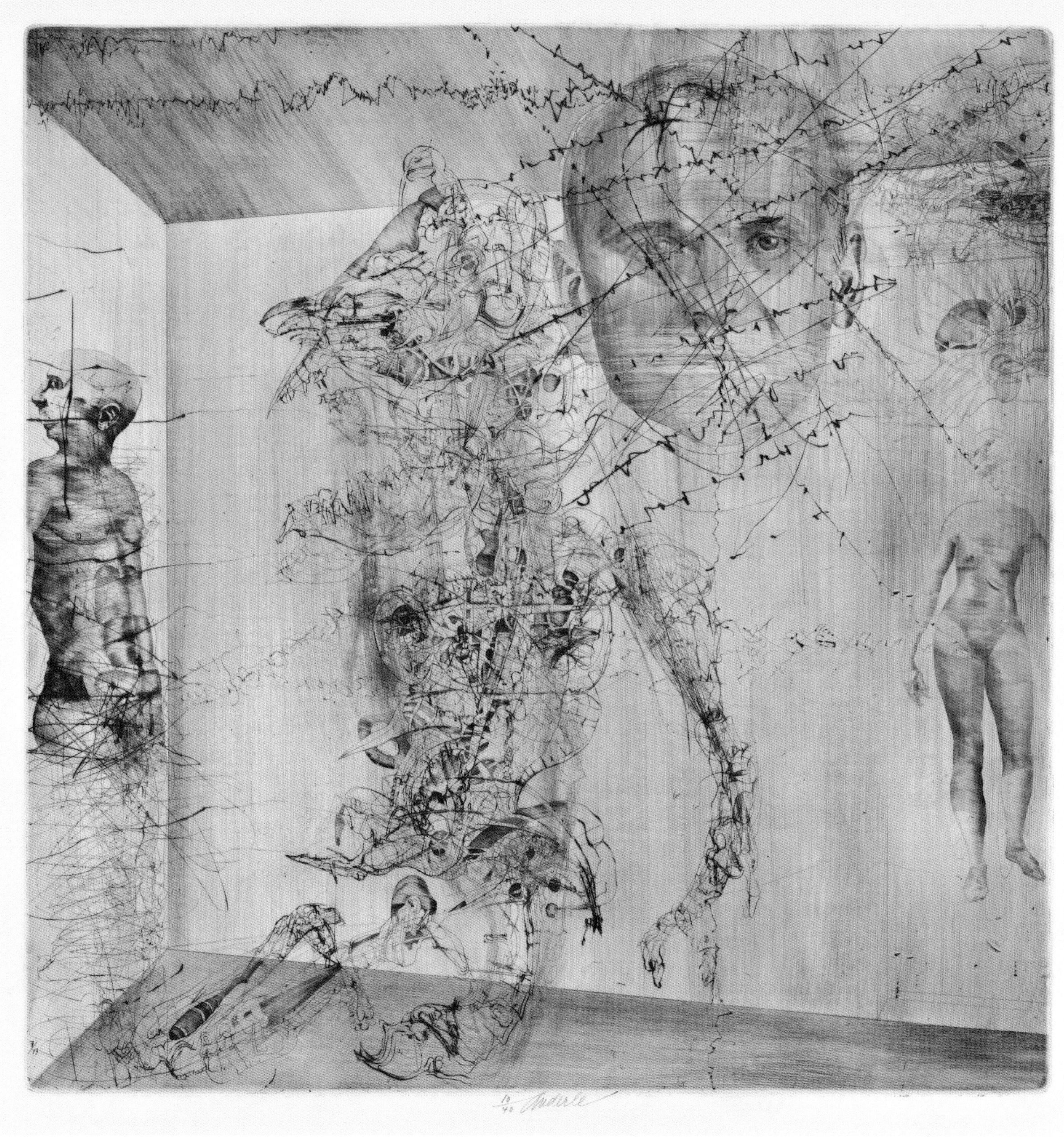

50 *Closed Door, Jiří*

1979, WV 157 third state (2005.577)

Ceiling: After Kafka's Metamorphosis
1979, WV 160 (2005.581)

51

52 *Vox Humana*
1979, WV 168 (2005.586)

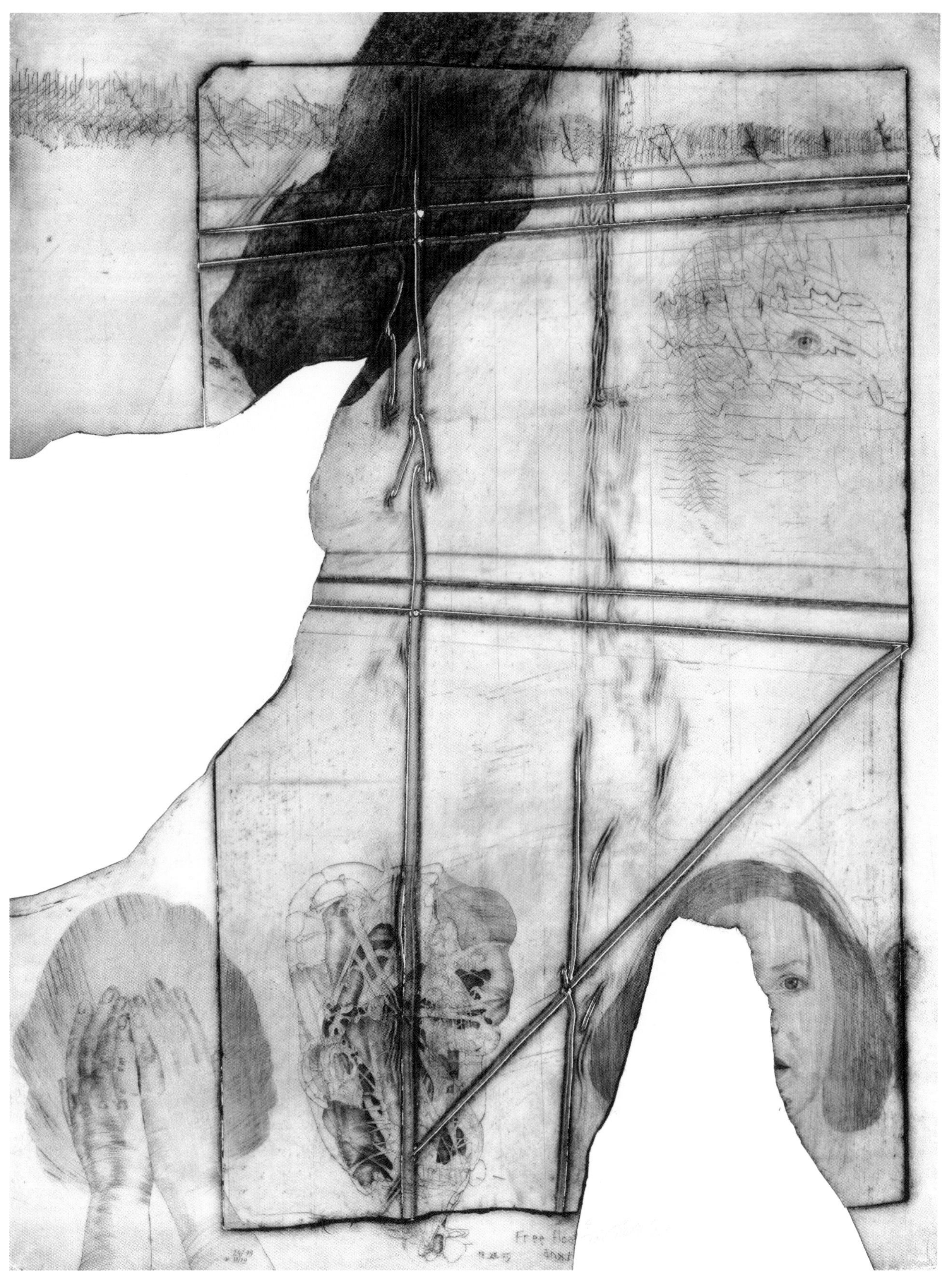

Free Floating Anxiety
1979, WV 169B second state (2005.588)

53

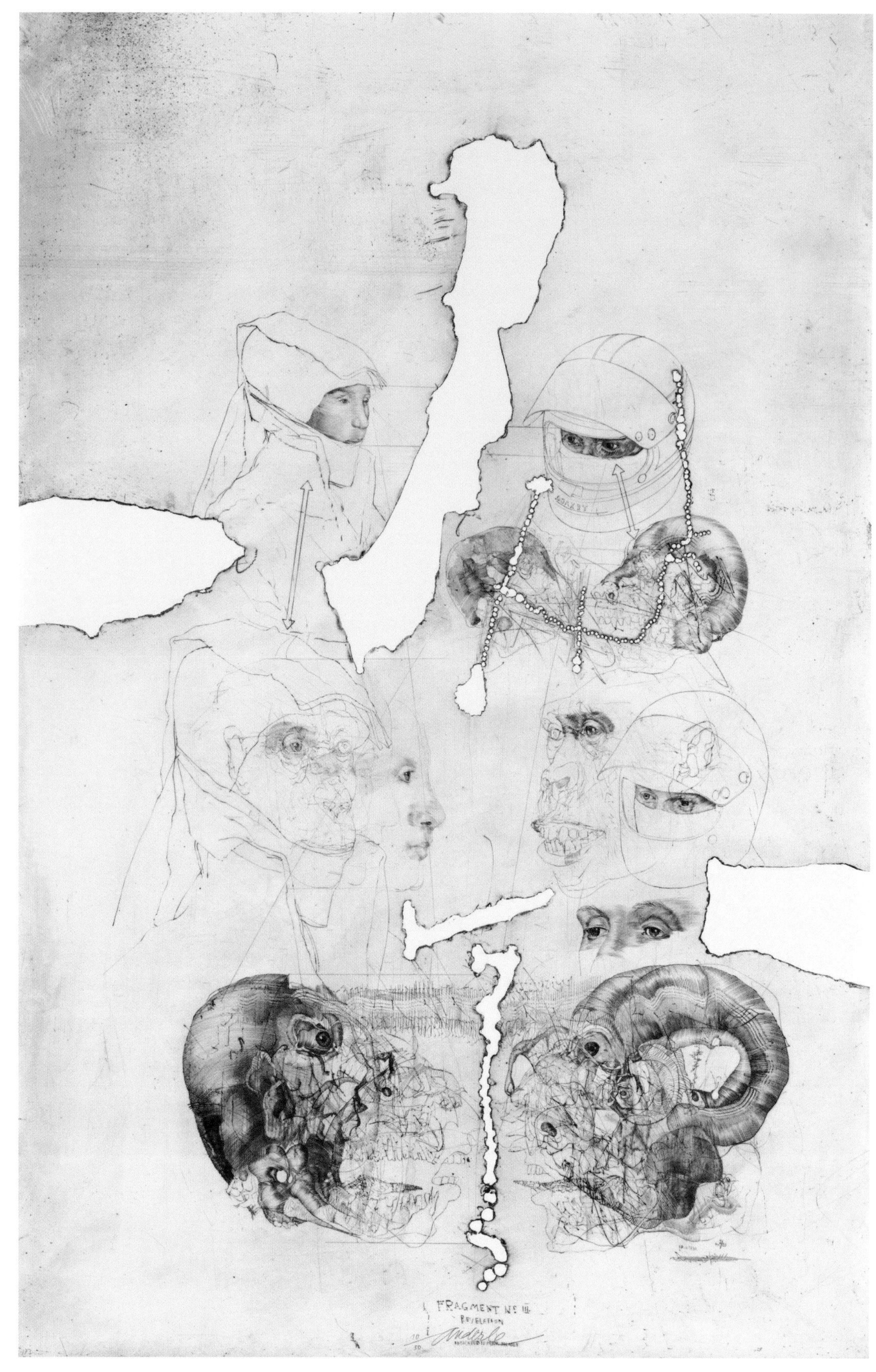

54 *Revelation*
1980, WV 173 (2005.591)

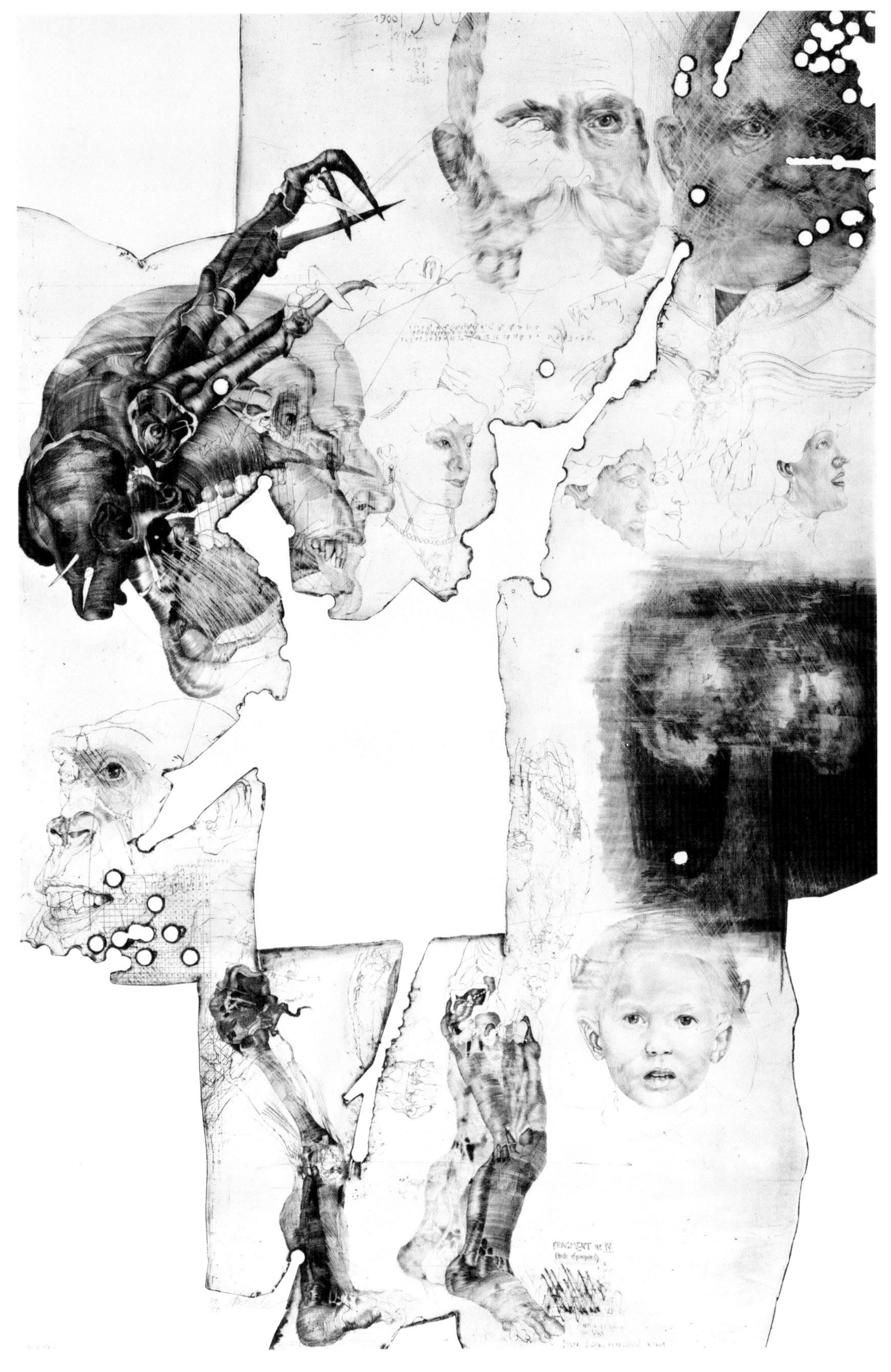

Belle Époque?
1980, WV 176 (1981.233)
55

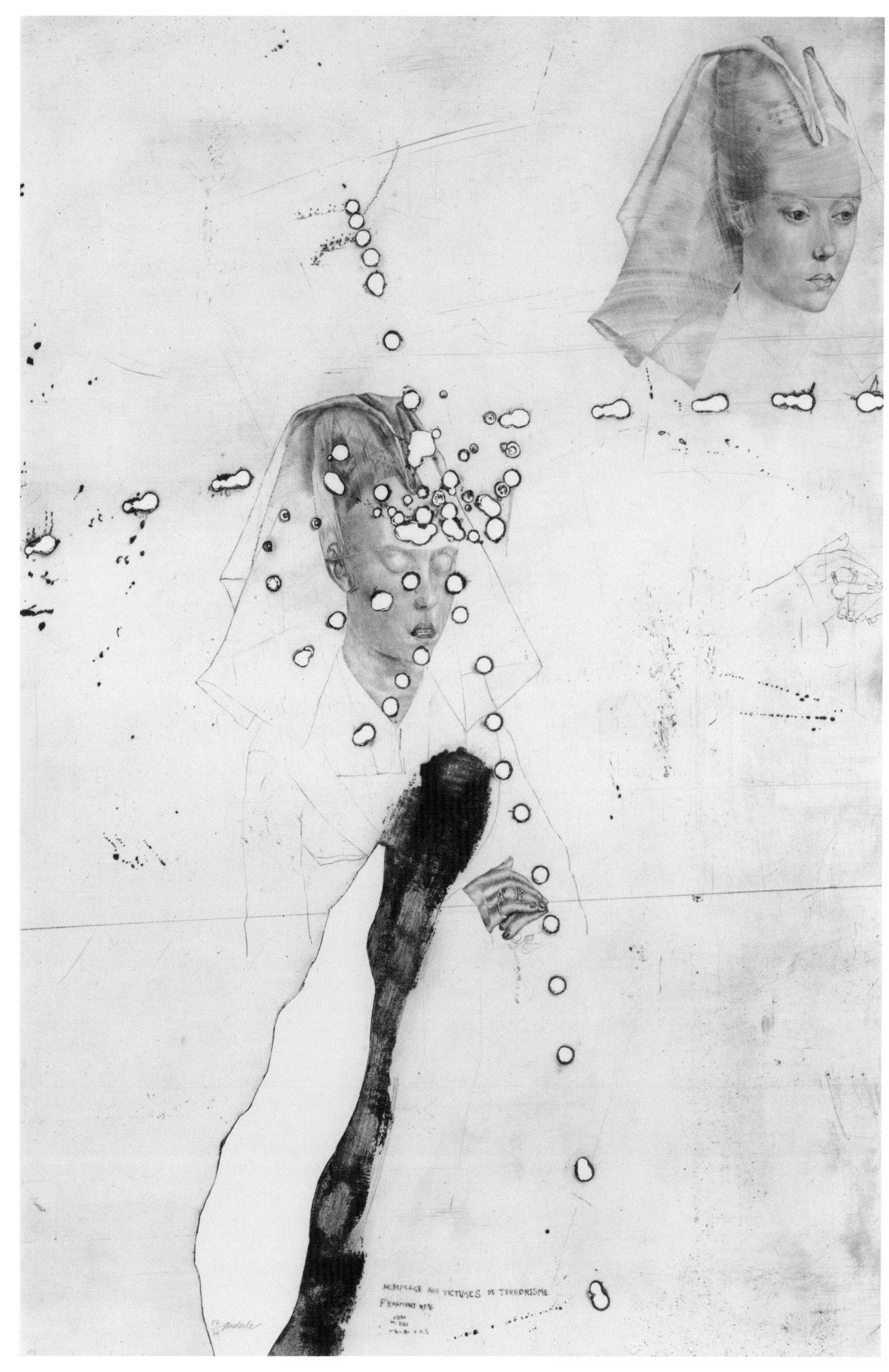

56 *Homage to Victims of Terrorism*
1980, WV 178 (2005.592)

Collioni and Isabella d'Este
1979, WV 171 (2005.590)

57

58 *Salomé*
1980, WV 191 (2005.600)

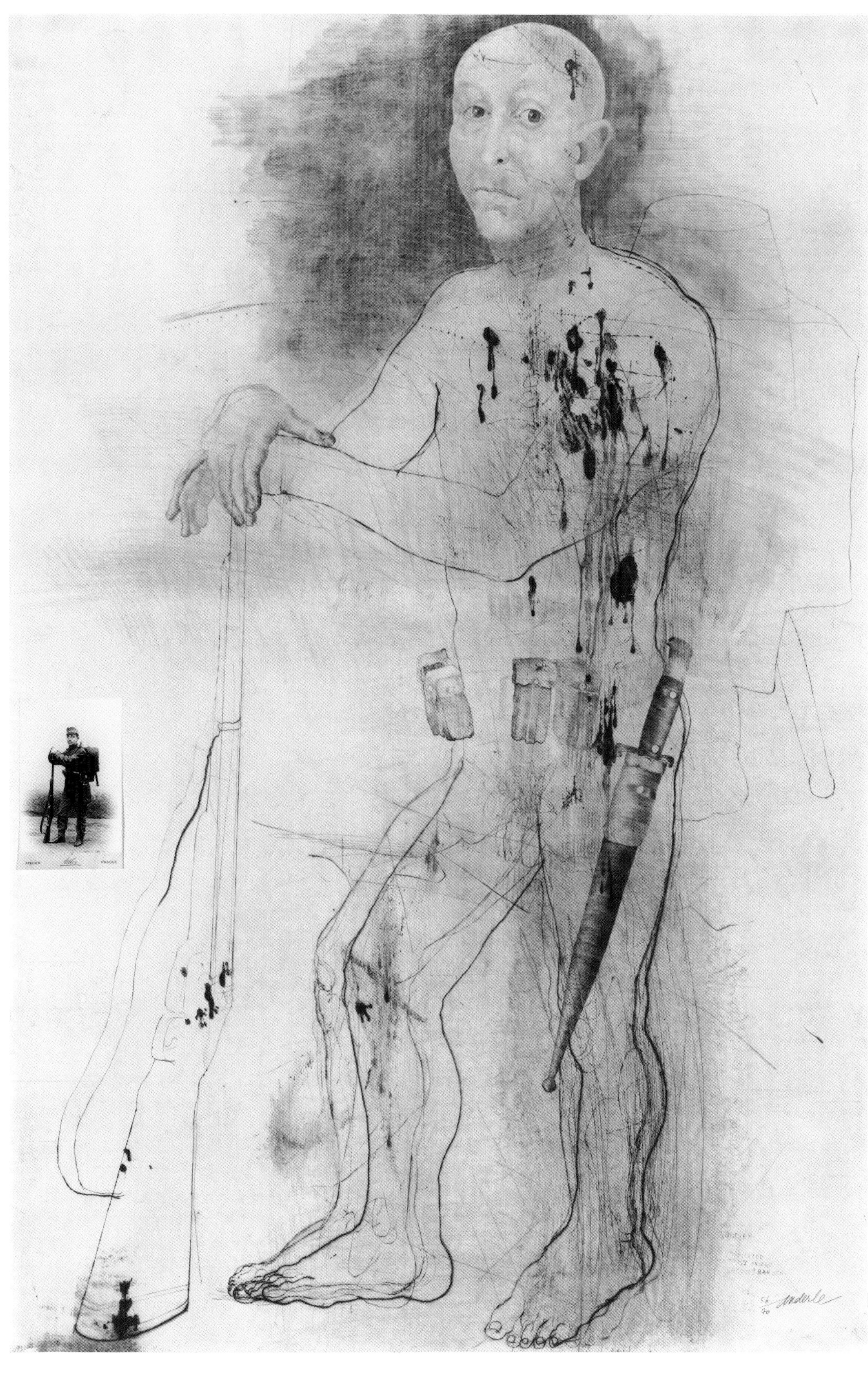

Soldier
1980, WV 183 (1983.251)

59

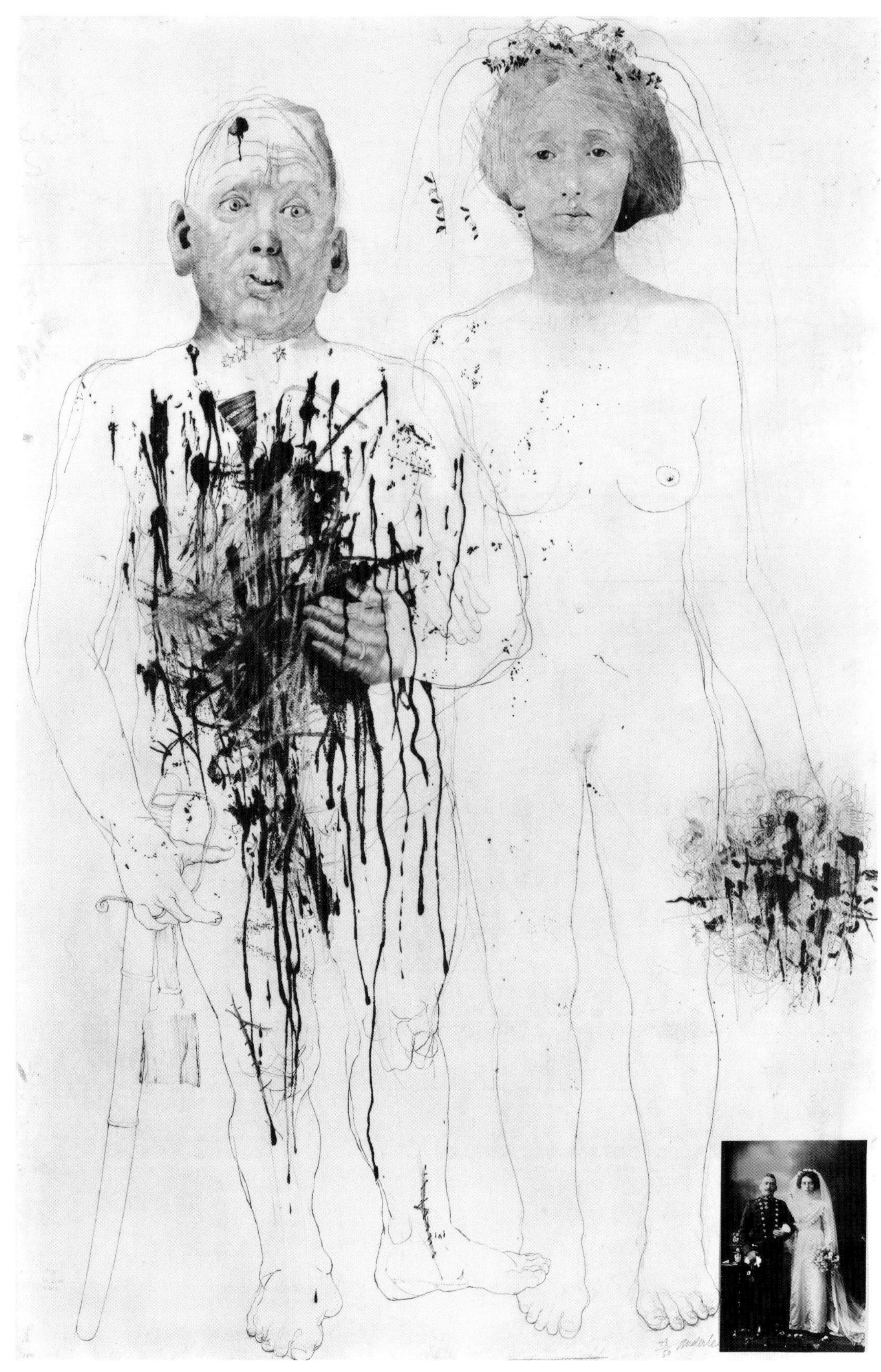

60 | *Soldier and Bride*
1980, WV 184 (2005.594)

Elite (Kaiser and Crown Prince)
1981, WV 192 (2005.120)

61

62 *Pan, Syrinx, and Old Woman*

1981, WV 193 second state (2005.121)

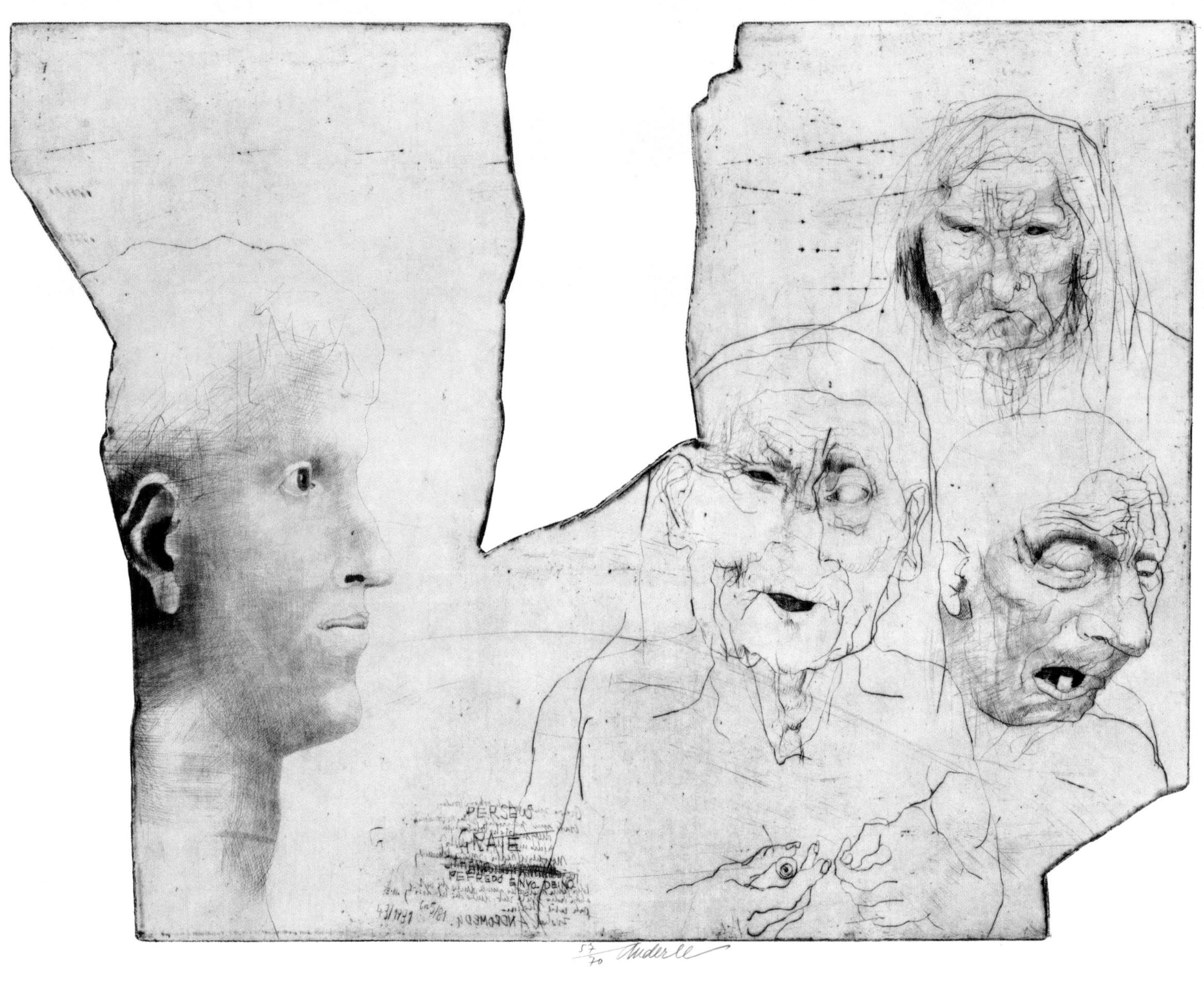

Perseus and the Graeae
1981, WV 196 second state (2005.124)

63

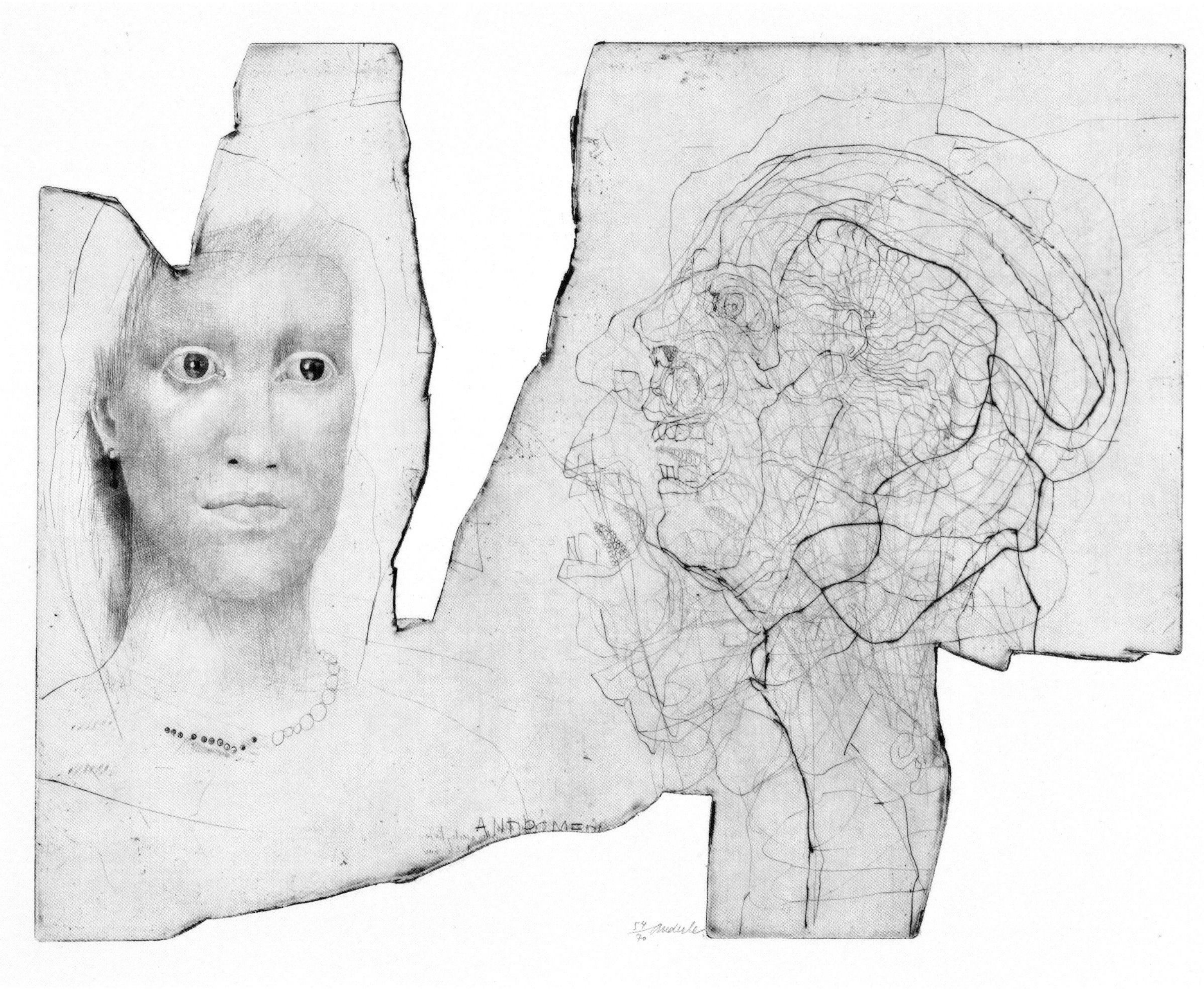

64 *Andromeda and Medusa*
1981, WV 195 second state (2005.123)

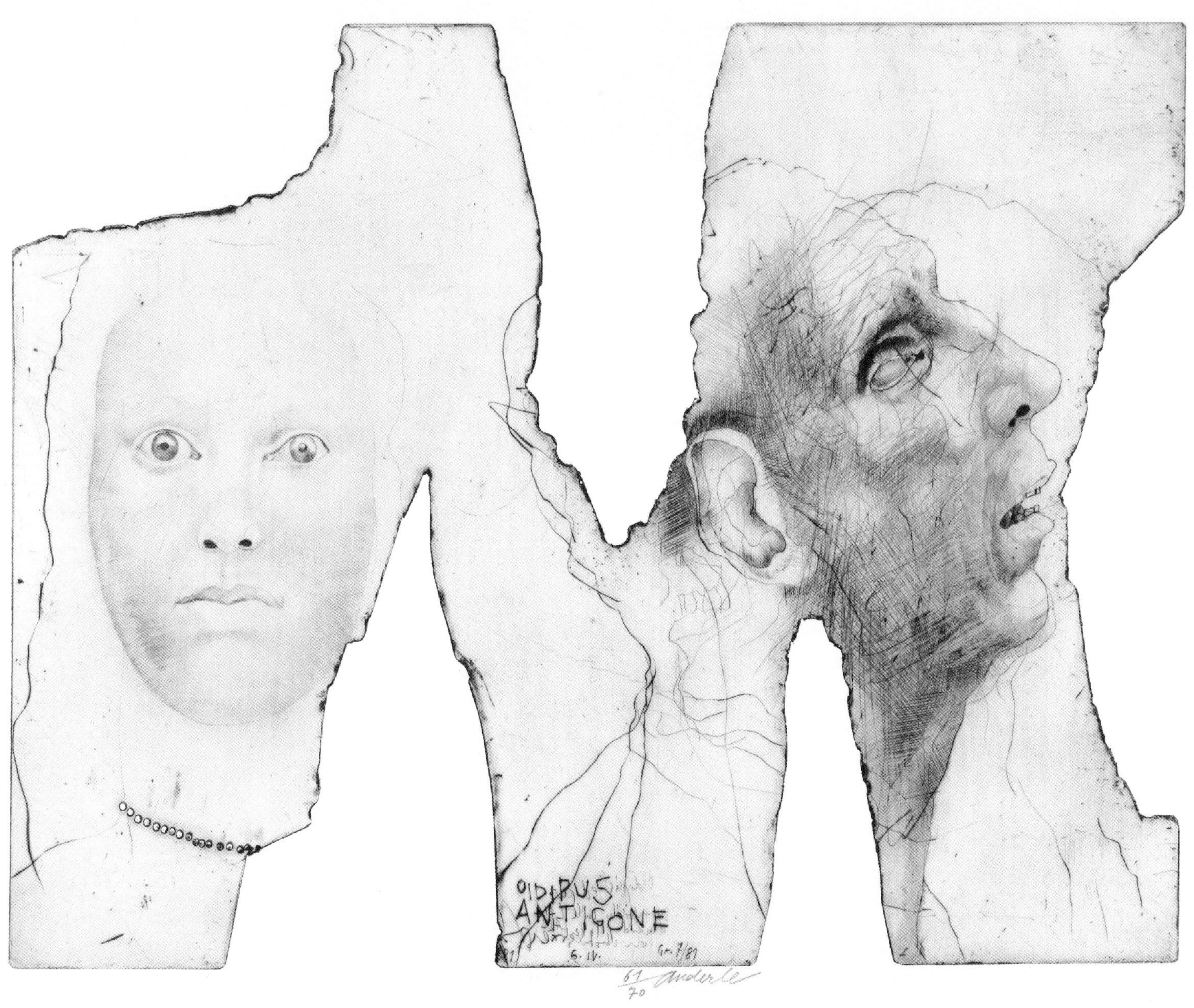

Oedipus and Antigone
1981, WV 198 second state (2005.126)

65

66 | *Ecce Homo*
1982, WV 236 (2005.149)

Riders of the Apocalypse: Death, Hunger, War, and Pestilence

1982, WV 237 (2005.150)

67

68 *Fortuna*

1984, WV 294 (2005.183)

Promenade – Lovers and Death
1982, WV 221 (2005.138)

69

70 *Simonetta Vespucci*
1982, WV 207 third state (2005.128)

Diana of Poitiers
1982, WV 222 (2005.139)
71

72 *Taste*
1983, WV 245 (2005.154)

Touch
1983, WV 241 (2005.152)

73

74 *Sight*
1983, WV 243 (2005.153)

Sight
1983 (2005.209)

75

76 | *Bacchus*
1982, WV 230 second state (2005.146)

Boy Bitten by a Lizard
1982, WV 233 (2005.148)

77

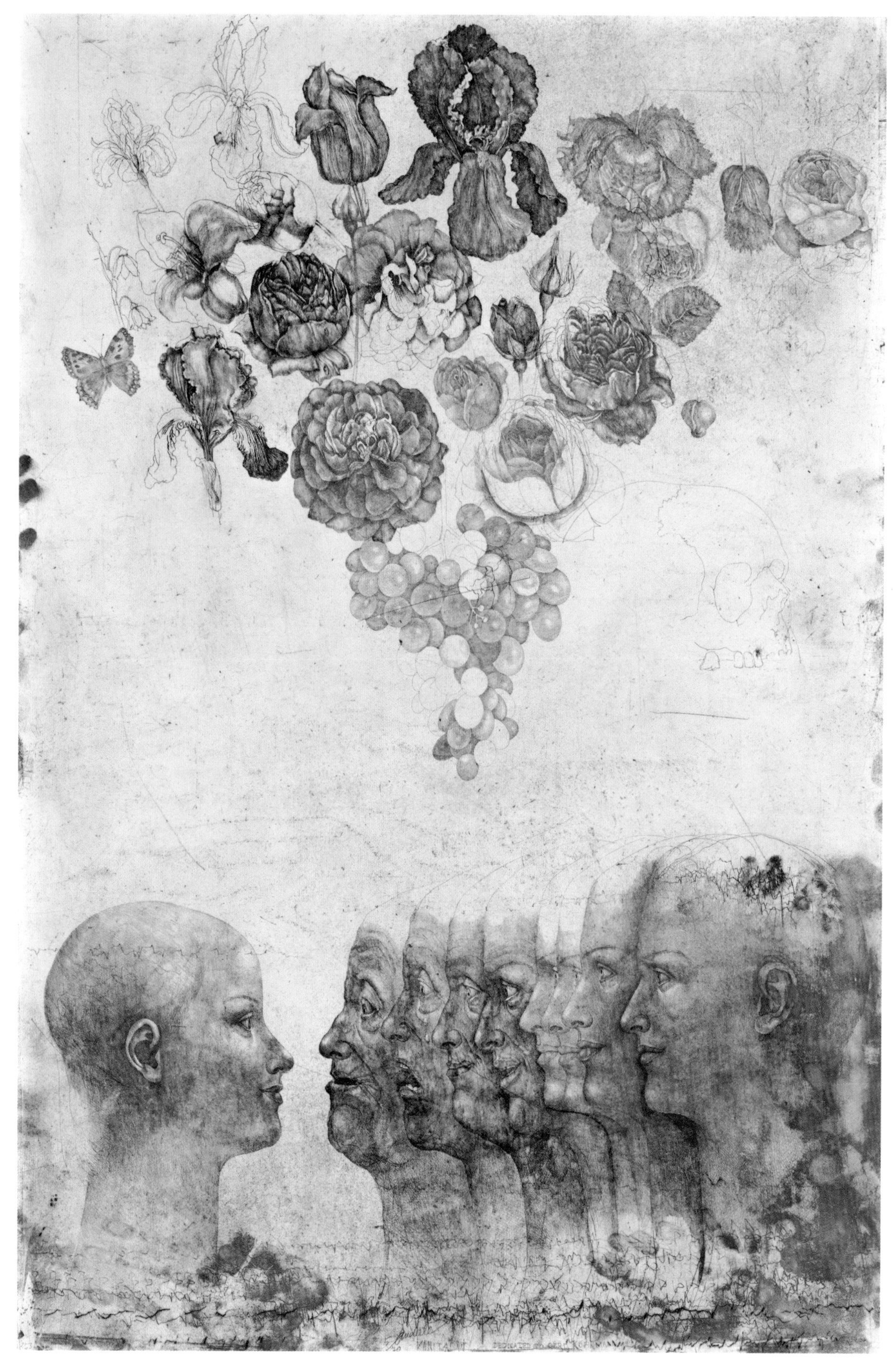

78 *Vanitas VI*
1983, WV 253 second state (2005.159)

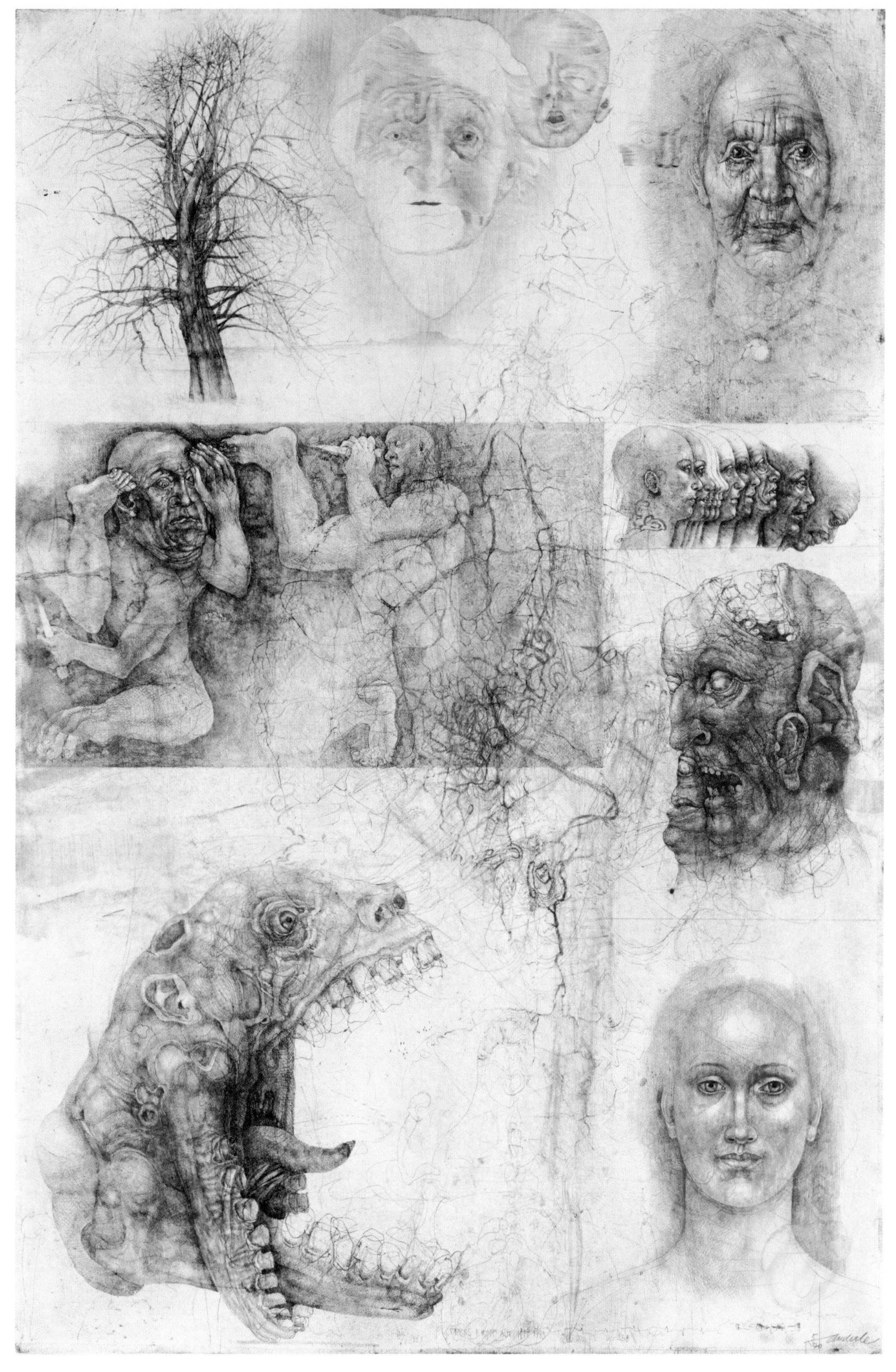

Beware of Asking What Tomorrow May Bring I
1983, WV 258 (2005.160)

79

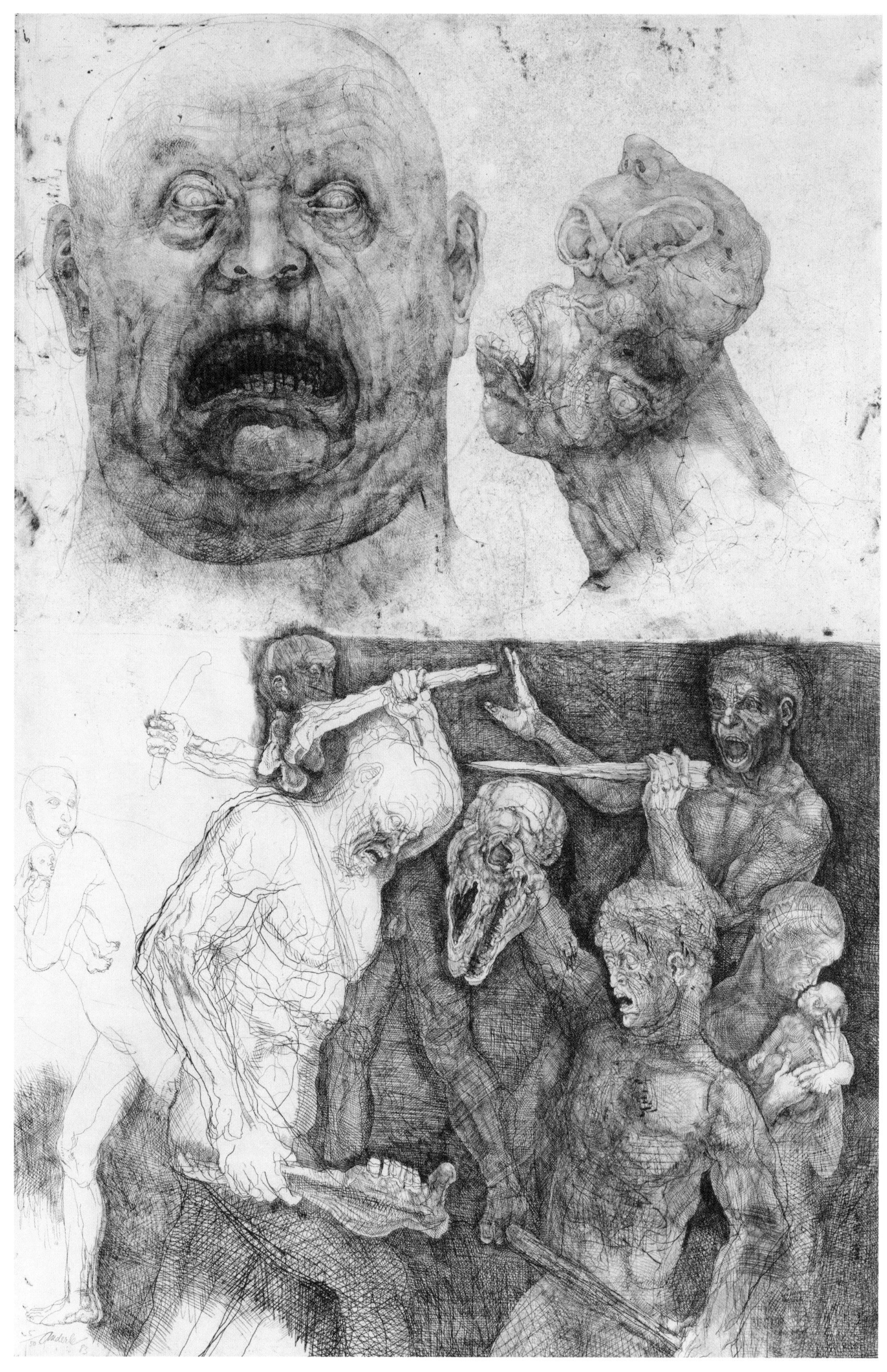

80 | *Remember That You Are Human! I*
1983, WV 261 (2005.161)

Triumphant Beast III
1984, WV 274 second state (2005.171)

81

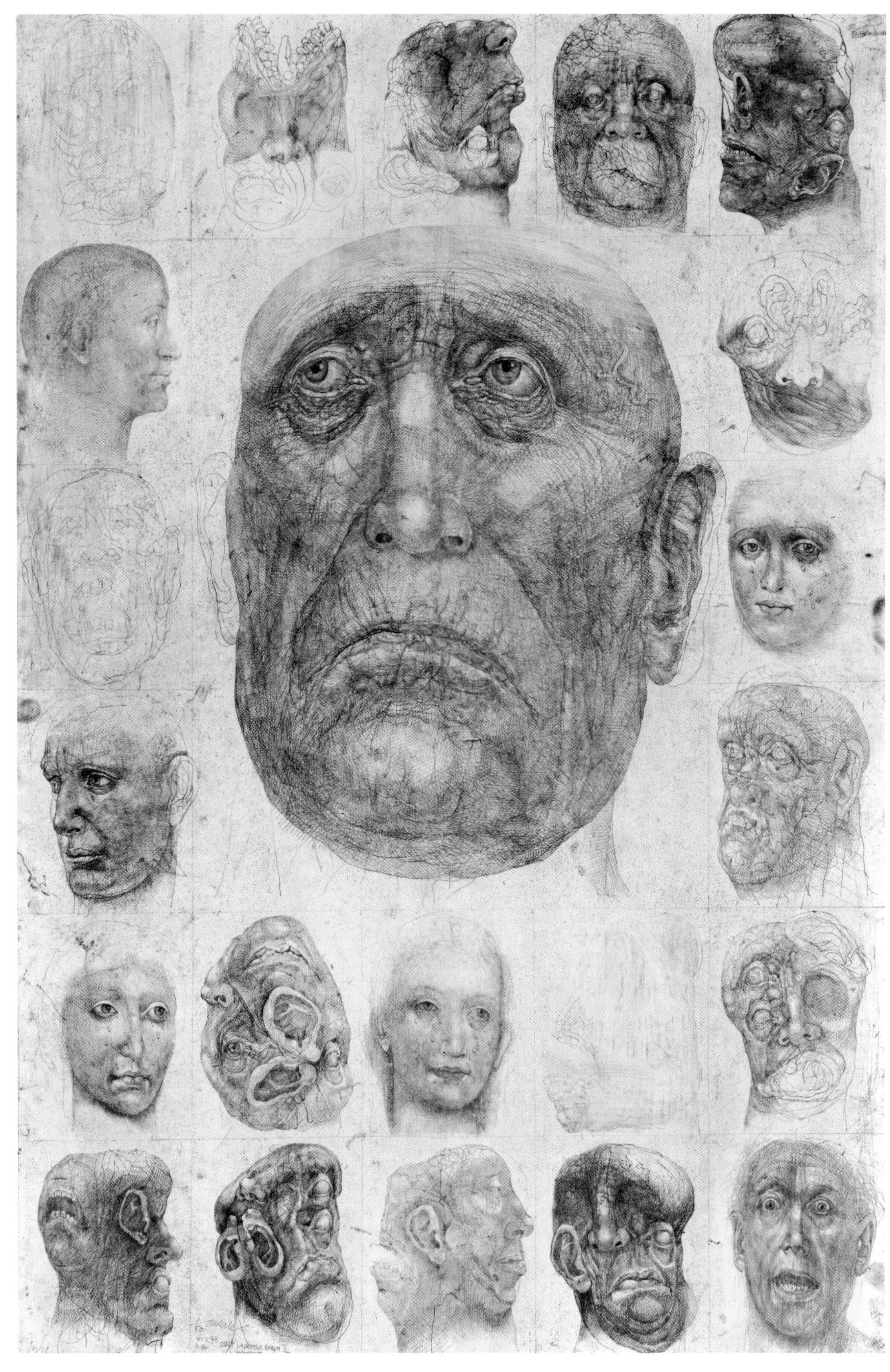

82 *And Now Only Tears II – Emperor*
1984, WV 278 (2005.173)

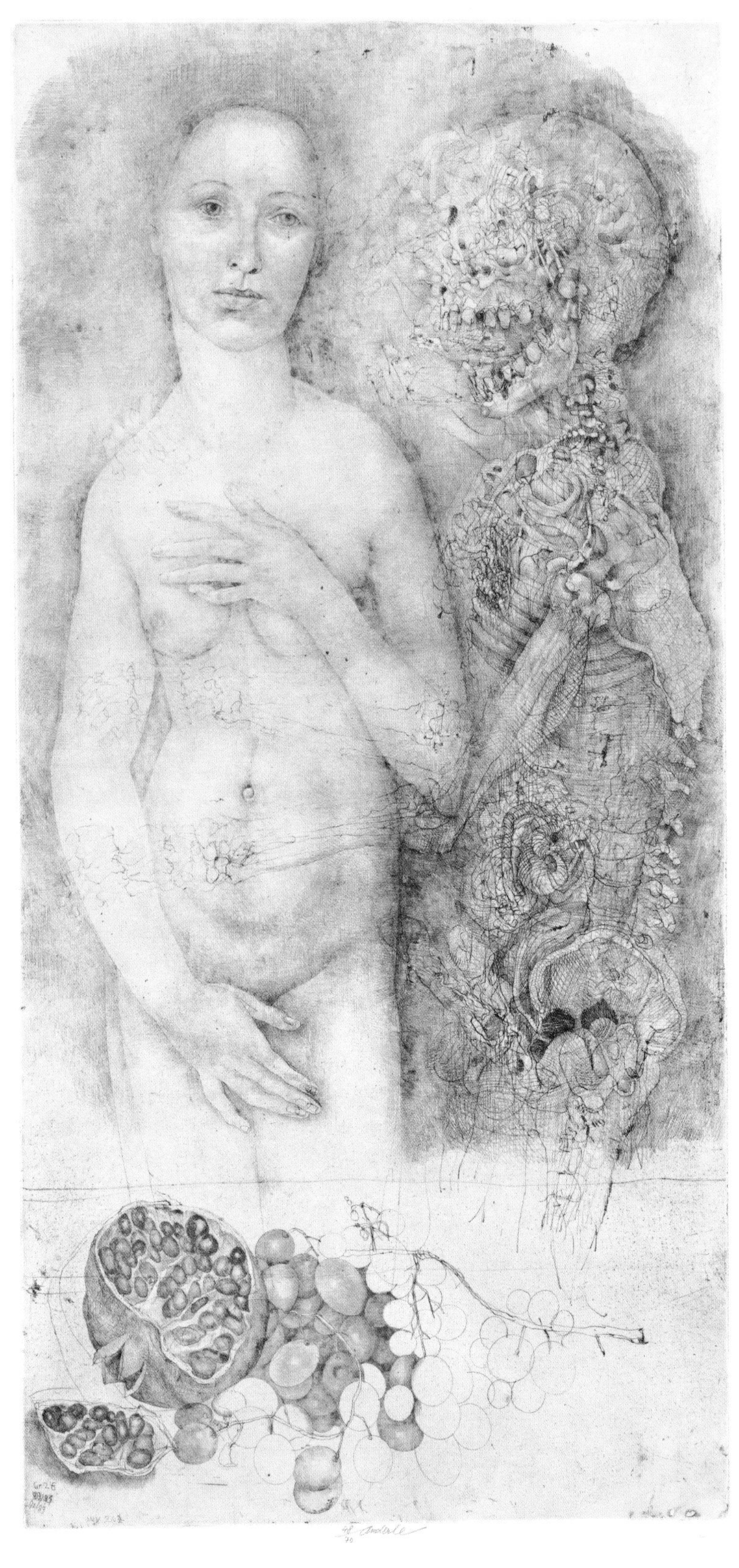

Girl and Death
1983, WV 264 (2005.164)

83

84 | *Carpe diem, carpe noctem I*
1984, WV 281 (2005.175)

Head of Athena
1984, WV 284 (2005.176)

85

86 | *Sick Bacchus*
1984, WV 285 second state (2005.177)

Rembrandt and Saskia
1984, WV 287 (2005.178)

87

88 *Dürer and Raphael*
1984, WV 289 (2005.179)

The Three Duchesses
1985, WV 293 (2005.182)

89

90 *Goodbye*

1985, WV 309 (2005.188)

Non omnium dierum sol occidit
1985, WV 341 (2005.193)

91

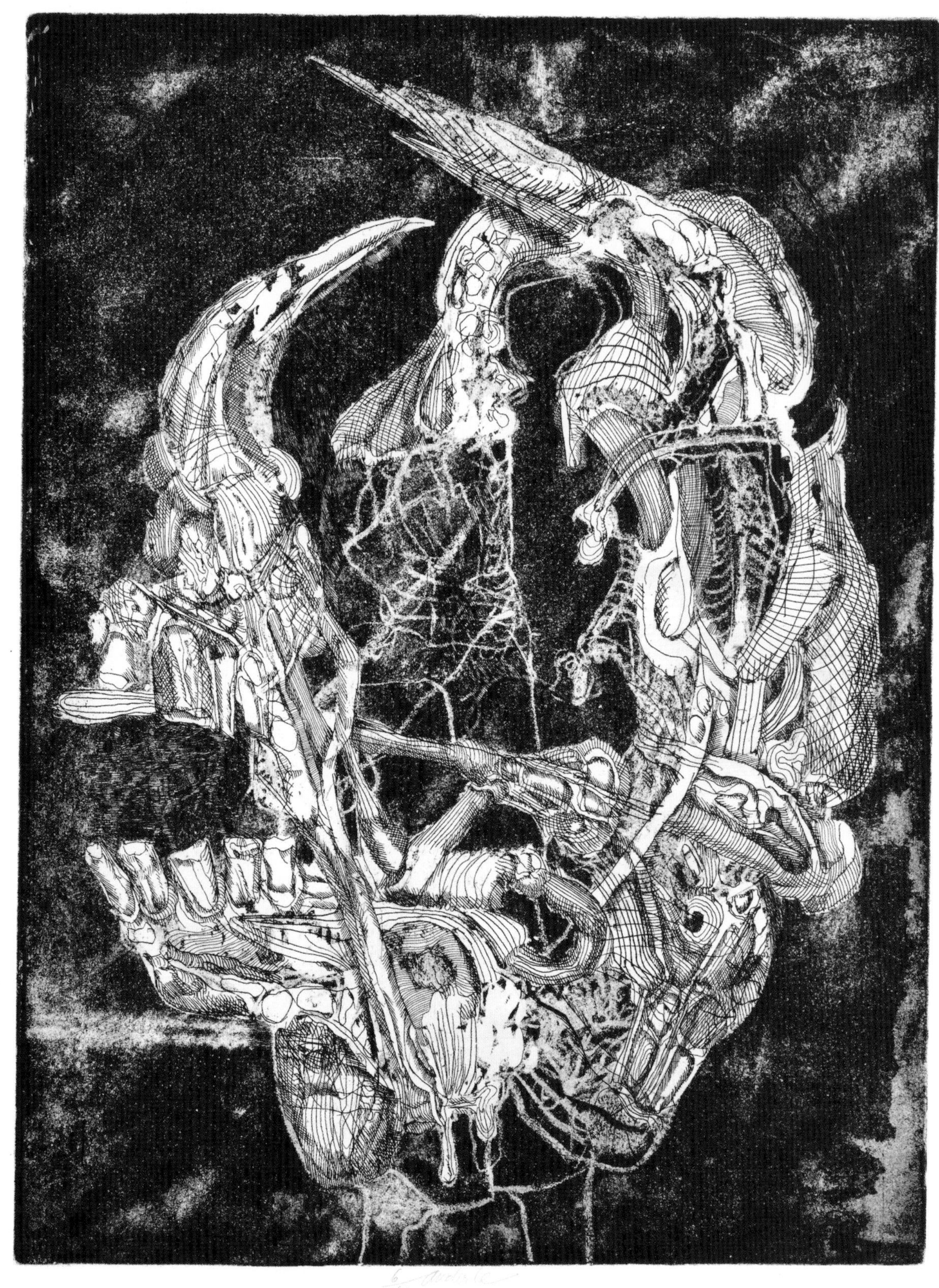

92 | *Jester's Head I – Full Face*
1985, WV 321 (2005.190)

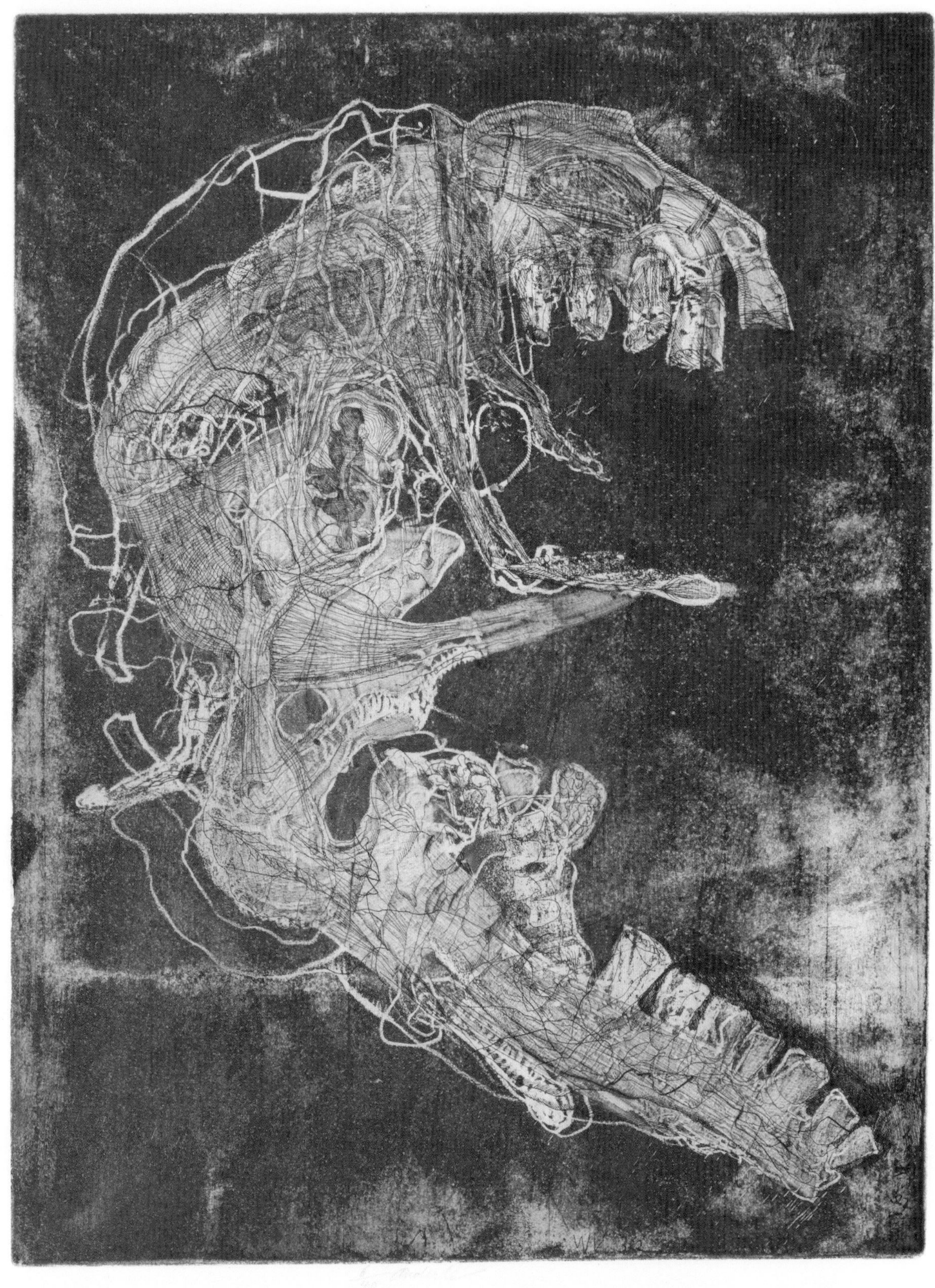

Jester's Head II – Profile
1985, WV 322 (2005.191)

93

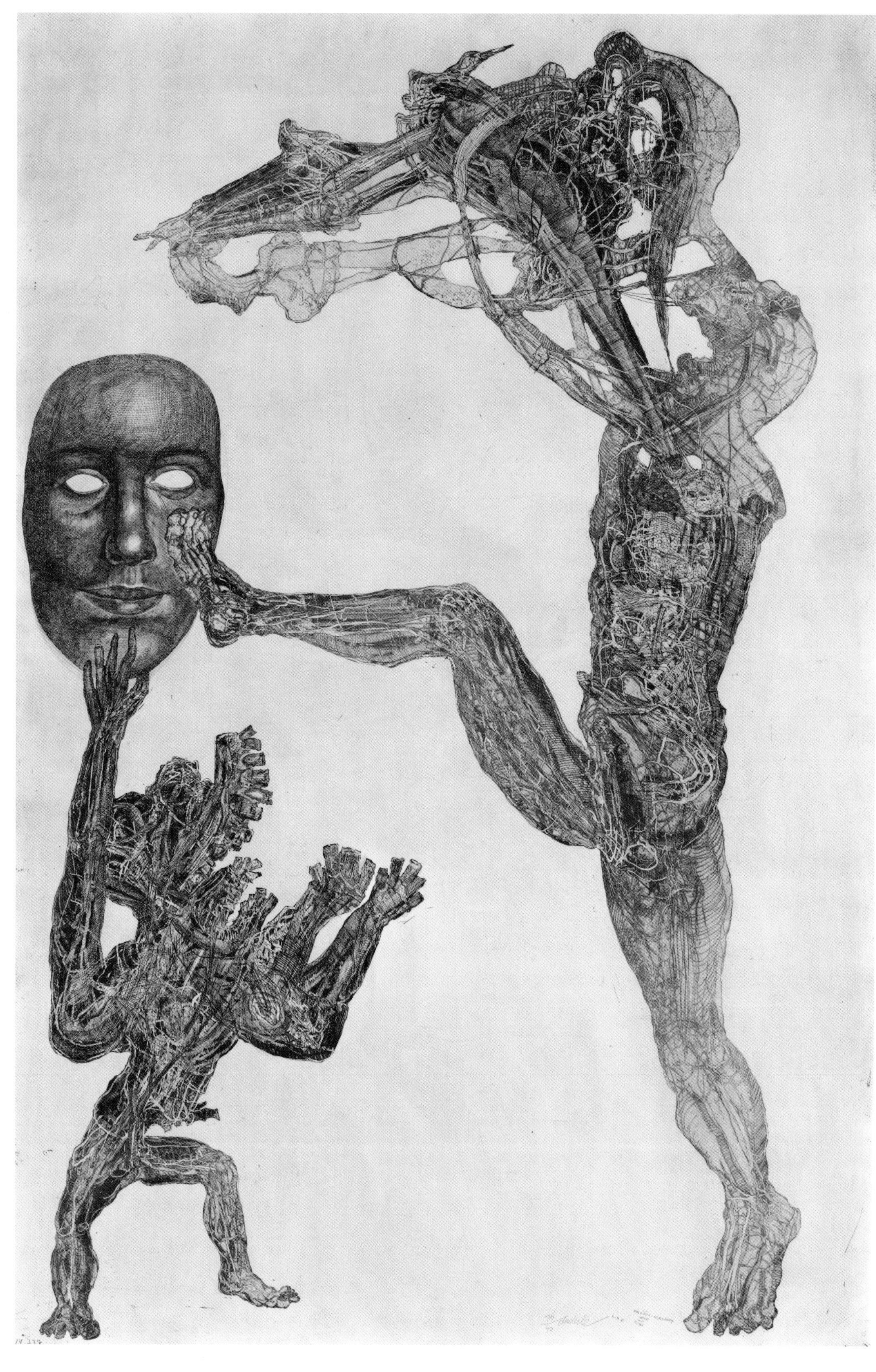

94 | *The King and Jester with Beautiful Mask*
1985, WV 337 (2005.192)

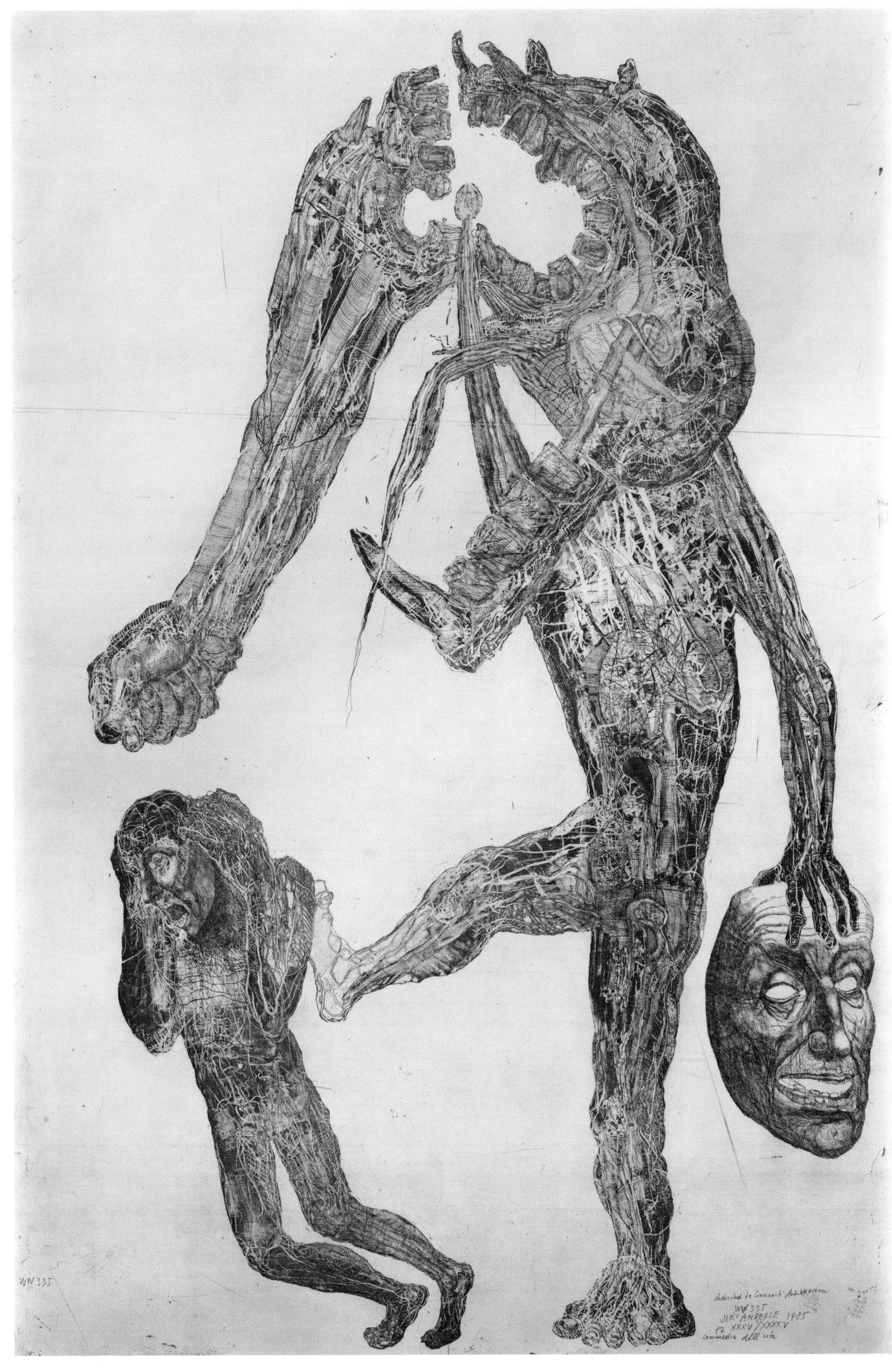

The King Kicks the Jester
1985, WV 335 (2008.19)

95

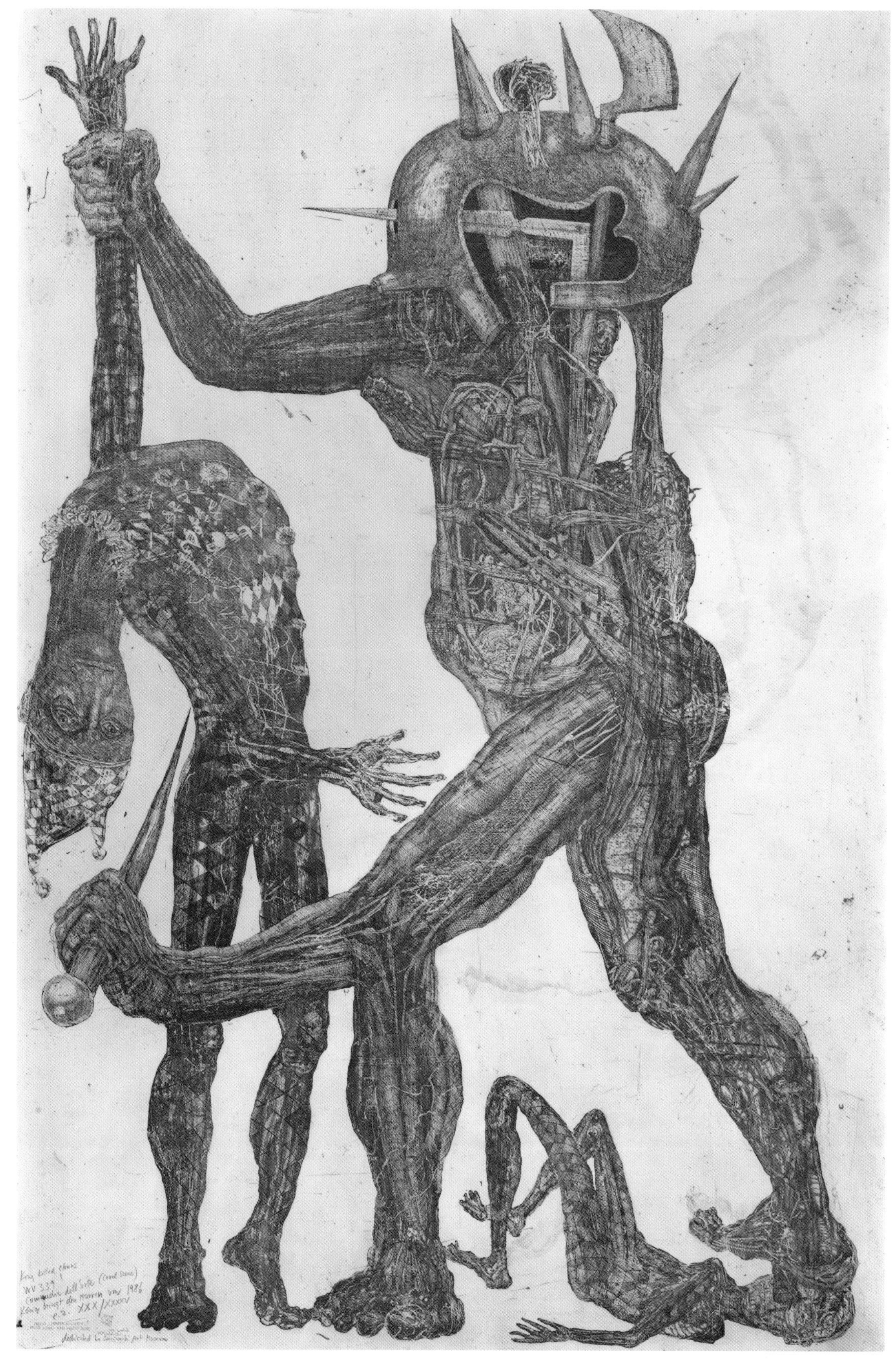

96 *The King Kills the Jesters*
1985–86, WV 339 (2008.20)

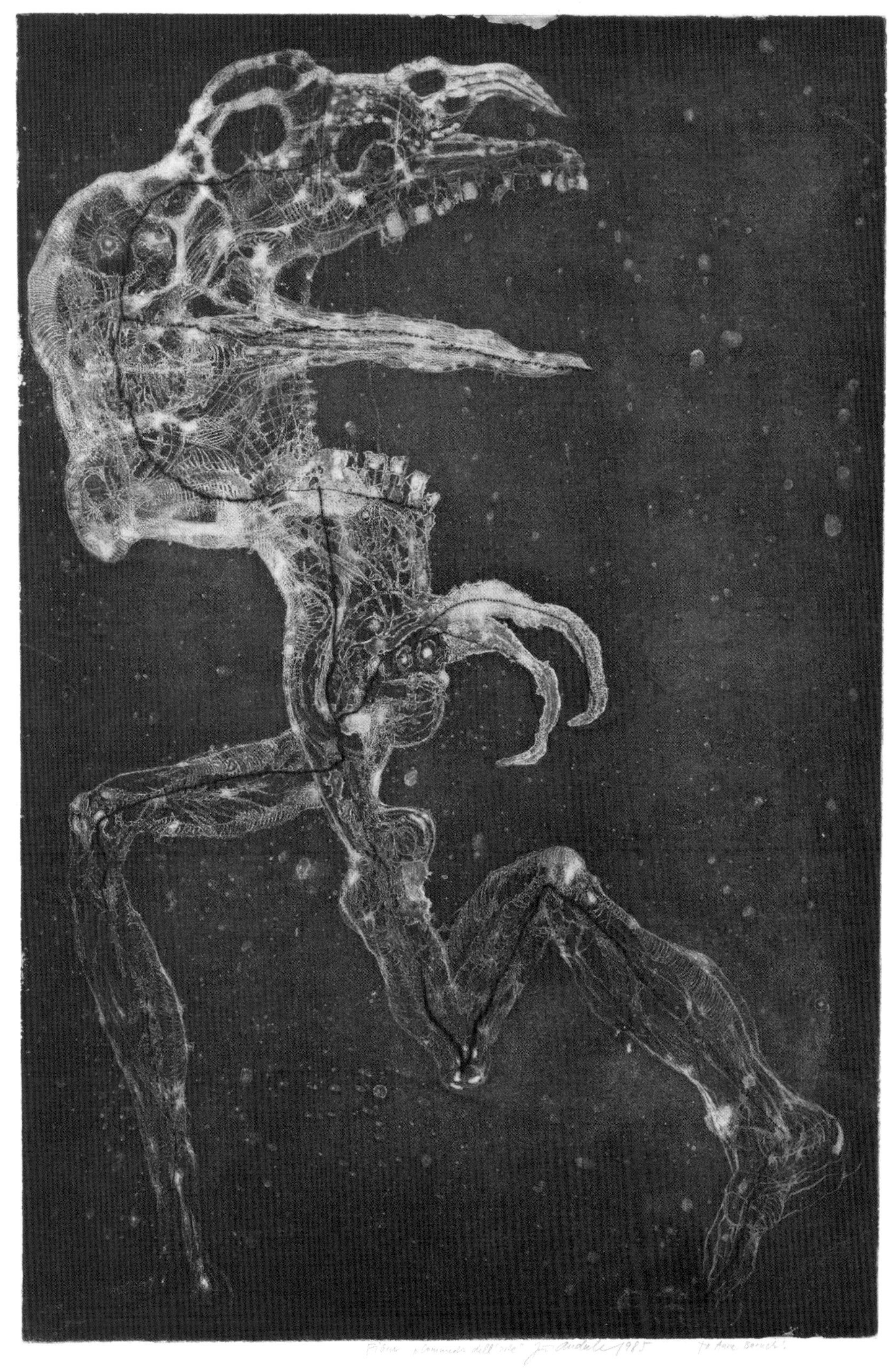

Figure on Dark Ground I
1990, WV 400 (2005.196)

97

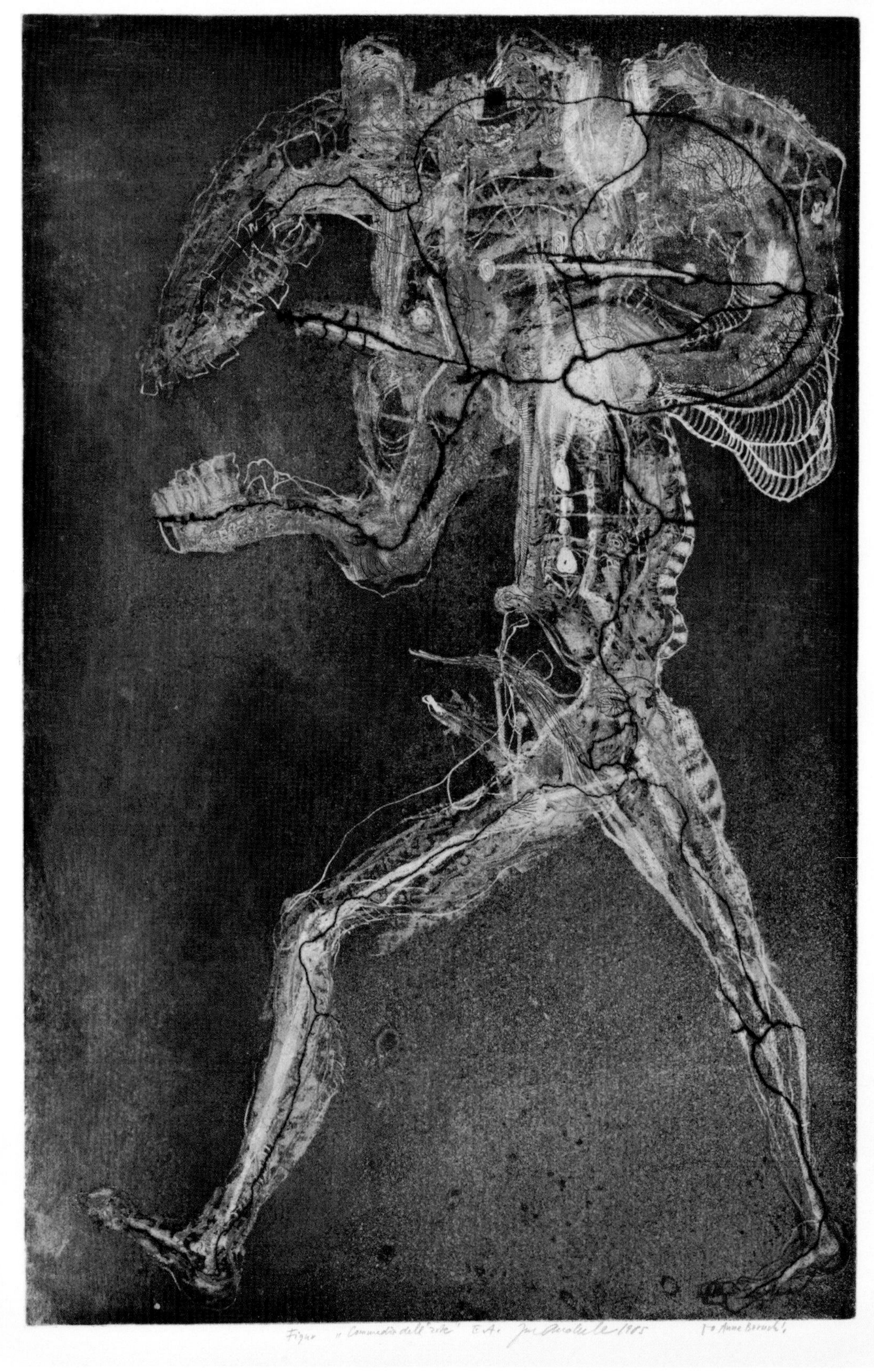

98 | *Figure on Dark Ground II*
1990, WV 401 (2005.197)

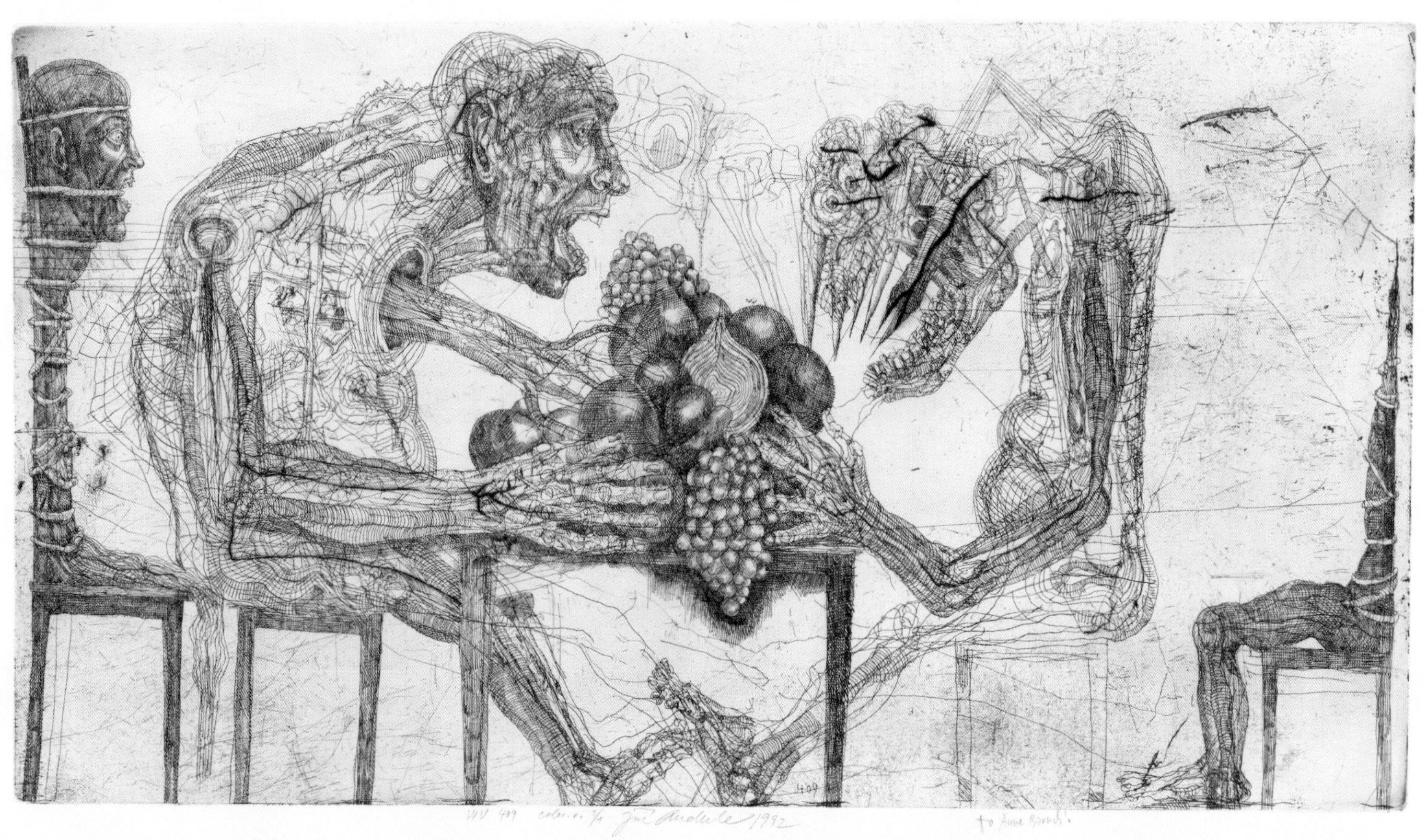

The Festival Eater
1992, WV 409 (2005.198)

99

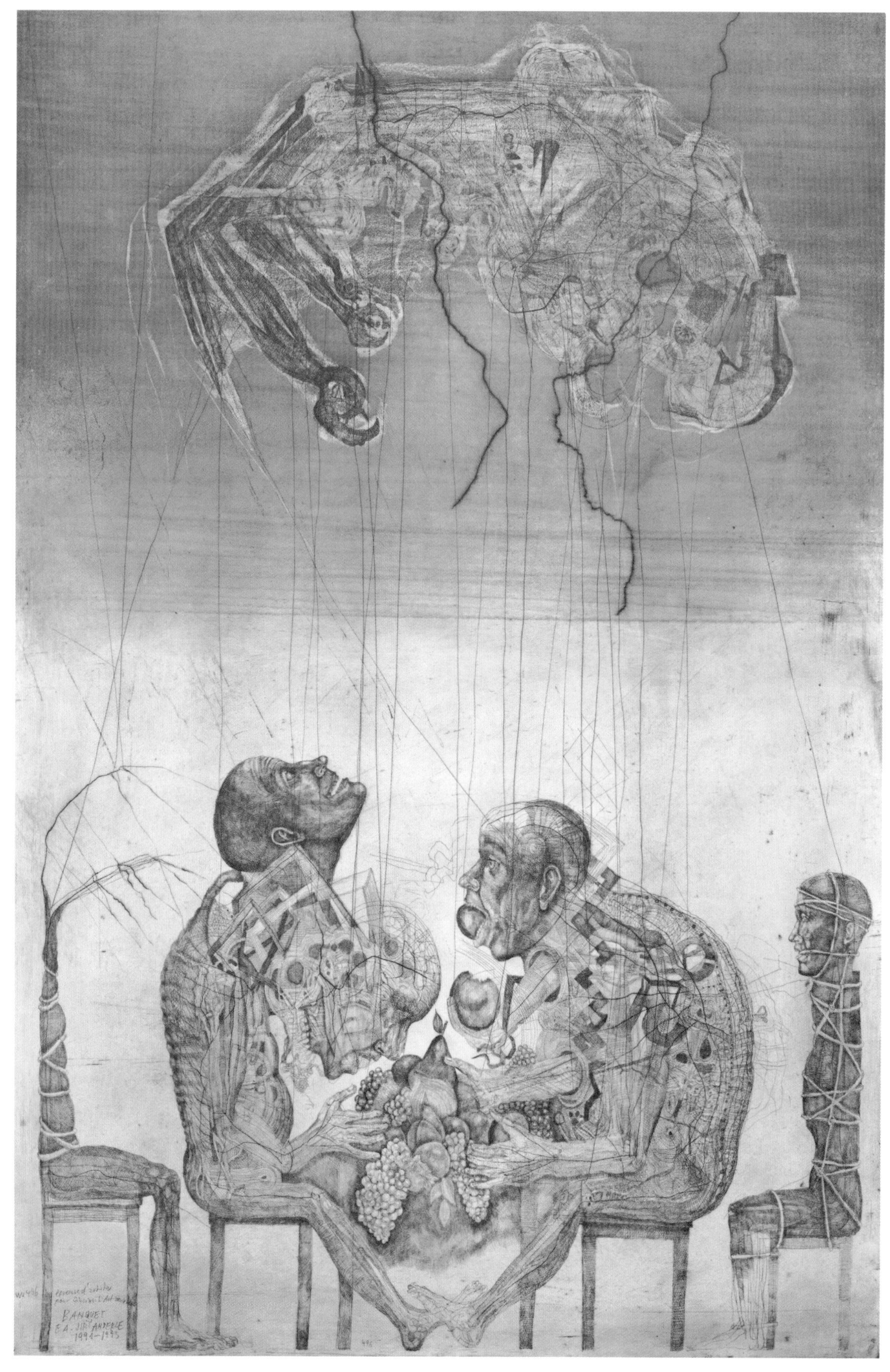

100 *Banquet*
1991–93, WV 496 (2008.21)

1954
Prize for drawing, *Shankar's Weekly*, New Delhi, India

1968
Ex aequo Prize, *2nd Międzynarodowe biennale grafiki*, Cracow, Poland

1969
Grand Prix, *1st Biennale Internationale de Gravure*, Liège, Belgium

Prize, *8th mednarodni grafični bienale*, Ljubljana, Yugoslavia

1970
Prize, *3rd Międzynarodowe biennale grafiki*, Cracow, Poland

1972
Medal, *2nd Internationale Graphik-Biennale*, Frechen, West Germany

1976
Second Prize, *5th British International Print Biennale*, Bradford, England

Second Prize, *3rd Norwegian International Print Biennale*, Fredrikstad, Norway

Medal, *4th Internationale Graphik-Biennale*, Frechen, West Germany

1978
Medal, *5th Internationale Graphik-Biennale*, Frechen, West Germany

Gold Medal, *4th Listowel International Graphic Art Open Exhibition*, Listowel, Ireland

1979
Third Prize, *1st Biennale der europäischen Graphik*, Heidelberg, West Germany

Purchase Prize, *13th mednarodni grafični bienale*, Ljubljana, Yugoslavia

1980
First Prize, *5th Norwegian International Print Biennale*, Fredrikstad, Norway

Medal of Honor and Purchase Prize, *World Print III*, San Francisco, California

Honorary Medal, *8th Międzynarodowe biennale grafiki*, Cracow, Poland

1981
Second Prize, *Graphica Creativa '81*, Jyväskylä Summer Festival, Jyväskylä, Finland

Grand Prize and Purchase Prize, *14th mednarodni grafični bienale*, Ljubljana, Yugoslavia

1982
Special Prize, *7th British International Print Biennale*, Bradford, England

Grand Prize for Graphic Art, *5th Triennale for Painting, Drawing and Graphics*, New Delhi, India

Grand Prize for Graphic Art, *2nd medjunarodna izložba portreta u crtežu i grafici*, Tuzla, Yugoslavia

1983
Grand Prize /Silver Plaque, *2nd Biennale internationale de gravure*, Varna, Bulgaria

1984
J. C. Editions Prize, *8th British International Print Biennale*, Bradford, England

Prize, *9th Międzynarodowe biennale grafiki*, Cracow, Poland

Diploma for Graphic Art and Purchase Prize, *3rd medjunarodna izložba portreta u crtežu i grafici*, Tuzla, Yugoslavia

1987
Grand Prix, *4th Biennale internationale de gravure*, Varna, Bulgaria

1991
Grand Prize, 1st *Triennale Europea dell'Incisione*, Udine, Italy

Prize, *1st grafične trienale Hexagonale*, Sežana, Slovenia

1993
Medal of Honor, *Trienále evropské volné grafiky*, Prague, Czech Republic

1998
Special Award for a lifetime contribution to graphic art, *Inter-Kontakt-Grafik '98, 2nd Mezinárodní trienále grafiky*, Prague, Czech Republic

Diploma for prints and Purchase Prize, *9th medjunarodna izložba portreta u crtežu i grafici*, Tuzla, Bosnia-Herzegovina

2004
Boudink prize for graphic work, Czech Republic

* *denotes exhibitions known to have publications, which can be found in the bibliography.*

1966
* Oblastní galerie, Liberec, Czechoslovakia
* Galerie na Karlově naměstí, Prague, Czechoslovakia

1967
Galerie im Zentrum, Göttingen, West Germany

1968
Galerie Bel Étage, Berlin, West Germany
Galerie Paul Bruck, Luxembourg, Luxembourg
Viola, Prague, Czechoslovakia
Konstallen, Uppsala, Sweden

1969
Galerie l'Angle-Aigu, Brussels, Belgium
Baukunst Galerie, Cologne, West Germany
* Oblastní galerie, Olomouc, Czechoslovakia

1970
Baukunst Galerie, Cologne, West Germany
Kunstverein, Göttingen, West Germany
Galerie Václava Špály, Prague, Czechoslovakia

1971
Galerie Walther, Düsseldorf, West Germany
Galerie Hardy Schneider-Sato, Karlsruhe, West Germany
Moderna galerija, Ljubljana, Yugoslavia
Galerie Alfermann, Solingen, West Germany

1972
Jacques Baruch Gallery, Chicago, IL, US
* Baukunst Galerie, Cologne, West Germany
* Galerie Walther, Düsseldorf, West Germany

1974
Baukunst Galerie, Cologne, West Germany

1975
* Jacques Baruch Gallery, Chicago, IL, US
Galerie Koch, Hanover, West Germany
Baukunst Galerie, Cologne, West Germany
Galerie Nickel und Zadow, Nuremberg, West Germany
Kunstsalon Wolfsberg, Zurich, Switzerland

1976
Galerie la taille douce, Brussels, Belgium
Galerie Commeter, Hamburg, West Germany
Galerie Elias, Wieze, Belgium

1977
Jacques Baruch Gallery, Chicago, IL, US
Galerie Walther, Düsseldorf, West Germany

1978
* University of North Dakota Art Galleries, Grand Forks, ND, US
Baukunst Galerie, Cologne, West Germany

1979
Galerie am Kübelmarkt, Bruchsal, West Germany
Carneol-Galerie, Gothenburg, Sweden
Idea-Galerie, The Hague, The Netherlands
* Baukunst Galerie, Cologne, West Germany
* Výstavní síň Fronta, Prague, Czechoslovakia
Galerie Bäumler, Regensburg, West Germany
Jacques Baruch Gallery, Chicago, IL, US

1980
* Jacques Baruch Gallery, Chicago, IL, US
Kunstverein, Gütersloh, West Germany
Galerie Happy Joss, Hamburg, West Germany
Galerie Konfrontation, Heidelberg, West Germany
Galerija Ars, Ljubljana, Yugoslavia
Institut für moderne Kunst, Nuremberg, West Germany
* Stadtgeschichtlichen Museen, Nuremberg, West Germany
* Galerie Götz, Stuttgart, West Germany
Galerie Walther, Düsseldorf, West Germany
Baukunst Galerie, Cologne, West Germany

1981
* Galerija Grafički kolektiv, Belgrade, Yugoslavia
Galerie Walther, Düsseldorf, West Germany
* Kresge Art Center Gallery, Michigan State University, East Lansing, MI, US
* Baukunst Galerie, Cologne, West Germany
Galerie Rampoldt, Berlin, West Germany
Galerie Happy Joss, Hamburg, West Germany
Galerija Ars, Ljubljana, Yugoslavia
Collegium artisticum, Sarajevo, Yugoslavia
Galerija Josip Račić, Zagreb, Yugoslavia
* Galerija Meblo, Nova Gorica, Yugoslavia

1982
Galerie Schmiedel, Bergheim, West Germany
Galerie Rampoldt, Berlin, West Germany
Jacques Baruch Gallery, Chicago, IL, US
* Kulturni dom, Nova Gorica, Yugoslavia
Haus Amselreuth, Güglingen, West Germany
Galerie Maskenbildchen, Coblenz, West Germany
Galerie Schäfer, Radevormwald, West Germany
Kopparstickskabinettet, Stockholm, Sweden
* Nationalmuseum, Stockholm, Sweden
Malmö Konsthall, Malmö, Sweden
* Galerie Götz, Stuttgart, Germany
* Galleria TK, Trieste, Italy
Galerie Goltenhof, Witten, West Germany
Baukunst Galerie, Cologne, West Germany

1983

Kunsthandel Helga Paepcke, Karlsruhe, West Germany

Galerie Happy Joss, Hamburg, West Germany

Galerie Götz, Stuttgart, West Germany

* Pilonova galerija, Adjovščina, Yugoslavia

* Kulturni centar, Belgrade, Yugoslavia

Galerija Loža, Koper, Yugoslavia

* Baukunst Galerie, Cologne, West Germany

Cankarjev dom, Ljubljana, Yugoslavia

Razstavišče Riharda Jakopiča, Ljubljana, Yugoslavia

Equivalents Gallery, Seattle, WA, US

* Dům Kultury ROH, Budweis, Czechoslovakia

1984

Galerie Götz, Stuttgart, West Germany

Gallery 200, University of Missouri, St. Louis, MO, US

Jacques Baruch Gallery, Chicago, IL, US

Lahden Taede Museo, Lahti, Finland

* Sieň Laca Novomeského, Bratislava, Czechoslovakia

Nova síň, Prague, Czechoslovakia

* Krajská galerie, Hradec Králové, Czechoslovakia

* Dům umění – Galerie Jaroslava Krále, Brno, Czechoslovakia

1985

Severočeská galerie výtvarného umění, Litoměřice, Czechoslovakia

The University of Iowa Museum of Art, Iowa City, IA, US

The University of Arkansas Fine Arts Gallery, Little Rock, AR, US

* Pratt Manhattan Center Gallery, New York, NY, US

Baukunst Galerie, Cologne, West Germany

Galerie Schmiedel, Bergheim, West Germany

Stadthalle, Bergheim, West Germany

Stadtgalerie Kiel, West Germany

* Okresní muzeum a galerie, Rakovnik, Czechoslovakia

Galerie Benedikta Rejta a Okresní knihovna, Louny, Czechoslovakia

1986

* Brunswiker Pavillon, Stadtbilderei und Stadtgalerie, Kiel, West Germany

Baukunst Galerie, Cologne, West Germany

Jacques Baruch Gallery, Chicago, IL, US

* Galerie umění, Karlovy Vary, Czechoslovakia

* Galerie výtvarného uměni, Cheb, Czechoslovakia

* Západočeská galerie, Pilsen, Czechoslovakia

* Oblastní galerie, Liberec, Czechoslovakia

J. Noblett Gallery, Sonoma, CA, US

Mary Ryan Gallery, New York, NY, US

1987

* Galéria mesta Bratislavy, Bratislava, Czechoslovakia

* Galerie Platýz, Prague, Czechoslovakia

* Grinnell College, Grinnell, IA, US

* Ville de Luxembourg, Luxembourg

1988

Gonzaga University, Spokane, WA, US (with Albín Brunovský)

Jacques Baruch Gallery, Chicago, IL, US

* Mary and Leigh Block Gallery, Northwestern University, Evanston, IL, US

Northern Idaho College, Coeur d'Alene, ID, US

Galleri Ängeln, Lund, Sweden

Galéria mesta Bratislavy, Bratislava, Czechoslovakia

1990

* Rodný statek Václava Šolce, Sobotka, Czechoslovakia

Galleri Ängeln, Lund, Sweden

* The New Harmony Gallery of Contemporary Art, University of Southern Indiana, New Harmony, IN, US

Grafiska Sällskapet, Stockholm, Sweden

1991

Krajské vlastivědné muzeum, Olomouc, Czechoslovakia

* JKZ Galerie, Valašské Meziříčí, Czechoslovakia

*Rabasova galerie, Rakovnik, Czechoslovakia

Jacques Baruch Gallery, Chicago, IL, US

* Mount Prospect Public Library, Mount Prospect, IL, US

Galerie Jean Briance, Paris, France

Galerie grafiky - Centrum české grafiky, Prague, Czechoslovakia

1992

Siemens AG, Erlangen, Germany

Galerie Götz, Stuttgart, Germany

1993

Středoevropská galerie a Centrum české grafiky, Prague, Czech Republic

* Amarillo Art Center, Amarillo, TX, US

1994

Galerie Litera, Prague, Czech Republic

Výstavní síň reklamní agentury SAM promotion, Náchod, Czech Republic

Galerie Polyprint, Wuppertal, Germany

Galerie Hirmichel, Bad Kissingen, Germany

1995

* Nevada Museum of Art, Reno, NV, US

College of Creative Arts, West Virginia University, Morgantown, WV, US

Galerie Bode, Nuremberg, Germany

Galerie Hirmichel, Bad Kissingen, Germany

Cynthia Bourne Gallery, London, England

Národní galerie, Palác Kinských, Prague, Czech Republic

Okresní muzeum, Lanškroun, Czech Republic

1996

* Prague Castle Imperial Stables, Prague, Czech Republic

Panorama Museum, Bad Frankenhausen, Germany

National Institute for Printmaking, Calografia, Rome, Italy

* Arlington Heights Memorial Library, Arlington Heights, IL, US

1997

Kunstverein Coburg, Coburg, Germany

Dům Alšovy jihočeské galerie, U Černé věže, Budweis, Czech Republic

University of Missouri-Kansas City Gallery of Art, Kansas City, MO, US

1998

Galerie Vltavín, Prague, Czech Republic

Muzeum w Sosnowcu, Sosnowiec, Poland

1999

Miejska Galeria Sztuki, Lodz, Poland

Galerie Jiřího a Běly Kolářových, Prague, Czech Republic

Universtät Hohenheim, Stuttgart, Germany

Galerie Pyramida, Prague, Czech Republic

2000

Maloskalská Galerie, Malá Skála, Czech Republic

Galerie U Klicperů, Hradec Králové, Czech Republic

Rabasova galerie, Rakovnik, Czech Republic

2002

* Galeria Sztuki Wspólezesnej BWA, Cracow, Poland

2003

Galerie Anderle, Prague, Czech Republic

2006

* Međunarodna galerija portreta, Tuzla, Bosnia and Herzegovina

GROUP EXHIBITIONS (SELECTED)

* *denotes exhibitions known to have publications.*

1962

Výstava hostů Hollara, Hollar, Prague, Czechoslovakia

1966

Výstava mladých, Dům umění, Brno, Czechoslovakia

* *Aktuální tendence českého umění*, výstavní síň Mánes and Galerie Václava Špály, Prague, Czechoslovakia

Tschechoslowakische Grafiker, Holsteinisches Landesmuseum, Schleswig, West Germany

1967

* *Internationale Ausstellung der Graphik*, Europahaus, Vienna, Austria

Tschechoslowakische Graphik, Neue Sparkasse, Schloß Kiel, Hamburg, West Germany

Junge tschechische Graphik, Galerie Tangente, Karlsruhe, and Galerie Tangente, Heidelberg, West Germany

* *7th mednarodni grafični bienale*, Moderna galerija, Ljubljana, Yugoslavia

Modern Tjeckoslovakisk graphik, Lunds Konsthall, Lund, Sweden, and Stavanger Konsthall, Stavanger, Norway

* *Fantasijní aspekty současného českého umění*, Galerie Václava Špály, Prague, and Galerie Vysočiny, Jihlava, Czechoslovakia

Nové cesty II – mladá generace, Dům umění, Gottwald, Czechoslovakia

Jeden okruh volby – obrazy, sochy, objekty, grafika, kresby 1964 –1967, Okresní muzeum, Písek, Czechoslovakia

1968

Ehrengast der Gruppe Cap d'Encre, Brussels, Belgium

* *2nd Międzynarodowe biennale grafiki*, Cracow, Poland

* *10th Biennale Bianco e Nero*, Lugano, Switzerland

Internationale Graphik, Kunstverein, Oldenburg, West Germany

* *Contemporary Prints of Czechoslovakia*, National Gallery of Canada, Ottawa, Canada. Traveled 1969 to Oregon State University, Corvallis, OR, US.

300 malířů, sochařů, grafiků pěti generací k 50 létům republiky, výstavní síň Mánes, Prague, Czechoslovakia

* *Recent Graphics from Prague*, Corcoran Gallery, Washington D.C., US. Traveled 1969–1971 to Philadelphia Museum of Art, Philadelphia, PA; Bemidji State College, Bemidji, PA; Virginia Intermont College, Bristol, VA; Central Connecticut State College, New Britain, CT; Mercersburg Academy, Mercersburg, PA; Civic Center Museum, Philadelphia, PA; The Brooklyn Center, Long Island University, Brooklyn, NY; Fayette Bank and Trust Company, Uniontown, PA; and Virginia Polytechnic Institute, Blacksburg, VA, US.

1969

* *1st Biennale Internationale de Gravure*, Liège, Belgium

* *8th mednarodni grafični bienale*, Moderna galerija, Ljubljana, Yugoslavia

Salon de Mai, Paris, France

Nová figurace (New Figuration), výstavní síň Mánes, Prague, Czechoslovakia

1970

Zestien Tsjechische Kunstenaars, Galerie de Tor, Amsterdam, The Netherlands

* *2nd British International Print Biennale*, Bradford, England

Six graveurs tchećques, Galerie la taille douce, Brussels, Belgium

New Surrealism, Jacques Baruch Gallery, Chicago, IL, US

Grafica cecoslovacca, Biblioteca comunale, Correggio, Italy

* *3rd Międzynarodowe biennale grafiki*, Cracow, Poland

Modern Tjeckoslovakisk graphik, Lunds Konsthall, Lund, Sweden

Cien Grabodos, Cien Fotografias de Checoslovaquia, Museo Universitario, Mexico City, Mexico

* *2nd Biennale internationale de l'estampe*, Musée d'Art moderne, Paris, France

50 e uno grafici cecoslovacchi, 21 rassegna d'arte contemporanea, Turin, Italy

Eleven Printmakers from Czechoslovakia, Gekkoso Gallery, Tokyo, Japan

International Exhibition, Library of Congress, Washington, D.C., US

* *Graveurs tchécoslovaques contemporains*, Musée d'art et d'histoire, Geneva, Switzerland

1971

Premio Internazionale Biella per l'incisione, Museo Civico, Biella, Italy

Sieben Künstler aus Prag, Kunsthalle, Bielefeld, West Germany, and Konsthallen, Uppsala, Sweden

Výstava grafiky, Galéria Klub grafikov, Bratislava, Czechoslovakia

Nearly Black and White: An Exhibition of Outstanding Graphics, Jacques Baruch Gallery, Chicago, IL, US

* *Zeitgenössische Künstler aus der Tschechoslowakei*, Baukunst Galerie, Cologne, West Germany

* *9th mednarodni grafični bienale*, Moderna galerija, Ljubljana, Yugoslavia

Internazionale rassegna d'arte grafica, Lugano, Switzerland

22 Tjeckiske Kunstnere, Stadisblioteket, Ljungby, Sweden

* *Albrecht Dürer zu Ehren*, Albrecht Dürer Gesellschaft, Nuremberg, Germany

Výstava grafiky, Galerie d, Prague, Czechoslovakia

Contemporanea grafica Checoslováquia, Rio de Janeiro, Brazil

International Graphic Art, Sveagalleriet, Stockholm, Sweden

Werken van Tsjechoslowaakse grafici 1960–1970, Central Museum, Utrecht, The Netherlands

1972

* *36th Internazionale Biennale di Venezia, Aspetti della grafica europea*, Venice, Italy
* *3rd British International Print Biennale*, Bradford, England

Selected Acquisitions for 5 Years, The Art Institute of Chicago, Chicago, IL, US

* *2nd Internationale Graphik-Biennale*, Frechen, West Germany
* *4th Międzynarodowe biennale grafiki*, Cracow, Poland

Group Exhibition, Western Illinois University, Macomb, IL, US

* *Tschechoslowakische Druckgraphik der Gegenwart*, Albrecht Dürer Gesellschaft, Nuremberg, West Germany

Z bienále grafické tvorby v Lublani 1971, Národní galerie, Palác Kinských, Prague, Czechoslovakia

1973

* *Premio Internazionale Biella per l'incisione*, Museo Civico, Biella, Italy

Realism, Fantasy and Abstract in Graphics, Jacques Baruch Gallery, Chicago, IL, US

* *10th mednarodni grafični bienale*, Moderna galerija, Ljubljana, Yugoslavia

1974

* *4th British International Print Biennale*, Bradford, England

Art on Paper, Jacques Baruch Gallery, Chicago, IL, US

* *3rd Internationale Graphik-Biennale*, Frechen, West Germany
* *2nd Norwegian International Print Biennale*, Fredrikstad, Norway

1975

* *Premio Internazionale Biella per l'incisione*, Museo Civico, Biella, Italy
* *Eastern European Printmakers*, Cincinnati Art Museum, Cincinnati, OH, US

Eastern European Printmakers–Important Works by Outstanding Artists, Jacques Baruch Gallery, Chicago, IL, US

* *Fantasy and Surrealism*, Kresge Art Center Gallery, East Lansing, MI, US
* *11th mednarodni grafični bienale*, Moderna galerija, Ljubljana, Yugoslavia
* *Mir '75*, Umetnostni paviljon, Slovenj Gradec, Yugoslavia

1976

* *5th British International Print Biennale*, Bradford, England

Erotic Art Exhibition, Jacques Baruch Gallery, Chicago, IL, US

* *4th Internationale Graphik-Biennale*, Frechen, West Germany
* *3rd Norwegian International Print Biennale*, Fredrikstad, Norway

7th Triennale internationale pour gravures originales en couleur, Parktheater, Grenchen, Switzerland

Eastern European Printmakers, Rahr-West Museum, Manitowoc, WI, and William Benton Museum, Storrs, CT, US

Slavic Printmakers, New Visions Gallery, Marshfield, MA, US

Graphische Miniaturen, Albrecht Dürer Gesellschaft, Nuremberg, West Germany

Rassegna di grafica contemporanea cecoslovacca, Gallerie Alzaia, Rome, Italy

1977

* *Premio Internazionale Biella per l'incisione*, Museo Civico, Biella, Italy

Self-Portraits of 400 Years, The Art Institute of Chicago, Chicago, IL, US

The Printed Word: Printmakers as Critics and Satirists, Cincinnati Art Museum, Cincinnati, OH, US

Graphische Miniaturen, Galerie L, Hamburg, West Germany

* *12th mednarodni grafični bienale*, Moderna galerija, Ljubljana, Yugoslavia

Selected Acquisitions, Library of Congress, Washington, D.C., US

1978

Recent Gifts of Modern Prints and Drawings, Cincinnati Art Museum, Cincinnati, OH, US

Collector's Choice, Cincinnati Art Museum, Cincinnati, OH, US

* *4th Listowel International Graphic Art Open Exhibition*, Listowel, Ireland
* *5th Internationale Graphik-Biennale*, Frechen, West Germany
* *4th Norwegian International Print Biennale*, Fredrikstad, Norway
* *3rd Biennale européenne de la gravure*, Mulhouse, France

Umění vítězného lidu, Jízdárna Pražského hradu, Mánes, Středočeská galerie, Prague, Czechoslovakia

1979

* *Premio Internazionale Biella per l'incisione*, Museo Civico, Biella, Italy
* *6th British International Print Biennale*, Bradford, England
* *8th Triennale internationale pour gravures originales en couleur*, Parktheater, Grenchen, Switzerland
* *1st Biennale der europäischen Graphik*, Heidelberg, West Germany
* *13th mednarodni grafični bienale*, Moderna galerija, Ljubljana, Yugoslavia
* *International Print Exhibition*, Rockford College, Rockford, IL, US
* *Contemporary Czechoslovakian Printmakers*, Smithsonian Institution Traveling Exhibition Service [SITES], 1979–1983: Cedar Rapids Art Center, Cedar Rapids, IA; Idaho State University Transition Gallery, Pocatello, ID; Squires Student Center Art Gallery, Virginia Polytechnic Institution and State University, Blacksburg, VA; University Art Museum, University of Texas, Austin, TX; Yale University School of Art Gallery, New Haven, CT; Prints and Photographs Division, The Library of Congress, Washington, D.C.; Wabash College Art Gallery, Crawfordsville, IN; University of Puerto Rico Art Museum, San Juan, PR; Salina Art Center, Salina, KS; University of Arkansas at Little Rock, Little Rock, AR; Culver Stockton College, Canton, MO; Meridian House International Building, Washington, D.C.; Carroll Reece Museum, East Tennessee State University, Johnson, TN; Montgomery College, Department of Art, Rockville, MD; Kansas State University, Manhattan, KS; Columbus Museum of Arts and Sciences, Columbus, GA; Santa Fe Community College Art Gallery, Gainesville, FL; Asheville School, Asheville, NC; and Morton College, Cicero, IL, US.

1980

* *World Print III*, traveling exhibition 1980–83: San Francisco Museum of Modern Art, San Francisco, CA; Anchorage Historical and Fine Art Museum, Anchorage, AK; Roanoke College, Salem, VA; El Paso Museum of Art, El Paso, TX; Memorial Art Gallery of the University of Rochester, Rochester, NY, US; Mount Saint Vincent College, Halifax, Nova Scotia, Canada; Michigan State University, East Lansing, MI; Springfield Art Museum, Springfield, Missouri; University of Southern Mississippi, Hattiesburg, Mississippi; Albrecht Art Museum, St. Joseph, MO; Western Kentucky University, Bowling Green, KY, US; University of Guelph, Guelph, Ontario, Canada; Toledo Museum of Art, Toledo, OH, US; Ring House Gallery, Edmonton, Alberta, Canada; and Beaumont Art Museum, Beaumont, TX, US
* *39th Internazionale Biennale di Venezia*, Venice, Italy

3rd Biennale internationale de la gravure, Bonsecours, Belgium

* *5th Norwegian International Print Biennale*, Fredrikstad, Norway
* *6th Internationale Graphik Biennale*, Frechen, West Germany

Biennale Internationale de la Gravure, Gerpinnes, Belgium

Members Purchase Exhibition, Museum of Art, The University of Iowa, Iowa City, IA, US

* *8th Międzynarodowe biennale grafiki*, Cracow, Poland
* *5th Listowel International Graphic Art Open Exhibition*, Listowel, Ireland

4th Biennale européenne de la gravure, Mulhouse, France

Výtvarní uměěk 35 výročí osvobození Československa Sovětskou armádou, Mánes, Jízdárna Pražského hradu, Prague, Czechoslovakia

1981

* *2nd Biennale der europäischen Graphik*, Baden-Baden, West Germany

Gallery Artists: Tapestries, Graphics, Photographs, Jacques Baruch Gallery, Chicago, IL, US

Recent Acquisitions of Prints and Drawings Department, The Art Institute of Chicago, Chicago, IL, US

Master Prints and Drawings from the Collection of the Cincinnati Art Museum, Cincinnati, OH, US

Triennale europea dell'incisione, Grado, Italy

* *Graphica Creativa '81*, Jyväskylä Summer Festival, Jyväskylä, Finland

Internationale Graphik-Biennale, Albertina, Vienna, Austria

9th Triennale internationale pour gravures originales en couleur, Parktheater, Grenchen, Switzerland

* *14th mednarodni grafični bienale*, Moderna galerija, Ljubljana, Yugoslavia

Printmaking in Czechoslovakia, The Print Club, Philadelphia, PA

Svědectví dějin, Mánes, Prague, Czechoslovakia

1st Biennale internationale de gravure, Varna, Bulgaria

* *Rockford International '81*, Rockford College Art Gallery, Rockford, IL, US

1982

Images of Arms and Armor, Cincinnati Art Museum, Cincinnati, OH, US

* *40th Internazionale Biennale di Venezia / Art as an Art: The Continuity of the Work*, Venice, Italy
* *5th Norwegian International Print Biennale*, Fredrikstad, Norway
* *7th British International Print Biennale*, Bradford, England

Sonderschau der Internationalen Buchkunst-Ausstellung, Leipzig, East Germany

* *6th Listowel International Graphic Art Open Exhibition*, Listowel, Ireland
* *5th Triennale for Painting, Drawing and Graphics*, New Delhi, India

Artist's Protest, Pratt Manhattan Center Gallery, New York

Künstler gegen den Krieg, Foyer der Kongresshalle, Saarbrücken, West Germany

8th tsjechoslowaakse graphici, International Exlibriscentrum, Saint Nicholas, Belgium

* *2nd medjunarodna izložba portreta u crtežu i grafici*, Tuzla, Yugoslavia

Recent Acquisitions of Prints and Drawings, The Art Institute of Chicago, Chicago, IL, US

Graphica Creativa '82, Jyväskylä, Finland

Autoritratti artistici, Galleria degli Uffizi, Florence, Italy

Současná grafika pražských členů SČVU, Mánes, Prague, Czechoslovakia

Boje a zápasy, Jízdárna Pražského hradu, Prague, Czechoslovakia

1983

Czechoslovakian Prints, Gonzaga University, Spokane, WA, US

Prints from Eastern Europe, Fred P. Giles Gallery, Eastern Kentucky University, Richmond, KY, US

Twentieth Century Drawings Acquired Since 1958, The Art Institute of Chicago, Chicago, IL, US

The Pennell Legacy, Two Centuries of Printmaking, The Library of Congress, Washington, D.C., US

Czech Drawings of the 20th Century, Musée nationale d'art moderne, Centre Georges Pompidou, Paris, France

Master Drawings from the Permanent Collection, Grand Rapids Art Museum, Grand Rapids, MI, US

Group Exhibition – Prints and Drawings, Jacques Baruch Gallery, Chicago

Eastern European Art, Fermi National Accelerator Laboratory Art Gallery, Batavia, IL, US

Portfolios from Czechoslovakia, Gonzaga University Art Gallery, Spokane, WA, US

Selected Acquisitions, Library of Congress, Washington, D.C., US

* *7th International Graphik-Triennale*, Frechen, West Germany
* *15th mednarodni grafični bienale*, Moderna galerija, Ljubljana, Yugoslavia

2nd Biennale internationale de gravure, Varna, Bulgaria

* *42nd Internazionale Biennale di Venezia*, Venice, Italy

1984

New Acquisitions of Prints, Drawings and Photographs, Cincinnati Art Museum, Cincinnati, OH, US

* *41st Internazionale Biennale di Venezia, Art in the Mirror*, Main Pavilion, Venice, Italy
* *8th British International Print Biennale*, Bradford, England

Graphica Creativa '84, Jyväskylä, Finland

Triennale Europea dell'Incisione de Grado, Grado, Italy

3rd medjunarodna izložba portreta u crtežu i grafici, Tuzla, Yugoslavia

* *9th Międzynarodowe biennale grafiki*, Cracow, Poland

Současná česká grafika 1977–1983, Galerie Vincence Kramáře, Prague, Czechoslovakia

1985

Contemporary Czechoslovakian Printmakers, Kendall Gallery, Kendall School of Design, Grand Rapids, MI, and Chicago Bar Association, Chicago, IL, US

Themes on Mythology: Graphics, Jacques Baruch Gallery, Chicago, IL, US

Greek Myths Updated, Carleton Art Gallery, Carleton College, Northfield, MN

* *Contemporary Prints, Contemporary Visions*, University of Southern California Art Galleries, Fisher Gallery, Los Angeles, CA, US

Gifts to the Art Institute of Chicago from Mr. And Mrs. Joseph Randall Shapiro, The Art Institute of Chicago, Chicago, IL, US

* *Graphica Creativa '85*, Jyväskylä, Finland
* *Selections from the Mesaros Collection*, The Butler Institute of American Art, Youngstown, OH, US

Vyznání životu a míru, Jízdárna Pražského hradu, Prague, Czechoslovakia

* *16th mednarodni grafični bienale*, Moderna galerija, Ljubljana, Yugoslavia

1986

Summer Show: Gallery Artists, Jacques Baruch Gallery, Chicago, IL, US

Uncovering the Past: Tribute and Parody, Long Beach Museum of Art, Long Beach, CA, US

New Acquisitions: Prints, Drawings, Photographs, Cincinnati Art Museum, Cincinnati, OH, US

New Acquisitions: Prints, Ad Gallery, Gonzaga University, Spokane, WA, US

* *Selections from the Mesaros Collection*, West Virginia University Art Galleries and Collection, Creative Art Centre, Morgantown, WV, US

Hommage à Seifert, 10 Tsjechoslowaakse grafici, Museum Dhondt-Dhaemens, Deurle, The Netherlands

Grafické techniky II: Tisk z hloubky, Galerie d, Prague, Czechoslovakia

Umění pro mír Výstava grafiky, kreseb, plakátů, fotografií, plastik, poštovních známek, Galerie d, Prague, Czechoslovakia

1987

Recent Acquisitions of Prints and Drawings, The Art Institute of Chicago, Chicago, IL, US

Post-War Czechoslovakian Printmakers in the Permanent Collection, Smart Museum of Art, University of Chicago, Chicago, IL, US

* *Catalogue and Exhibition of the Permanent Art Collection*, Board of Governors of the Federal Reserve System, Washington, D.C., US

4th Biennale internationale de gravure, Varna, Bulgaria

Obrazy a sochy, Výstava pražských členů SČVU, výstavní síň Mánes, Prague, Czechoslovakia

* *17th mednarodni grafični bienale*, Moderna galerija, Ljubljana, Yugoslavia

1988

Review and Preview: Drawings, Fiber, Paintings, Photographs and Prints, Jacques Baruch Gallery, Chicago, IL, US

Czech Prints: The Baruch Collection, Ad Gallery, Gonzaga University, Spokane, WA, US

* *Twenty Years of Czechoslovak Art 1968–1988, A Tribute to Jacques Baruch*, Jacques Baruch Gallery, Chicago, IL, US

The Nude, Cincinnati Art Museum, Cincinnati, OH, US

1989

New Acquisitions: Prints, Ad Gallery, Gonzaga University, Spokane, WA, US

Contemporary Czechoslovak Printmakers for the Washington Print Club, The Czechoslovak Embassy, Washington, D.C., US

* *Under Pressure: Western Printmaking from the 15th Century to the Present*, Center for the Arts, Vero Beach, FL; Mississippi Museum of Art, Jackson, MS; Dixon Gallery and Gardens, Memphis, TN; and Roanoke Museum of Fine Arts, Roanoke, WV, US

The Washington Print Club: 25 Years of Collecting, The George Washington University, The Dimock Gallery, Washington, D.C., US

* *18th mednarodni grafični bienale*, Moderna galerija, Ljubljana, Yugoslavia

1990

Contemporary Czechoslovakian Prints from the Werksman Collection, Fairfield Public Library, Fairfield, CT, US

Review and Preview – Drawings, Photography, Prints, Fiber, and Sculpture, Jacques Baruch Gallery, Chicago, IL, US

Reflections: Religion and Mythology, Prints and Drawings, Jacques Baruch Gallery, Chicago, IL, US

* *Creativity in the Shadow of Political Oppression: Recent Czechoslovakian Graphic Art from the Werksman Collection and the Jacques Baruch Gallery*, Art Gallery, Los Angeles Valley College, Van Nuys, CA, US

Dialog '90, Prague – Paris, výstavní síň Mánes, Prague, Czechoslovakia

1991

Contemporary Art from Czechoslovakia and Poland, The Kansas City Artists Coalition, Kansas City, KS, US

Papier aus Prag, Tschechische Graphik, Stadtgalerie – Landeshauptstadt, Saarbrücken, Germany

Collecting Portrait Prints: The Washington Print Club Biennial, National Portrait Gallery, Smithsonian Institution, Washington, D.C., US

The International Prints Exhibition Kanagawa '91, Kanagawa Prefectural Gallery, Kanagawa, Japan

1st Triennale Europea dell'Incisione, Undine, Italy

1st grafične trienale Hexagonale, Sežana, Slovenia

1992

Conflict – Real and Imagined, Lawrence Collection, Rolling Meadows Library, Rolling Meadows, IL, US

Creativity in the Shadow of Political Oppression – Recent Czechoslovakian Graphic Art from the Werksman Collection and the Jacques Baruch Gallery, Rockford College Art Gallery, Clark Art Center, Rockford, IL, US

In Celebration of Our 25th Anniversary and in Memory of Jacques Z. Baruch, We pay Tribute to Our Collectors with a Special Exhibition from Private Collections, Jacques Baruch Gallery, Chicago, IL, US

1993

* *From Oppression to Freedom: Eastern European Prints and Drawings*, Bruce Gallery, Edinboro University of Pennsylvania, Edinboro, PA, US

Public Tragedy–Personal Concern, Union Gallery, North Idaho College, Coeur d'Alene, ID, US

A Personal Selection, The Anne and Jacques Baruch Collection, Chicago, IL, US

Grafičanka five o'clock, výstava Hudebního sdružení českých umělců grafiků, výstavní síň Atrium, Prague, Czech Republic

Dante Alighieri v českém výtvarném umění, Galerie moderního umění, Roudnice nad Labem and Národní galerie, klášter sv. Anežky České, Prague, Czech Republic

Inter-Kontakt-Grafik-Praha '93, výstava v rámci nultého ročníku Trienále evropské grafiky, výstavní síň Mánes, Prague, Czech Republic

* *20th mednarodni grafični bienale*, Moderna galerija, Ljubljana, Slovenia

1994

New Works in the Collection, Amarillo Art Center, Amarillo, TX, US

Flesh and Spirit: Czech Art Before the Velvet Revolution, Laband Art Gallery, Loyola Marymount University, Los Angeles, CA, US

* *Contemporary Master Prints from Eastern Europe: The Gonzaga University Collection*, Nevada Museum of Art, Reno, NV, US

* *Recent Czech and Slovak Printmaking*, Samuel P. Harn Museum of Art, University of Florida, Gainesville, FL, US

Úzkost těla, Památník Terezí, Nadace Symposium, Terezín, Czech Republic

Ze současného českého umění, Muzeum a galerie, Litomyšl, Czech Republic

Quest for Quality, Cincinnati Art Museum, Cincinnati, OH, US

1995

The Lawrence Collection, Grinnell College, Grinnell, IA, US

1998

* *2nd Mezinárodní trienále grafiky*, Old Town Hall and Strahov Monastery, Prague, Czech Republic

2005

* *Strength and Will: Czech Prints from Behind the Iron Curtain, A Gift of the Anne and Jacques Baruch Collection*, Cincinnati Art Museum, Cincinnati, OH, US

COLLECTIONS (SELECTED)

AUSTRIA
Vienna:
Albertina

BELGIUM
Brussels:
Musée de l'Art Moderne,
Cabinet des Estampes

Liège:
Musée des Beaux Arts

BOSNIA-HERZEGOVINA
Sarajevo:
Collegium artisticum

CZECH REPUBLIC
Cheb:
Galerie výtvarného umění
(Gallery of Fine Art)

Hluboká nad Vltavou:
Alšova jihočeská galerie
(Aleš South Bohemian Gallery)

Hradec Králové:
Galerie moderního umění
(Gallery of Modern Art)

Karlovy Vary:
Galerie umění
(Gallery of Art)

Liberec:
Oblastní galerie

Litoměřice:
Severočeská galerie výtvarného
umění (North
Bohemian Gallery of Fine Art)

Prague:
České muzeum výtvarných umění
(Czech Museum of Fine Arts)

Galerie hlavního města Prahy
(City Gallery Prague)
Národní galerie (National Gallery)

Roudnice nad Labem:
Galerie moderního umění
(Gallery of Modern Art)

ENGLAND
Bradford:
Cartwright Hall Art Gallery

London:
The Victoria and Albert Museum

FRANCE
Paris:
Bibliothèque nationale de France

Centre Georges Pompidou

Musée National de l'Art Moderne

GERMANY
Berlin:
Nationalgalerie

Cologne:
Wallraf-Richartz Museum

Essen:
Folkwang Museum

Hamburg:
Kunsthalle

ITALY
Florence:
Galleria degli Uffizi

Turin:
Galleria Civica d'Arte Moderna

JAPAN
Osaka:
Osaka University of Art

LUXEMBOURG
Luxembourg:
Musée National d'Art et d'Historie

MACEDONIA
Skopje:
Muzej na sovremena umetnost
(Museum of Contemporary Art)

THE NETHERLANDS
Amsterdam:
Stedelijk Museum

RUSSIA
Moscow:
Gosudarstvennyi Muzei
Izobrazitelnykh Iskusstv Imeni A. S.
Pushkina (The Pushkin Museum of
Fine Arts)

SLOVAKIA
Banská Bystrica:
Oblastná galéria (Regional Gallery)

Bratislava:
Galéria hlavného mesta Bratislavy
(Bratislava City Gallery)

Slovenská národná galéria (Slovak
National Gallery)

SLOVENIA
Adjovščina:
Pilonova galerija

Ljubljana:
Moderna galerija

SWEDEN
Stockholm:
Nationalmuseum

UNITED STATES

Amarillo, Texas:
Amarillo Museum of Art

Berkeley, California:
Berkeley Art Museum and Pacific Film Archive, University of California

Cambridge, Massachusetts:
Harvard University Art Museums

Chicago, Illinois:
The Art Institute of Chicago

Smart Museum of Art, University of Chicago

Cincinnati, Ohio:
Cincinnati Art Museum

Cleveland, Ohio:
The Cleveland Museum of Art

Des Moines, Iowa:
Des Moines Art Center

Detroit, Michigan:
The Detroit Institute of Arts

East Lansing, Michigan:
Kresge Art Museum, Michigan State University

Evanston, Illinois:
Mary and Leigh Block Museum of Art, Northwestern University

Gainesville, Florida:
Samuel P. Harn Museum of Art, University of Florida

Grand Rapids, Michigan:
Grand Rapids Art Museum

Grinnell, Iowa:
Faulconer Gallery, Grinnell College

Iowa City, Iowa:
University of Iowa Museum of Art

Los Angeles, California:
Fisher Gallery, University of Southern California

Grunwald Center for the Graphic Arts, Hammer Museum, UCLA

Macomb, Illinois:
Western Illinois University Art Gallery

Madison, Wisconsin:
Chazen Museum of Art

Morgantown, West Virginia:
West Virginia University College of Creative Arts

New York, New York:
The Jewish Museum

The Museum of Modern Art

The Metropolitan Museum of Art

The New York Public Library

Oakland, California:
California College of Arts and Crafts

Portland, Oregon:
Portland Art Museum

Reno, Nevada:
Nevada Museum of Art

San Francisco, California:
Achenbach Foundation for Graphic Arts, Fine Arts Museums of San Francisco

Spokane, Washington:
Jundt Art Museum, Gonzaga University

Tampa, Florida:
Tampa Museum of Art

Washington D.C.:
Library of Congress
National Gallery of Art

Williamstown, Massachusetts:
Sterling and Francine Clark Art Institute

Albrecht Dürer zu Ehren. Nuremberg: Albrecht Dürer Gesellschaft, 1971.

Anderle, Jiří. *Jiří Anderle—Werkverzeichnis der Graphik,* Cologne, Edition Baukunst, 1972-84.

———. *Anderle: Drawings, Prints, Paintings, Objects 1954 / 1995.* Introduction by Jiří Machalický. Translated by Anna Bryson. Prague: Slovart Publishing, Ltd., 1995.

Baruch, Anne. *Twenty Years of Czechoslovak Art: 1968–1988, A Tribute to Jacques Baruch.* Chicago: Jacques Baruch Gallery, 1988.

Beall, Karen F. *Contemporary Czechoslovakian Printmakers.* Foreword by Jacques Z. Baruch. Washington, D.C.: Smithsonian Institution, 1979.

———. "Prints from Eastern Europe: The Last 20 Years." *The Quarterly Journal of the Library of Congress* 37, no. 1 (Winter 1980): 74–113.

———. "The Uncontrolled Press: Eastern European Prints." *Art News* 80, no. 3 (March 1981): 112–115.

Bénézit, E. *Dictionnaire critique et documentaire des peintres, sculpteurs, dessinateurs et graveurs.* Paris: Gründ, 1999, vol. 1, 287.

Boone, Elizabeth. *Jiri Anderle: A Selection from the Werksman Collection.* Chicago: Mary and Leigh Block Gallery, Northwestern University, 1987.

Bornstein, Karen. "Jiri Anderle." *The New Art Examiner,* Midwest Edition 8, no. 4 (January 1981): 16.

Bruce, Deborah. "Passages in Time: The Prints of Jiří Anderle." *Print News* 7, nos. 3–4 (May–August 1985): 3, 23.

Castelman, Riva. "News of the Print World." *The Print Collectors Newsletter* 2, no. 3 (July–August 1971): 54.

Chasson, Timothy. *Dialogues with the Grand Masters: Selected Prints of Jiří Anderle.* Grinnell, IA: Grinnell College, 1987.

Cox, William M. *From Oppression to Freedom: Eastern European Prints and Drawings.* Edinboro: Bruce Gallery, Edinboro University of Pennsylvania, 1993.

Drury, Richard, Gerd Köhrmann, and Jan Kříž. *Jiří Anderle – At the Close of the Millennium: Paintings, Prints, Drawings 1950–2000.* Translated by Anna Bryson and Richard Drury. Prague: Slovart Publishing, Ltd., 1995.

Drury, Richard. *Jiří Anderle: View Back and Forward.* Translated by Maciej Głogoczowski and Richard Drury. Cracow: Galeria Sztuki Wspólezesnej BWA [BWA Contemporary Art Gallery], 2002.

Ferondell, Michele. "Anderle's Moments in Time." *California Printmaker,* October 1986: 2–3.

Forsling, Stephen. "Fizzles, Savage, Breeze, Kitty Hawk and a Message from Degas." *Art News* 79, no. 7 (September 1980): 124–128.

Georg, Charles, Antonín Hartmann, and Vaněk. *Graveurs tchécoslovaques contemporains.* Geneva: Musée d'art et d'histoire, 1970.

Goldscheider, Irena. *Czechoslovak Prints from 1900 to 1970.* London: British Museum, 1986.

"Graphica Creativa." *Print News* 7, no. 5 (September–October 1985): 14.

Graphica Creativa '81. Jyväskylä, Finland: The Museum of Central Finland – Alvar Aalto Museum, 1981.

Hartmann, Antonín. "Eastern European Printmaking, Part 2: Czechoslovakia, 1950 to the Present." *Print Review* 7 (1977): 62–74.

Henry, Clare. "1984 Bradford Biennale Assessed." *Print News* 7, no. 1 (January–February 1985): 7–10.

Holten, Ragnar von. *Jiří Anderle grafik från 1967–82.* Stockholm: Nationalmuseum, 1982.

Hošková, Simeona. "Jiří Anderle." In *Papier aus Prag, Tschechische Grafik.* Saarbrücken: Stadtgalerie, 1990.

Hrabal, Bohumil. *Domácí úkoly z pilnosti: Grafické listy a Jiří Anderle a Vysvlékání očima a ocelovým perem.* Prague: Československý spisovatel, 1982.

———. *Jiří Anderle Grafika.* Sobotka: Rodný statek Václava Šolce, 1990.

———. *Jiří Anderle – Grafika.* Valašské Meziříčí: JKZ Galerie, 1991.

———. *Jiří Anderle – Werkverzeichnis der Graphik.* Cologne: Edition Baukunst, 1979.

Hrabal, Bohumil, Jiří Kotalík, Jiří Mašín, and Gerd Köhrmann. *Jiří Anderle.* Ljubljana: Mladinska kniga, 1985.

———. *Jiří Anderle*. Translated by Jan Čulik and Milan Mlačnik. New York: Alpine Fine Arts Collection, Ltd., 1985.

Jiří Anderle. 26 Neue graphien 1981/82. Cologne: Baukunst Galerie, 1981.

Jiří Anderle. Stuttgart: Galerie Götz, 1982.

Jiří Anderle. Cologne: Baukunst Galerie, 1983.

Jiří Anderle: Obrazy a grafika 1962–1984. Hradec Králové: Krajská galerie, 1984.

Katzenstein, Marjorie. "Surrealism and the Contemporary Print." In *Print Review 20*. New York: Pratt Graphics Center, 1985, 78–91.

Klein, Henry F. *Creativity in the Shadow of Political Oppression: Recent Czechoslovakian Graphic Art from the Werksman Collection and the Jacques Baruch Gallery*. Los Angeles: Los Angeles Valley College, 1990.

Köhrmann, Gerd. *Jiří Anderle*. Kiel: Städtische Galerie, 1986.

Koschatzky, Walter. *Mit Nadel und Säure*. Vienna: Edition Tusch, 1982.

Kotalík, Jiří. *Jiří Anderle*. Düsseldorf: Galerie Walther, 1972.

———. *Jiří Anderle—Werkverzeichnis der Graphik*. Cologne: Baukunst Galerie, 1972-84. Essay for ongoing work catalogue.

———. *Jiří Anderle – výběr z graficlých cyklů*. Prague: Výstavni siň Fronta, 1979.

Kotalík, Jiří, and Bohumil Hrabal. *Jiří Anderle Master Graphics: 10th Anniversary Exhibition*. Chicago: Jacques Baruch Gallery, 1980.

Kotalík, Jiří, Jiří Mašín, Bohumil Hrabal, and Gerd Köhrmann. *Jiří Anderle*. Rakovnik: Okresní muzeum a galerie, 1985.

Krátký, Čestmír. *Jiří Anderle*. Liberec: Oblastní galerie, 1966.

Kříž, Jan. "Grafika Jiřího Anderla." *Výtvarná práce*, 1966, no. 14.

Kudrna, Miroslav. *Jiří Anderle: Výber z obrazových cyklov 1981–1983, Fragmenty grafickej tvorby 1978–1984*. Bratislava: Sieň Laca Novomeského, 1984.

Kudrna, Miroslav, and Zdeněk Čubrda. *Jiří Anderle*. Brno: Dům umění – Galerie Jaroslava Krále, 1984.

Lundquist, Svenrobert. "The 1980 Frechen Biennale of Graphics." *Print News* 3, no. 1 (February–March 1981): 1.

———. "Report from the Ljubljana Print Biennale." *Print News* 3, no. 4 (August–September 1981): 12–13.

———. "The Ljubljana Biennale–A Good Concept in Need of a Revised Structure." *Print News* 5, no. 5 (September–October 1983): 4–7.

Mašin, Jiří. *Jiří Anderle*. Olomouc: Oblastní galerie, 1969.

———. *Jiří Anderle*. Stockholm: Nationalmuseum, 1982.

———. *Jiří Anderle, obrazy grafika*. Karlovy Vary: Galerie umění, 1986.

Mašín, Jiří, and Simeona Hošková. *Jiří Anderle, Appassionata humana*. Rakovnik: Rabasova galerie, 1991.

McCracken, Patrick. *Jiri Anderle: Prints*. Amarillo, TX: Amarillo Art Center, 1993.

Mende, Matthias. *Dürer A-Z: Zeitgenössische Dürer – Variationen von Anderle bis Zimmermann*. Nuremberg: Hans Carl, 1980. Published in conjunction with the exhibit at the Stadtgeschichtlichen Museen Nürnberg and Albrecht Dürer Haus Stiftung e.V.

Míčko, Miroslav. *Aktuální tendence českého umění*. (Prague: Galerie Václava Špály and Galerie Mánes, 1966).

Morrison, C. L. "Chicago." *Artforum* 17, no. 8 (April 1979): 75.

Moser, Joann. *Passages in Time: The Prints of Jiří Anderle*. New York: Pratt Graphics Center, 1985.

Perkins, Larry David. *Recent Czech and Slovak Printmaking*. Gainesville: University of Florida, Harn Museum of Art, 1994.

Pregl, Tatjana. *Jiří Anderle*. Belgrade: Galerija Grafički kolektiv, 1981.

———. *Jiří Anderle: Razstava grafik*. Nova Gorica: Galerija Meblo, 1981.

———. *Jiří Anderle*. Zagreb: Galerija Josip Račić, 1981.

———. *Jiří Anderle*. Trieste: Gallerie TK, 1982.

———. *Jiří Anderle*. Gorzia: Kulturni dom, 1982.

———. *Anderle*. Belgrade: Kulturni centar Beograda, 1983

———. *Jiří Anderle: pregledna razstava*. Ajdovščina: Pilonova galerija, 1983.

Reuter, Laurel J. *Jiří Anderle*. Foreword by Harold Joachim. Grand Forks: University of North Dakota, 1978.

Risatti, Howard. "Descending from Olympus, 1980 Venice Biennale: Art in the Seventies." *The New Art Examiner* (December 1980): 10.

Saur, K. G. *Allgemeines Künstler-Lexikon: Die Bildenden Künstler aller Zeiten und Völker* (Munich and Leipzig: K. G. Saur, 1992, vol. 3, 357–358.

Šefčáková, Eva, and Eva Petrová. *Contemporary Prints of Czechoslovakia*. Introduction by Jean-Paul Morisset. Ottawa: The National Gallery of Canada, 1968.

"7th International Grafik Triennale." *Print News* 6, no. 4 (July–August 1984): 15.

Simoncic, Klement. "Venice Biennale 77." *Print Review* 8, no. 8 (1978): 69–71.

Šmejkal, František. *Fantasijní aspekty současného českého umění*. Prague: Oblastní galerie Vysočiny and Galerie Václava Špály, 1967.

Sokolová-Mládkova, Meda. *Recent Graphics from Prague*. Introduction by Walter Hopps. Washington, D.C.: Corcoran Gallery, 1968.

Spangenberg, Kristin L. *Eastern European Printmakers*. Cincinnati: Cincinnati Art Museum, 1975.

Spencer, Howard DaLee. *Contemporary Master Prints from Eastern Europe: The Gonzaga University Collection*. Reno: Nevada Museum of Art / E. L. Wiegand Gallery, 1994.

———. *Dialogue With the Grand Masters: Prints by Jiri Anderle*. Reno: Nevada Museum of Art / E. L. Wiegand Gallery, 1995.

"Surrealism from Eastern Europe." *Kresge Art Center Bulletin*, Michigan State University 9, no. 2 (December 1975): 14–15.

Tetiva, Vlastimil. *Jiří Anderle – grafika*. Budweis: Dům Kultury ROH, 1983.

Tschechoslowakische Druckgraphik der Gegenwart. Nuremberg: Albrecht Dürer Gesellschaft, 1972.

Vachtová, Ludmila. *Jiří Anderle – grafické cykly*. Prague: Galerie na Karlově námǒstí, 1966.

Weichandt, Jürgen. "The Norwegian Biennal – Two Reports, Two Views." *Print News* 4, no. 6 (November–December, 1982): 8–9.

Weinzapfel, Connie A. *Beauty & Truth: The Graphic Works of Jiří Anderle*. New Harmony, IN: New Harmony Gallery of Contemporary Art, 1990.

Winn, Steven. "Helping Artists Hear Each Other." *Art News* 79, no. 7 (September 1980): 138–140.

"World Print III." *Print News* 2, no. 3 (June–July 1980): 18–20.

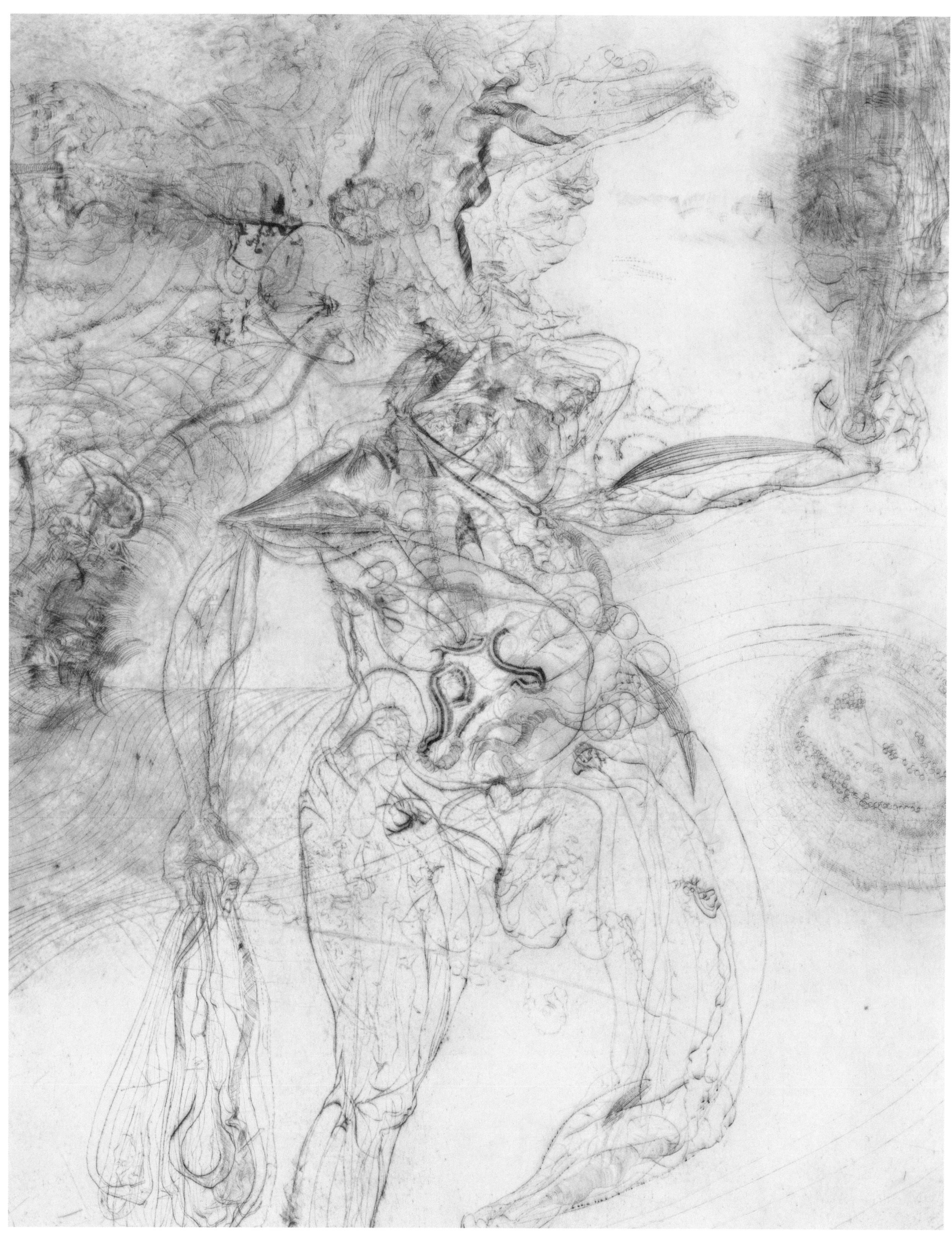

GLOSSARY OF TECHNICAL TERMS AND ABBREVIATIONS

after Indicates that the artist has executed a work after another artist.

à la poupée (French, "with a dolly"). A technique for printing several colors at one time from a single plate.

aquatint Aquatint is an intaglio method of etching with tone. A porous ground of particles of finely powdered asphaltum or resin is applied to the plate. The acid bites the plate where it is unprotected between the particles, thereby pitting the metal to give it a grainy texture when printed.

artist's proof Proofs outside the edition reserved for the artist. These proofs are identified by Roman numerals.

bon à tirer (French, "good to pull"). Inscription by the artist indicating that the printer should take this particular impression as the guide for the edition.

collagraph A print pulled from a surface that has been built up in the collage manner.

crayon resist The artist draws with a lithographic crayon directly on the bare plate. These stopped-out areas prevent the biting of the plate by the acid, resulting in areas that do not print in the final image.

drypoint An intaglio process in which the plate is scored with a pointed tool or needle, inked, wiped, and printed. The burr created by the cut of the pointed tool provides a warm, velvety line that breaks down if not steel faced.

edition The total number of prints pulled by the artist for distribution. The 11th print in an edition of seventy is numbered 11/70.

épreuve d'artiste [e.a.] (French). See "artist's proof."

etching An intaglio process in which an acid-resistant ground is applied to a plate, an image is cut into the ground with a needle, and acid is applied to bite the image into the plate.

hors commerce [h.c.] (French). Proof outside the commercial edition.

intaglio In intaglio processes the image, i.e., the printing surface, is either cut or bitten below the surface of a metal plate. The ink is forced into the grooves or pits of the image, the surface is wiped clean, and the print is made under pressure on paper in an etching press, which pulls the ink out of the grooves.

lithography One of the four major divisions of printmaking, in which a drawing is made with a greasy substance on a stone or plate. The surface is then treated so that the image accepts ink and the non-image areas repel ink, and the print is made with a lithographic press.

mezzotint A tonal intaglio process in which the surface of the plate is methodically roughened with a rocker to produce a dark background. With various scrapers the printmaker lightens certain passages, working from black to white to clarify the design.

soft ground etching A method with which the effect of a pencil drawing or any other texture can be imitated. A grease is added to the protective ground on the plate so that it does not harden.

state A particular stage in the development of a work. Any alteration to the printing surface, after a proof has been taken, involves the creation of a new state.

Variation on Dürer's The Great Fortune *(Nemesis)* (detail, plate 9)
1966, WV 24 (2005.514)

Catalogue order: This list records all the prints and drawings by Jiří Anderle donated to the Cincinnati Art Museum by the Anne and Jacques Baruch Collection in 2005, plus those previously donated to the Museum by the Baruchs, Granvil I. and Marcia Specks, and the promised bequest of Dr. Paula S. Biren. The prints are listed following the numbering as published in *Jiří Anderle—Werkverzeichnis der Graphik* documenting the editions published by Baukunst Galerie, Cologne, beginning in 1972. The print documentation sheets are referred to as "WV." Baukunst published sheets documenting the prints from numbers WV 1 to WV300 covering the years 1962 to 1984. In 1984 Edition Götz, Stuttgart, took over the publication of the print documentation sheets running from WV301 to WV451 covering the years 1984 to 1991. According to the artist, to date he has executed 607 print editions. There are no published edition records for WV 452 to WV 607. The artist reviewed the worksheets on each print described in this catalogue.

Titles: Titles have been translated into English, followed by the title used in *Jiří Anderle—Werkverzeichnis der Graphik.*

Dates: Prints are dated on the plate, as part of the inscription or supplied by the artist.

Cycles: The artist works in cycles. See the separate list of cycles citing the date and media involved.

Edition: The artist recorded the print edition number in the margin in pencil. For example, a print numbered 25/70 indicates that it is the 25th impression from the plate of an edition limited to 70. The total number of impressions appears in parentheses, followed by the number of prints reserved by the artist (given in Roman numerals) and then the Arabic-numbered commercial edition. The artist retained the *épreuve d'artiste* [e.a.] designation following the Roman numerals. Edition Baukunst published print descriptions WV 1 to WV 300 unless otherwise indicated. The commercial editions published by Edition Baukunst are numbered in Arabic numerals preceded by "EB." Between WV 104 and WV 143 ten Roman-numeraled impressions were reserved for Art Centrum. These prints are described as "AC X." Edition Götz published print descriptions WV 301 to WV 451. Unless otherwise indicated Edition Götz published WV 301 to WV 451 and the editions are preceded by "EG."

Catalogues: WV number is given first, followed by numbers documented in the artist's yearly record book. In later years the artist added a work number (WN) on the plate. The yearly works completed read, for example, "WN 3/80" meaning the third work regardless of medium completed in 1980. For prints, a graphic number (Gr) is added; for example, "Gr 6/80" means the sixth print executed in 1980.

States: WV number is given first, followed by the state. The next state number is assigned for the published state cited in *Jiří Anderle—Werkverzeichnis der Graphik.*

Printer: Prints WV 1 through WV 38 were printed by the artist. Starting with WV 39 the fine art printers Pavel and Milan Dřímal of the Dřímal Workshop in Prague printed the editions unless otherwise indicated. The Dřímal Workshop continues to print for the artist today.

Publisher: Print editions WV 1 to WV 84 and WV 452 to WV 607 were published by the artist. Unless otherwise indicated, starting with WV 96 through WV 300, Edition Baukunst, of Baukunst Galerie, Cologne, published the editions, and editions WV 301 to WV 451 were published by Edition Götz, Stuttgart.

Medium: The methods used by the artist are described as accurately as possible in consultation with the artist.

Measurements: Dimensions are listed in inches followed by centimeters, height preceding width. Measurements are based on the impressions in the Museum collection. The first set of measurements represents the platemark. The second set of measurements represents the sheet size of the paper. For larger format prints the sheet size is recorded, as the actual plate size is larger in dimension than the sheet.

Accession number: The year of acquisition is followed by the number of the object. For example, 2005.1 would be the first work acquired in 2005.

Credit line: In 2005 the Anne and Jacques Baruch Collection gave the Museum 191 prints and drawings by Jiří Anderle, adding to their three previous gifts. The 2005 gift carries the credit line "Gift of the Anne and Jacques Baruch Collection." Those prints donated at other years carry a specific credit line. The list also includes the six prints given in 1986 by Granvil I. and Marcia G. Specks in honor of the Museum's centennial.

Illustrations: Asterisks appear before the prints selected for the exhibition, which are illustrated full page. The remaining prints are illustrated as thumbnails with the collection list.

* *Four Masks [Vier Masken]*, 1962
Cycle: *Village Dances*
Edition: 28/50
Catalogue: WV 1
Color drypoint and collagraph à la poupée
12 9/16 x 27 3/16 in. (31.9 x 69 cm) on sheet 25 5/8 x 32 5/16 in. (65.1 x 80 cm)
Museum Purchase, 1974.360
Plate 1

* *Large Dance [Großer Tanz]*, 1962
Cycle: *Village Dances*
Edition: 22/30
Catalogue: WV 3
Color drypoint and collagraph à la poupée
18 9/16 x 27 5/8 in. (47.2 x 70.1 cm) on sheet 25 5/8 x 32 5/16 in. (65.1 x 81 cm)
2005.505
Plate 2

^

Dance III, 1962
Cycle: *Village Dances*
Edition: 5/6
Catalogue: not recorded
Drypoint and collagraph
18 3/16 x 26 9/16 in. (46.2 x 67.5 cm) on sheet 20 9/16 x 27 7/16 in. (52.3 x 69.7 cm)
2005.506

* *Head with Violin [Kopf mit Geige]*, 1963
Edition: 9/50 (1/50-21/50 with color monotype)
Catalogue: WV 6
Drypoint with color monotype
11 9/16 x 15 5/16 in. (29.4 x 38.9 cm) on sheet 14 1/8 x 17 1/2 in. (35.9 x 44.5 cm)
2005.507
Plate 3

* *Instigator [Hetzer]*, 1965
Cycle: *Heads*
Edition: 8/16 (16 + variant edition 10)
Catalogue: WV 10
Color drypoint
17 11/16 x 13 13/16 in. (44.9 x 35.1 cm) on sheet 21 x 16 3/4 in. (53.3 x 42.5 cm)
2005.508
Plate 4

* *Nude [Nackte]*, 1965
Cycle: *Heads*
Edition: 4/40
Catalogue: WV 11
Color drypoint
19 13/16 x 6 1/2 in. (50.4 x 16.5 cm) on sheet 25 1/16 x 10 1/16 in. (63.7 x 25.5 cm)
2005.509
Plate 5

* *The Harried One, the Strong One Attack the Weak One Who Is Caught in His Own Net [Die Eilende, der Starke ergreift den Schwachen]*, 1965
Cycle: *Skinless*
Edition: 20/30
Catalogue: WV 20
Color drypoint à la poupée
16 1/2 x 23 7/16 in. (41.9 x 59.5 cm) on sheet 25 x 29 1/2 in. (63.5 x 74.9 cm)
2005.510
Plate 6

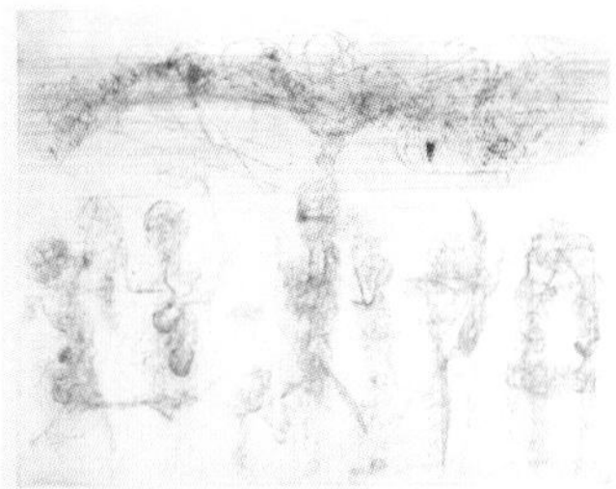

^

Fight Under a Cloud [Kampf unter der Wolke], 1965
Cycle: *Skinless*
Edition: 22/40 with various color tones
Catalogue: WV 21
Color drypoint à la poupée
18 1/16 x 23 7/16 in. (45.8 x 59.5 cm) on sheet 21 x 29 7/8 in. (53.4 x 75.9 cm)
2005.511

^

Secret Unrest [Geheime Unruhe], 1965–66
Cycle: *Skinless*
Edition: 22/45 with various color tones
Catalogue: WV 22
Color drypoint à la poupée
16 ⅝ x 25 ¼ in. (42.2 x 64.2 cm) on sheet 21 1/16 x 29 15/16 in. (53.5 x 76.1 cm)
2005.512

* *Conversation [Gespräch]*, 1966
Cycle: *Skinless*
Edition: 10/45 with various color tones
Catalogue: WV 23
Color drypoint à la poupée
16 ⅝ x 25 ¼ in. (42.3 x 64.2 cm) on sheet 20 1/16 x 28 7/16 in. (50.9 x 72.3 cm)
2005.513
Plate 7

* *Variation on Dürer's The Great Fortune (Nemesis) [Variante über Dürers "Große Fortuna"]*, 1966
After Albrecht Dürer (German, 1471–1528)
Cycle: *Skinless*
Edition: VIII/IX (69 imp. [e.a. IX + 45 red variant + 15 blue variant])
Catalogue: WV 24
Color drypoint à la poupée
23 ½ x 18 ⅛ in. (59.7 x 46 cm) on sheet 26 ⅞ x 21 ⅛ in. (68.3 x 53.6 cm)
2005.514
Plate 9

^

The Harried [Gehetzter], 1966
Cycle: *Skinless*
Edition: 19/20 (50 imp. [e.a. XV + 15 with color tones +20])
Catalogue: WV 25
Color drypoint à la poupée
23 7/16 x 16 7/16 in. (59.6 x 41.8 cm) on sheet 29 11/16 x 21 ⅛ in. (75.4 x 53.6 cm)
2005.515

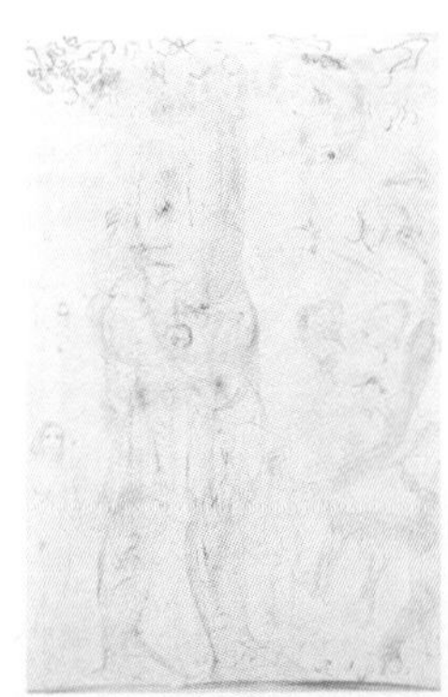

^

Alone [Allein], 1966
Cycle: *Skinless*
Edition: VIII/X (32 imp. [e.a. 13 + X red variant + 4 violet variant + 5 black variant])
Catalogue: WV 26
Color drypoint à la poupée
25 3/16 x 16 5/16 in. (64 x 41.4 cm) on sheet 30 x 25 in. (76.2 x 63.5 cm)
2005.516

* *Beasts of Prey [Raubtiere]*, 1966
Cycle: *Skinless*
Edition: IV/XI (31 imp. [e.a. XI + 20])
Catalogue: WV 28
Color drypoint
16 7/16 x 26 3/16 in. (41.8 x 64 cm) on sheet 20 x 28 ½ in. (50.8 x 72.2 cm)
2005.517
Plate 8

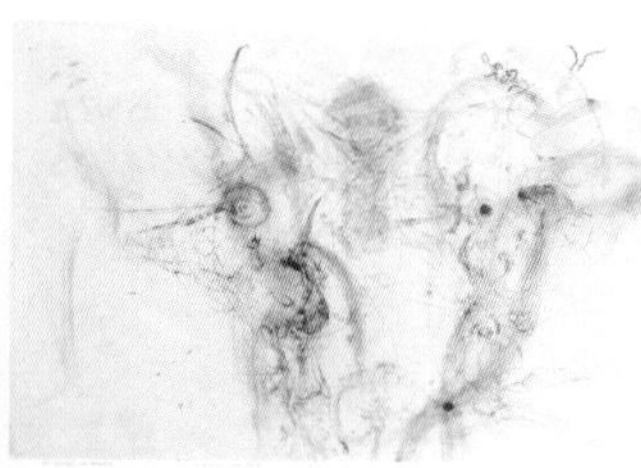

^

Look Forward and Backward II [Blick nach vorn und zurück II], 1967
Cycle: *Skinless*
Edition: 40
Catalogue: WV 30
Color drypoint à la poupée
16 7/16 x 25 ¼ in. (41.7 x 64.2 cm) on sheet 25 1/16 x 30 ⅜ in. (63.7 x 77.2 cm)
2005.518

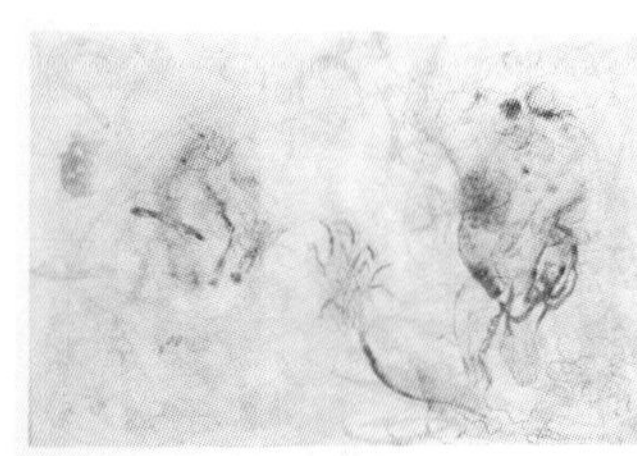

^

Delight and Wideness [Wonne und Weite], 1967
Cycle: *Skinless*
Edition: 29/30 (40 imp. [e.a. X + 30])
Catalogue: WV 31
Color drypoint à la poupée
16 ⅜ x 25 ¼ in. (41.6 x 64.2 cm) on sheet 24 ⅝ x 30 ⅛ in. (62.6 x 76.5 cm)
2005.519

^

You Are Your Own Worst Enemy [Des eigenen Ichs schlimmster Feind], 1967
Cycle: *Skinless*
Edition: 13/16 (32 imp. [e.a. XXV (plate destroyed after XVI) + 16])
Catalogue: WV 32
Color drypoint à la poupée
18 x 25 3/16 in. (45.7 x 63.9 cm) on sheet 21 ⅛ x 29 ⅛ in. (53.6 x 74 cm)
2005.520

* *Smile of Happiness [Lächeln des Glücks]*, 1967
Cycle: *Heads*
Edition: 10/40 (60 imp. [e.a. X + 10 blue variant + 40 black/brown variant])
Catalogue: WV 33
Color drypoint and mezzotint à la poupée
25 ¼ x 19 9/16 in. (64.2 x 49.7 cm) on sheet 30 x 19 9/16 in. (76.2 x 53.5 cm)
2005.521
Plate 10

* *Dawn [Morgengrauen]*, 1967
Cycle: *Comedy No. 1*
Edition: e.a. V/X (50 imp. [X + 40])
Catalogue: WV 34 (third state)
Color drypoint and mezzotint à la poupée
18 1/16 x 25 ¼ in. (45.8 x 64.1 cm) on sheet 25 1/16 x 30 ⅛ in. (63.7 x 76.5 cm)
2005.522
Plate 12

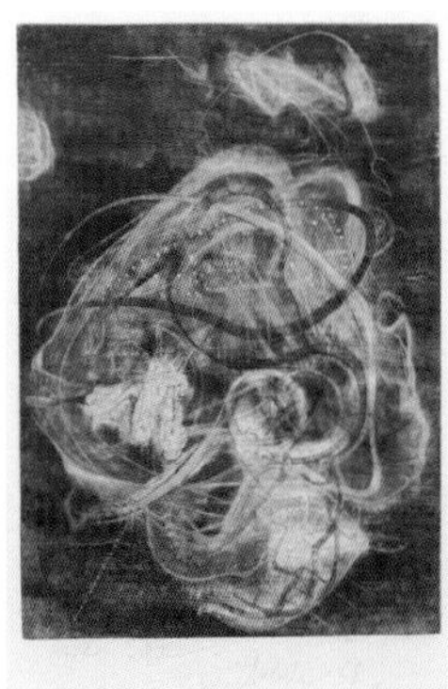

^

Head [Kopf], 1967

Edition: 17/50 (45 imp. [e.a. V + 40])

Catalogue: WV 35

Hand colored drypoint and mezzotint

12 13/16 x 9 1/16 in. (32.5 x 23 cm) on sheet 21 1/16 x 15 in. (53.5 x 38.1 cm)

2005.523

* *Eye of the Tortoise [Schildkrötenaugen]*, 1968

Cycle: *Comedy No. 5*

Edition: X/XX (78 imp. [e.a. X + 48 dark brown variant + XX indigo variant])

Catalogue: WV 39 (fifth state)

Color drypoint and mezzotint à la poupée

25 1/8 x 19 5/8 in. (63.8 x 49.8 cm) on sheet 30 1/4 x 25 1/4 in. (76.8 x 64.2 cm)

2005.524

Plate 11

* *Variation on Dürer's Knight, Death, and the Devil [Variante über Dürers "Ritter, Tod und Teufel"]*, 1968

After Albrecht Dürer (German, 1471–1528)

Cycle: *Comedy No. 6*

Edition: 16/65 (117 imp. [XX + 65 dark red variant + 32 blue variant])

Catalogue: WV 40 (third state)

Color drypoint and mezzotint à la poupée

25 3/8 x 19 1/2 in. (64.5 x 49.6 cm) on sheet 30 1/4 x 21 1/4 in. (76.9 x 53.9 cm)

2005.525

Plate 13

* *And There Is No Hope [Lasciate ogni speranza]*, 1968

Cycle: *Comedy No. 8*

Edition: 5/60 (96 imp. [e.a. VI + 60 black/brown variant + 30 violet/orange variant])

Catalogue: WV 42

Color drypoint and mezzotint

24 15/16 x 19 7/16 in. (63.4 x 49.3 cm) on sheet 30 11/16 x 25 1/16 in. (77.9 x 63.7 cm)

2005.526

Plate 14

^

Variation on the Theme of the School of Fontainebleau [Variante über Motiv "Ecole de Fontainebleau"], 1968

Edition: 90/91 (100 imp., [e.a. IX + 91])

Catalogue: WV 68 (third state)

Color drypoint and mezzotint à la poupée

14 x 8 7/8 in. (35.6 x 22.6 cm) on sheet 18 7/8 x 12 13/16 in. (48 x 32.5 cm)

2005.527

^

Variation on Lucas Cranach's Judith and the Head of Holofernes *[Variante über Lucas Cranachs "Judith mit dem Haupt des Holofernes"]*, 1968

After Lucas Cranach (German, 1472–1533)

Edition: 6/60 (71 imp. [e.a. V + e.a. VI + 60])

Catalogue: WV 69 (second state)

Color drypoint and mezzotint à la poupée

12 15/16 x 8 15/16 in. (32.9 x 22.7 cm) on sheet 18 7/8 x 12 5/8 in. (47.9 x 32 cm)

2005.528

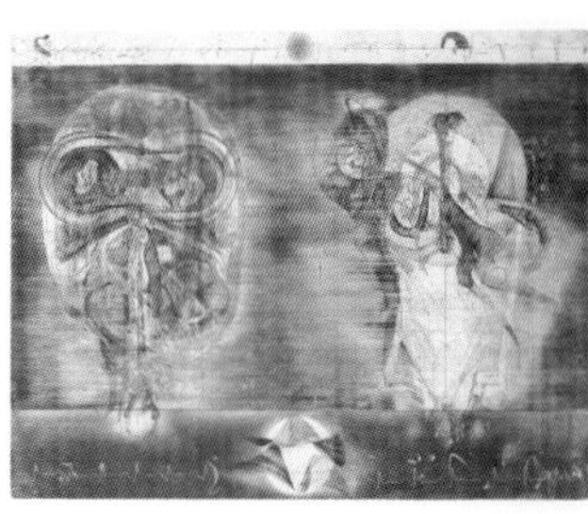

^

Superego – Man [Superego – Mann], 1969

Cycle: *Comedy No. 11*

Edition: 3/50 (58 imp. [e.a. VIII + 50])

Catalogue: WV 72 (fifth state)

Color drypoint and mezzotint à la poupée

19 1/16 x 24 3/4 in. (48.4 x 62.9 cm) on sheet 25 1/2 x 30 1/16 in. (64.8 x 76.4 cm)

2005.529

^

Superego – Woman [Superego – Frau], 1969

Cycle: *Comedy No. 11*

Edition: 27/80 (58 imp. [e.a. VIII + 50])

Catalogue: WV 73

Color drypoint and mezzotint à la poupée

19 1/8 x 24 7/8 in. (48.5 x 63.4 cm) on sheet 25 x 10 1/4 in. (63.5 x 76.8 cm)

2005.530

* *Superego – Man and Woman [Superego – Mann und Frau]*, 1969

Cycle: *Comedy No. 11*

Edition: 20/50 (76 imp. [e.a. VIII Turkish red variant + 50 Turkish red variant + e.a. VIII warm red variant + 10 grayish violet variant])

Catalogue: WV 74

Color drypoint and mezzotint

19 1/8 x 24 7/8 in. (48.5 x 63.2 cm) on sheet 25 1/4 x 30 1/4 in. (64.2 x 76.8 cm)

2005.531

Plate 15

^

As It Should Be – Party [Comme il faut – Gesellschaft], 1969

Cycle: *Comedy No. 12*

Edition: 14/30 (38 imp. [e.a. VIII + 30 various colors])

Catalogue: WV 75

Color drypoint and mezzotint

19 x 24 ¾ in. (48.3 x 62.9 cm) on sheet 19 x 24 ¾ in. (48.3 x 62.9 cm)

2005.532

* *As It Should Be – Meal [Comme il faut – Speise]*, 1969

Cycle: *Comedy No. 12*

Edition: 26/30 (38 imp. [e.a. VIII + 30 various colors])

Catalogue: WV 76

Color drypoint and mezzotint à la poupée

19 x 24 11/16 in. (48.2 x 62.7 cm) on sheet 25 ⅜ x 30 3/16 in. (64.5 x 76.6 cm)

2005.533

Plate 16

* *Monkey [Äffchen]*, 1969

Cycle: *Comedy No. 13*

Edition: 15/40 (48 imp. [e.a. VIII + 40])

Catalogue: WV 79

Color drypoint and mezzotint

26 ⅞ x 20 1/16 in. (68.3 x 51 cm) on sheet 30 ¼ x 24 15/16 in. (76.9 x 63.3 cm)

2005.534

Plate 17

* *Girl [Mädchen]*, 1969

Cycle: *Comedy No. 13*

Edition: VI/VIII (48 imp. [e.a. VIII + 40])

Catalogue: WV 80

Color drypoint and mezzotint

23 1/16 x 20 1/16 in. (58.6 x 51 cm) on sheet 30 ⅛ x 25 ¼ in. (76.5 x 64.2 cm)

2005.535

Plate 18

* *Monkey and Girl [Äffchen und Mädchen]*, 1969

Cycle: *Comedy No. 13*

Edition: 38/47 B variant (68 imp. red background [e.a. VIII + 13 + 47])

Catalogue: WV 81B variant

Color drypoint and mezzotint

26 11/16 x 20 1/16 in. (67.8 x 50.9 cm) on sheet 30 ¼ x 25 1/16 in. (76.8 x 63.6 cm)

2005.536

Plate 19

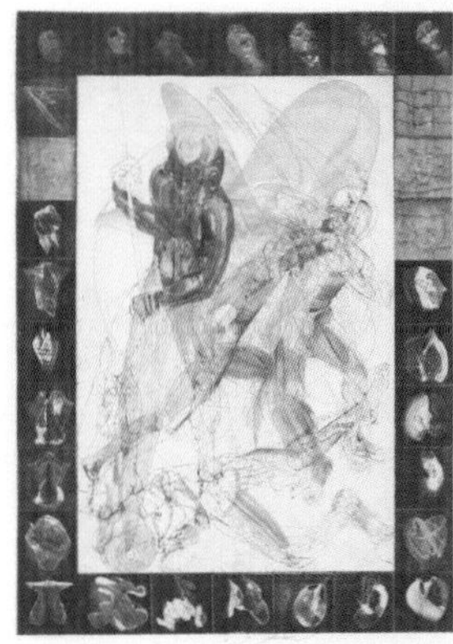

^

Survival, 1969

Edition: For Pragensis IX/XX (200 imp. [e.a. XX olive green/ brown violet variant + 148 dark brown variant + 32 olive green/ brownish violet variant])

Catalogue: WV 82

Color drypoint and mezzotint

14 9/16 x 10 ⅝ in. (37 x 27 cm) on sheet 25 ½ x 18 ⅞ in. (64.8 x 47.9 cm)

2005.537

* *Homage to Watteau [Fêtes galantes de Watteau]*, 1970

Cycle: *Perspectives No. 1*

Edition: unique proof (88 imp. [e.a. VIII + 80])

Catalogue: WV 83

Color drypoint and mezzotint à la poupée

36 13/16 x 24 3/16 in. (93.5 x 61.5 cm) on sheet 41 ⅞ x 29 15/16 in. (106.3 x 76 cm)

2005.538

Plate 20

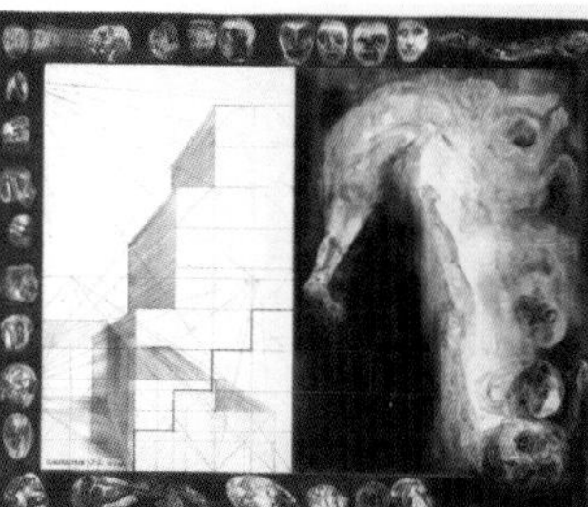

^

The Leap [Le saut], 1970

Cycle: *Perspectives No. 2*

Edition: 65/70 (80 imp. [e.a. X + 70])

Catalogue: WV 84

Color drypoint and mezzotint à la poupée

19 ½ x 23 11/16 in. (49.5 x 60.2 cm) on sheet 25 ⅜ x 30 ⅛ in. (64.5 x 76.5 cm)

2005.539

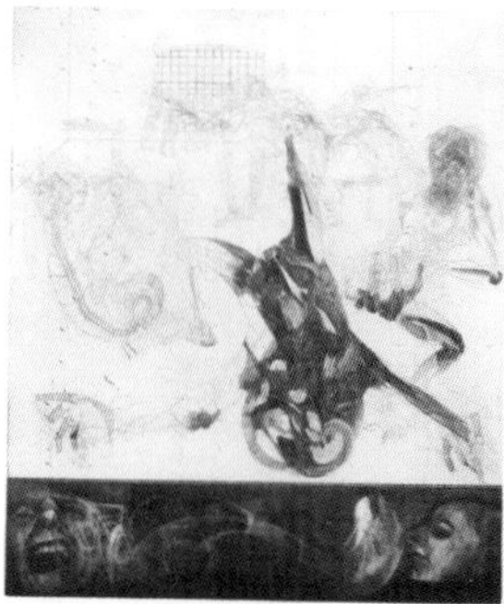

^

Interior [Interieur], 1970

Publisher: Jacques Ludovicy, Brussels

Portfolio: *Adventures of the Mind: New Trends in Czechoslovak Graphic Art*

Edition: 31/65 (82 imp. [h.c. 10 + e.a. VII + 65])

Catalogue: WV 85

Color drypoint and mezzotint à la poupée

13 11/16 x 11 11/16 in. (34.7 x 29.7 cm) on sheet 25 11/16 x 18 ⅞ in. (65.3 x 47.9 cm)

2005.504.1

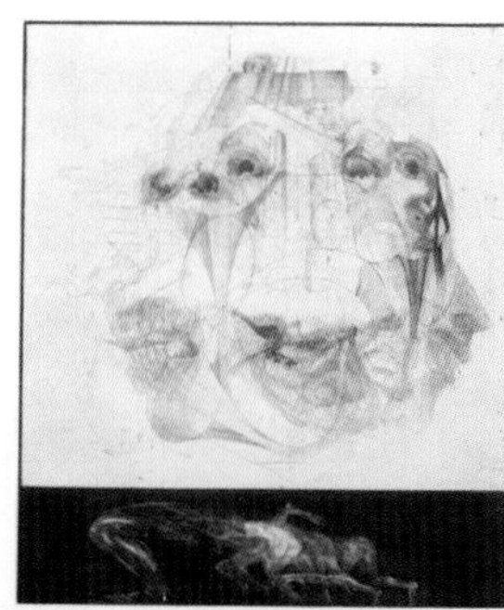

^

Head [Kopf], 1970

Publisher: Jacques Ludovicy, Brussels

Portfolio: *Adventures of the Mind: New Trends in Czechoslovak Graphic Art*

Edition: 31/65 (82 imp. [h.c. 10 + e.a. VII + 65])

Catalogue: WV 86

Color drypoint and mezzotint à la poupée

13 11/16 x 11 ¾ in. (34.7 x 29.8 cm) on sheet 25 11/16 x 18 ⅞ in. (63.5 x 47.9 cm)

2005.504.2

* *Cogito ergo sum [I Think Therefore I Am]*, 1971

Cycle: *Perspectives No. 4*

Edition: 36/91 (100 imp. [e.a. IX various colors + EB 91])

Catalogue: WV 96

Color drypoint and mezzotint à la poupée

23 3/16 x 17 1/2 in. (58.9 x 44.5 cm) on sheet 30 5/16 x 24 3/8 in. (77 x 61.9 cm)

2005.540

Plate 21

* *Space for Two [Espace pour deux]*, 1971

Cycle: *Perspectives No. 6*

Edition: 57/91 (100 imp. [e.a. IX + EB 91])

Catalogue: WV 98 (third state)

Color drypoint and mezzotint à la poupée

25 3/16 x 19 1/2 in. (63.9 x 49.6 cm) on sheet (29 5/16 x 25 1/16 in. (74.4 x 63.7 cm)

2005.541

Plate 22

* *Self Image*, 1971

Cycle: *Perspectives No. 7*

Edition: 27/91 (100 imp. [e.a. IX + EB 91])

Catalogue: WV 99 (third state)

Color drypoint and mezzotint à la poupée

21 7/16 x 17 5/8 in. (54.4 x 44.7 cm) on sheet 29 5/8 x 25 1/16 in. (75.3 x 63.7 cm)

Centennial Gift of Granvil I. and Marcia G. Specks

1986.317

Plate 23

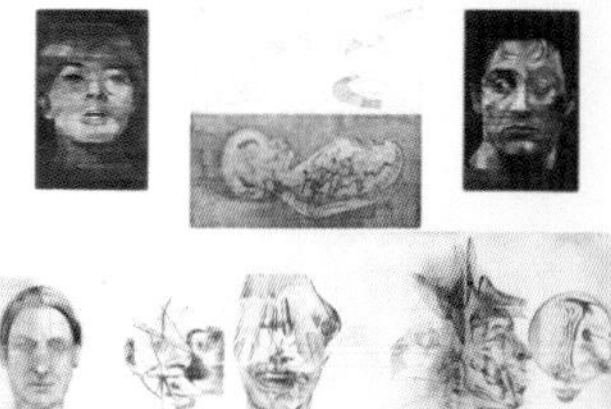

^

Our Generation [Generatio nostra], 1972

Cycle: *Perspectives No. 8*

Edition: 15/91 (100 imp. [e.a. IX + EB 91])

Catalogue: WV 100 (third state)

Color drypoint and mezzotint à la poupée

22 1/16 x 28 in. (56 x 71.1 cm) on sheet 25 1/4 x 29 3/4 in. (64.1 x 75.5 cm)

2005.542

* *Gravitation*, 1972

Cycle: *Perspectives No. 9*

Edition: 36/70 (100 imp. [e.a. XX + AC X + EB 70])

Catalogue: WV 104 (eighth state)

Color drypoint and mezzotint à la poupée

17 9/16 x 21 3/8 in. (44.6 x 54.3 cm) on sheet 25 1/16 x 29 13/16 in. (63.6 x 75.7 cm)

2005.543

Plate 24

^

Where Are Those Madmen Rushing [Qui qui ruitis scedentes], 1973

Cycle: *Perspectives No. 10*

Edition: 47/70 (100 imp. [e.a. X + e.a. 1/XX – X/XX + AC XI–XX + EB 70])

Catalogue: WV 105

Color drypoint and mezzotint à la poupée

25 3/16 x 19 9/16 in. (63.9 x 49.7 cm) on sheet 29 3/4 x 25 1/8 in. (75.5 x 63.8 cm)

2005.544

^

El Loulabi II, 1973

Cycle: *Kamasutra*

Edition: III/X (100 imp. [e.a. XX + AC X + EB 70])

Catalogue: WV 108

Color drypoint and mezzotint à la poupée

25 3/16 x 19 1/2 in. (64 x 49.5 cm) on sheet 29 1/2 x 25 3/8 in. (75 x 64.4 cm)

2005.545

* *El Motadani*, 1973

Cycle: *Kamasutra*

Edition: e.a. (100 imp. [e.a. X + e.a. 1/XX–X/XX + AC XI/XX–XX + EB 70])

Catalogue: WV 109

Color drypoint and mezzotint à la poupée

25 3/16 x 19 9/16 in. (63.9 x 49.7 cm) on sheet 30 1/4 x 24 15/16 in. (76.8 x 63.3 cm)

2005.546

Plate 25

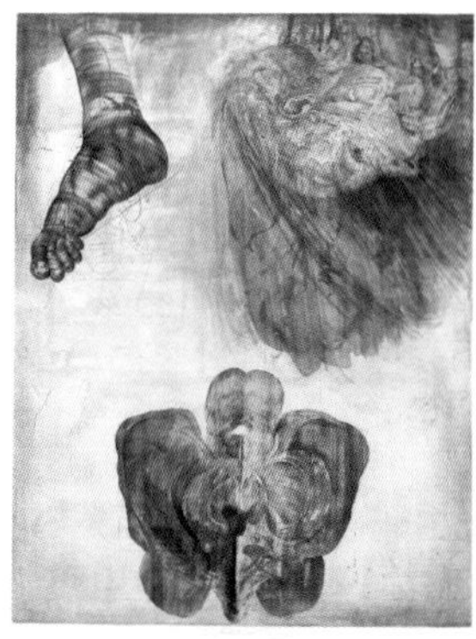

^

El Ladid, 1973

Cycle: *Kamasutra*

Edition: VI/X (100 imp. [e.a. XX + AC X + EB 70])

Catalogue: WV 110 (fifth state)

Color drypoint and mezzotint à la poupée

25 1/4 x 19 1/2 in. (64.1 x 49.6 cm) on sheet 29 11/16 x 25 3/8 in. (75.4 x 64.4 cm)

2005.547

* *Game for 122 Persons*, 1974

Cycle: *Games No. 1 – Free Space*

Edition: 4/20

Catalogue: WV 112D (fourth state)

Color drypoint and mezzotint à la poupée

24 13/16 x 19 9/16 in. (63.1 x 49.7 cm) on sheet 29 5/8 x 25 1/16 in. (75.2 x 63.6 cm)

2005.549

Plate 26

^

Game for 122 Persons, 1974

Cycle: *Games No. 1 – Free Space*

Edition: 10/17

Catalogue: WV 112E (fifth state)

Color drypoint and mezzotint á la poupée

24 ⅞ x 19 ⅝ in. (63.2 x 49.8 cm) on sheet 29 ¾ x 25 1/16 in. (75.5 x 63.7 cm)

2005.550

* *Game for 122 Persons*, 1974

Cycle: *Games No. 1 – Free Space*

Edition: VIII/X (100 imp. [e.a. XX + AC X + EB 70])

Catalogue: WV 112 (sixth state)

Color drypoint and mezzotint à la poupée

24 15/16 x 19 ⅝ in. (63.3 x 49.9 cm) on sheet 29 11/16 x 25 ⅜ in. (75.4 x 64.4 cm)

2005.548

Plate 27

^

Game in the Car, 1974

Cycle: *Games*

Edition: VIII/X (100 imp. [e.a. XX + AC X + EB 70])

Catalogue: WV 115 (fifth state)

Color drypoint and mezzotint à la poupée

24 ⅞ x 19 9/16 in. (63.2 x 49.7 cm) on sheet 29 ½ x 25 7/16 in. (75 x 64.6 cm)

2005.551

^

David I, 1975

Edition: VIII/X (100 imp. [e.a. XX + AC X + EB 70])

Catalogue: WV 120

Color drypoint and mezzotint à la poupée

24 15/16 x 19 11/16 in. (63.4 x 49.9 cm) on sheet 29 ½ x 25 ⅜ in. (75 x 64.5 cm)

Centennial Gift of Granvil I. and Marcia G. Specks

1986.318

^

David II, 1975

Edition: VII/X (100 imp. [e.a. XX + AC X + EB 70])

Catalogue: WV 121

Color drypoint and mezzotint à la poupée

19 13/16 x 24 15/16 in. (50.3 x 63.4 cm) on sheet 25 7/16 x 29 ¾ in. (64.4 x 75.5 cm)

2005.552

* *Cruel Game for a Man*, 1975

Cycle: *Games*

Publisher: Jacques Baruch Gallery, Chicago

Edition: 32/60 (84 imp. [4 proofs + e.a. XX + JBG 60])

Catalogue: WV 122

Color drypoint and mezzotint à la poupée

36 ⅛ x 24 ⅜ in. (92 x 62 cm) on sheet 41 ⅝ x 30 ⅞ in. (105.7 x 78.5 cm)

Gift of Anne and Jacques Baruch

1976.332

Plate 28

^

Madame Rivière Among Us [Madame Rivière entre nous], 1975

After Jean Auguste Dominique Ingres (French, 1780–1867)

Cycle: *Rivière Family Triptych*

Edition: XX (100 imp. [e.a. XX + AC X + EB 70])

Catalogue: WV 124

Color drypoint and mezzotint à la poupée

19 9/16 x 24 13/16 in. (49.7 x 63 cm) on sheet 25 3/16 x 29 15/16 in. (64 x 76 cm)

2005.553

^

Monsieur Rivière Among Us [Monsieur Rivière entre nous], 1975

After Jean Auguste Dominique Ingres (French, 1780–1867)

Cycle: *Rivière Family Triptych*

Edition: III/X (100 imp. [e.a. XX + AC X + EB 70])

Catalogue: WV 125

Color drypoint and mezzotint à la poupée

19 11/16 x 24 7/16 in. (50 x 62.1 cm) on sheet 25 ⅜ x 29 9/16 in. (64.4 x 75.1 cm)

Centennial Gift of Granvil I. and Marcia G. Specks

1986.319

TV – Game, 1975

Cycle: *Games*

Edition: VIII/X (100 imp. [e.a. XX + AC X + 70 (EB 1/70–20/70)])

Catalogue: WV 126 (second state)

Color drypoint and mezzotint à la poupée

19 5/8 x 25 7/8 in. (49.8 x 65.8 cm) on sheet 25 5/16 x 29 3/8 in. (64.3 x 74.6 cm)

2005.554

Follow Me [Sequere me], 1975

Edition: 45/70 (100 imp. [e.a. XX + AC X + EB 70])

Catalogue: WV 127 (second state)

Color drypoint and mezzotint à la poupée

25 11/16 x 19 11/16 in. (65.2 x 50 cm) on sheet 29 7/16 x 24 7/8 in. (74.7 x 63.2 cm)

2005.555

Mr. Reversible [Monsieur Reversible], 1975

Publisher: Galerie Platýz, Prague

Edition: 34/130 (140 imp. [e.a. X + GP 130])

Catalogue: WV 128

Color drypoint and mezzotint à la poupée

12 1/2 x 10 9/16 in. (31.7 x 26.8 cm) on sheet 25 1/16 x 29 5/8 in. (63.6 x 75.2 cm)

Centennial Gift of Granvil I. and Marcia G. Specks

1986.320

* *Dialogue with Myself [Dialogue avec moi même]*, 1975

Cycle: *Relations No. 1*

Edition: 43/70 (100 imp. [ea. XX + AC X + EB 70])

Catalogue: WV 129

Color drypoint and mezzotint à la poupée

19 5/8 x 26 in. (49.8 x 66.1 cm) on sheet 25 1/16 x 29 5/8 in. (63.6 x 75.2 cm)

2005.556

Plate 31

Acis and Galathea [Acis und Galathea], 1975

After Claude Gellée, called Claude Lorrain (French, 1600–1682)

Edition: 68/70 (100 imp. [e.a. XX + AC X + EB 70])

Catalogue: WV 130

Color drypoint and mezzotint à la poupée

19 3/4 x 26 in. (50.2 x 66.1 cm) on sheet 25 3/8 x 29 13/16 in. (64.4 x 75.7 cm)

2005.557

Mutual Agreement on a Condemnation [Vereinbarung über eine Verurteilung], 1975

Cycle: *Relations No. 2*

Edition: 12/70 (100 imp. [e.a. XX + AC X + EB 70)]

Catalogue: WV 131

Color drypoint and mezzotint à la poupée

19 5/8 x 26 1/8 in. (49.9 x 66.3 cm) on sheet 25 3/16 x 29 5/8 in. (63.9 x 75.2 cm)

2005. 558

* *Confrontation [Konfrontation]*, 1976

Cycle: *Relations No. 3*

Edition: 13/70 (100 imp. [e.a. XX + AC X + EB 70])

Catalogue: WV 132

Color drypoint and mezzotint à la poupée

19 1/2 x 26 1/8 in. (49.6 x 66.3 cm) on sheet 24 13/16 x 30 3/16 in. (63 x 76.7 cm)

2005.559

Plate 30

* *Appassionata*, 1977

Edition: 18/70 (100 imp. [e.a. XX + AC X + EB 70])

Catalogue: WV 133 (fourth state)

Color drypoint and mezzotint à la poupée

24 13/16 x 36 3/4 in. (63 x 93.3 cm) on sheet 30 x 41 15/16 in. (76.2 x 106.5 cm)

2005.560

Plate 29

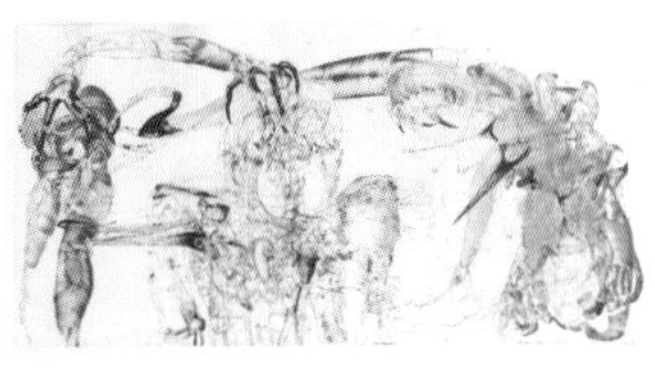

Manipulation I, 1976

Cycle: *Relations No. 4*

Edition: 17/70 (100 imp. [e.a. XX + AC X + EB 70])

Catalogue: WV 134 (second state)

Color drypoint and mezzotint à la poupée

12 13/16 x 25 11/16 in. (32.5 x 65.3 cm) on sheet 16 9/16 x 30 7/8 in. (42.1 x 78.4 cm)

2005.561

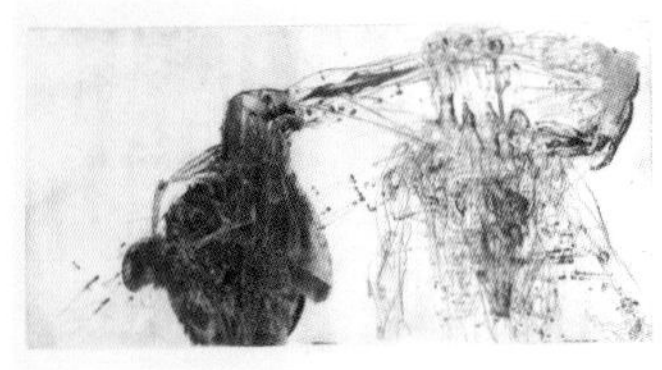

^

Manipulation III, 1976
Cycle: *Relations No. 6*
Edition: 26/70 (100 imp. [e.a. XX + AC X + BG 70])
Catalogue: WV 136 (second state)
Color drypoint and mezzotint à la poupée
12 ⅞ x 25 13⁄16 in. (32.7 x 65.6 cm) on sheet 16 ⅝ x 31 1⁄16 in. (42.2 x 78.9 cm)
2005.562

^

Profile [Profil], 1977
Edition: 13/70 (100 imp. [e.a. XX + AC X + EB 70])
Catalogue: WV 138
Color drypoint and mezzotint à la poupée
26 ⅛ x 19 9⁄16 in. (66.3 x 49.7 cm) on sheet 31 ⅛ x 25 1⁄16 in. (79 x 63.6 cm)
Centennial Gift of Granvil I. and Marcia G. Specks
1986.321

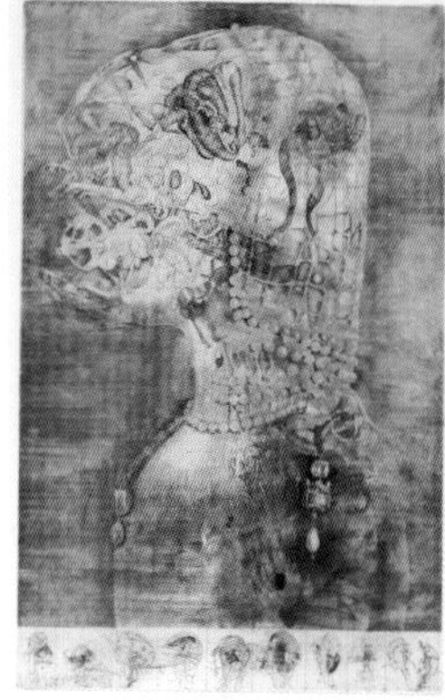

^

Portrait of a Renaissance Girl [Portrait eines Renaissance-Mädchens], 1977
After Ambrogio de Predis (Italian, ca. 1450–1460, d. post 1520)
Publisher: Galerie Walther, Düsseldorf
Edition: 63/100 (120 imp. [e.a. XX + GW 100])
Catalogue: WV 139
Color drypoint and mezzotint à la poupée
19 3⁄16 x 12 3⁄16 in. (48.7 x 31 cm) on sheet 27 15⁄16 x 20 ⅞ in. (71 x 53.1 cm)
2005.563

* *The Hazards of the Swing [Les hasards heureux de l'escarpolette]*, 1978
After Jean-Honoré Fragonard (French, 1732–1806)
Edition: 15/70 (100 imp. [e.a. XX + AC X + EB 70])
Catalogue: WV 140
Color drypoint and mezzotint à la poupée
26 5⁄16 x 19 9⁄16 in. (66.8 x 49.7 cm) on sheet 29 ⅞ x 25 ⅛ in. (75.9 x 63.8 cm)
Centennial Gift of Granvil I. and Marcia G. Specks
1986.322
Plate 45

* *The Smile [Il Sorriso]*, 1976–78
After Alesso Baldovinetti (Italian, 1426–1499)
Cycle: *Portraits in the Passage of Time*
Edition: proof outside edition (113 imp. [e.a. XX + e.a. X indigo variant + 13 black variant + EB 70])
Catalogue: WV 142 (proof)
Drypoint and mezzotint in brown
36 ½ x 24 ½ in. (92.7 x 62.4 cm) on sheet 37 ⅝ x 24 ½ in. (95.5 x 62.4 cm)
Gift of the artist in memory of Anne and Jacques Baruch
2008.18
Plate 32

* *The Smile [Il Sorriso]*, 1976–78
After Alesso Baldovinetti (Italian, 1426–1499)
Cycle: *Portraits in the Passage of Time*
Edition: e.a. (113 imp. [e.a. XX + e.a. X indigo variant + EB 70 + 13 black variant])
Catalogue: WV 142
Drypoint and mezzotint
37 ⅜ x 25 ⅞ in. (94.9 x 65.4 cm)
Promised Bequest of Paula S. Biren, M.D.
Plate 33

* *Leonardo and Isabella d'Este [Leonardo und Isabella d'Este]*, 1978
Edition: 12/70 (100 imp. [e.a. XX + AC X + EB 70])
Catalogue: WV 143
Color drypoint and mezzotint à la poupée
17 ½ x 26 3⁄16 in. (44.5 x 66.5 cm) on sheet 25 ¼ x 31 ⅛ in. (64.2 x 79 cm)
2005.564
Plate 47

* *Saskia*, 1978
After Rembrandt van Rijn (Dutch, 1606–1669)
Cycle: *Portraits in the Passage of Time*
Edition: 44/50 (60 imp. [e.a. X + EB 50])
Catalogue: WV 145A
Color drypoint and mezzotint à la poupée
20 5⁄16 x 26 7⁄16 in. (51.6 x 67.2 cm) on sheet 25 5⁄16 x 31 ¼ in. (64.3 x 79.3 cm)
2005.565
Plate 34

^

Portrait of Venetians, 1978
After Domenico Ghirlandaio (Italian, 1449–1494)
Cycle: *Portraits in the Passage of Time*
Edition: h.c. (no edition)
Catalogue: WV CXXXVI A (proof)
Color drypoint and mezzotint à la poupée
17 3⁄16 x 12 ⅞ in. (43.6 x 32.7 cm) on sheet 24 ⅞ x 18 ¼ in. (63.2 x 46.4 cm)
2005.566

Woman in Fur [Dame im Pelz], 1978
After Peter Paul Rubens (Flemish, 1577–1640)
Cycle: *Portraits in the Passage of Time*
Edition: 54/70 (100 imp. [e.a. XXX + EB 70])
Catalogue: WV 147
Color drypoint and mezzotint à la poupée
26 ½ x 20 ¼ in. (67.3 x 51.4 cm) on sheet 31 7/16 x 25 1/8 in. (79.8 x 63.8 cm)
2005.567
Plate 46

^
My Wife [Meine Frau], 1978
Cycle: *Portraits in the Passage of Time*
Edition: 5/10 (15 imp. [e.a. V + EB 10])
Catalogue: WV 148A (second state)
Color drypoint and mezzotint à la poupée
20 ½ x 20 3/8 in. (52.1 x 51.8 cm) on sheet 31 5/16 x 25 3/8 in. 79.5 x 64.4 cm)
2005.568

My Wife [Meine Frau], 1978
Cycle: *Portraits in the Passage of Time*
Edition: 8/30 (50 imp. [e.a. XX + EB 30])
Catalogue: WV 148B (third state)
Color drypoint and mezzotint à la poupée
20 ½ x 20 ¼ in. (52.1 x 51.1 cm) on sheet 31 7/16 x 25 3/16 in. (79.9 x 63.9 cm)
2005.569
Plate 35

^
Girl and Man with Spectacles A [Mädchen und Mann mit Brille A], 1978
Cycle: *Portraits in the Passage of Time*
Edition: 8/45 (55 imp. [e.a. X + EB 45])
Catalogue: WV 150A (first state)
Color drypoint and mezzotint à la poupée
19 7/16 x 26 in. (49.3 x 66.1 cm) on sheet 25 1/8 x 31 3/16 in. (63.8 x 79.2 cm)
2005.570

Girl and Man with Spectacles B [Mädchen und Mann mit Brille B], 1978
Cycle: *Portraits in the Passage of Time*
Edition: 7/15 (35 imp. [e.a. XX + EB 15])
Catalogue: WV 150B (second state)
Color drypoint and mezzotint à la poupée
19 7/16 x 26 1/16 in. (49.3 x 66.2 cm) on sheet 25 ¼ x 31 3/16 in. (64.2 x 79.2 cm)
2005.571
Plate 37

Arnolfini Portrait, 1978–79
After Jan van Eyck (Flemish, ca. 1390–1441)
Cycle: *Portraits in the Passage of Time*
Edition: 8/40 (70 imp. [e.a. XXX + EB 40 (only 1/40–10/40 and e.a. I/VI–VI/VI, X/XXX printed)])
Catalogue: WV 151
Drypoint
35 9/16 x 26 1/16 in. (90.3 x 66.2 cm) on sheet 41 ¾ x 30 ¾ in. (106 x 78.1 cm)
2005.572
Plate 42

Arnolfini Portrait, 1978/79–1981
After Jan van Eyck (Flemish, ca. 1390–1441)
Cycle: *Portraits in the Passage of Time*
Edition: 6/50 (80 imp. [XXX + EB 50])
Catalogue: WV 151 / 1981 (second state)
Color drypoint with perforated and cut plate à la poupée
35 5/8 x 26 in. (90.5 x 66 cm) on sheet 41 7/8 x 31 in. (106.3 x 78.7 cm)
2005.573
Plate 43

^
Loud Monologue of Bohumil Hrabal [Lauter Monolog des Bohumil Hrabal], 1979
Edition: 15/40 (100 imp. [e.a. LX + EB 40])
Catalogue: WV 152 (fifth state)
Color drypoint and mezzotint à la poupée
19 ½ x 25 3/16 in. (49.5 x 63.9 cm) on sheet 25 ¼ x 31 ¼ in. (64.1 x 79.3 cm)
2005.574

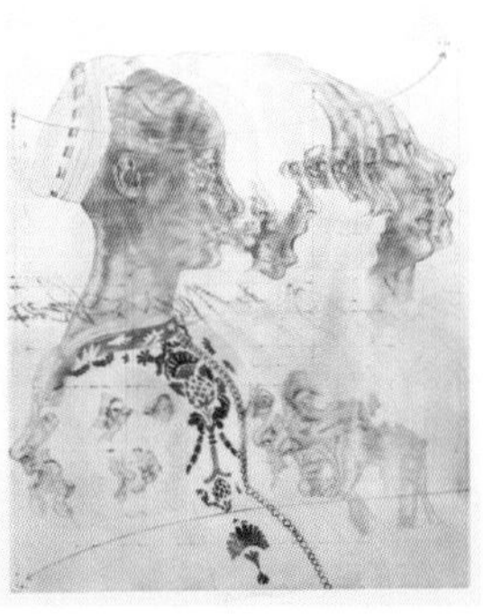

^
Portrait of a Girl after Veneziano [Portrait eines Mädchens nach Veneziano], 1979
After Domenico Veneziano (Italian, ca. 1400–1461)
Cycle: *Portraits in the Passage of Time*
Edition: XXVIII/LXXX (150 imp. [e.a. LXXX + EB 70])
Catalogue: WV 153 (third state)
Color drypoint, mezzotint, and wire brush à la poupée
25 15/16 in. x 19 5/16 in. (65.9 x 49.1 cm) on sheet 31 ¼ x 25 3/16 in. (79.4 x 64 cm)
2005.575

Open Door, Milada [Offene Türen, Milada], 1979
Cycle: *Rooms*
Edition: 10/70 (100 imp. [e.a. XXX + EB 70])
Catalogue: WV 156
Color drypoint, mezzotint, and wire brush à la poupée
19 5/8 x 19 ½ in. (40.8 x 49.5 cm) on sheet 31 7/16 x 25 3/8 in. (79.8 x 64.4 cm)
2005.576
Plate 49

Closed Door, Jiří [Geschlossene Türen, Jiří], 1979

Cycle: *Rooms*

Edition: 10/40 (100 imp. [LX + EB 40])

Catalogue: WV 157 (third state)

Color drypoint, mezzotint, and wire brush à la poupée

19 ⅝ x 19 5⁄16 in. (49.8 x 49.1 cm) on sheet 30 ⅝ x 25 ¼ in. (77.8 x 64.2 cm)

2005.577

Plate 50

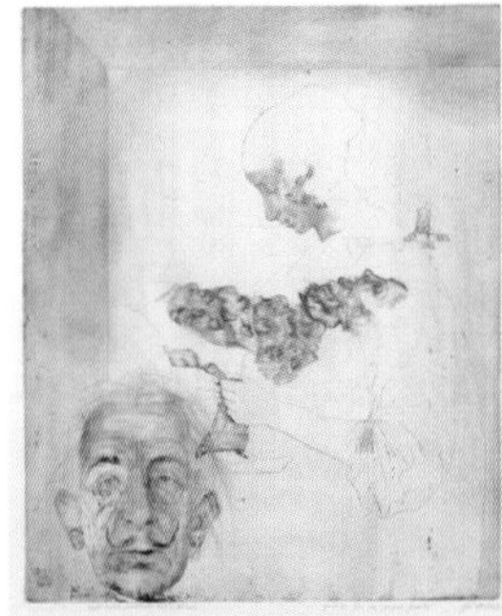

^

Sad Letter from Salvador Dali to Vermeer [Carta tristes de Salvador Dali à Vermeer], 1978–79

Cycle: *Portraits in the Passage of Time*

Edition: LXXX (special edition for exhibition at Galerie Fronta and Galerie Platýz, Prague)

Catalogue: WV 158D (fourth state)

Color drypoint and wire brush à la poupée

23 ½ x 19 ⅜ in. (59.7 x 49.2 cm) on sheet 31 ¼ x 25 3⁄16 in. (79.3 x 63.9 cm)

2005.579

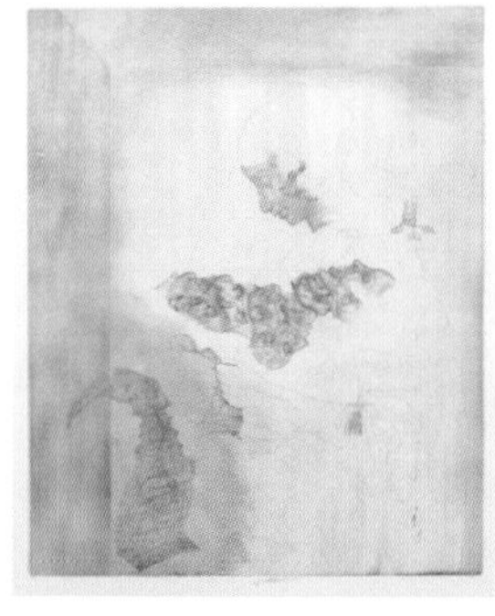

^

Girl Reading Letter II [Brieflesendes Mädchen II], 1978–79

After Jan Vermeer (Dutch, 1632–1675)

Cycle: *Portraits in the Passage of Time*

Edition: 3/50 (70 imp. [e.a. XX + EB 50])

Catalogue: WV 158 (fifth state)

Color drypoint and wire brush à la poupée

23 7⁄16 x 19 ⅜ in. (59.6 x 49.2 cm) on sheet 31 7⁄16 x 25 3⁄16 in. (79.9 x 64 cm)

2005.578

Portrait of My Friend [Portrait meines Freundes], 1979

Cycle: *Portraits in the Passage of Time*

Edition: 16/20 (45 imp. [e.a. XXV + EB 20])

Catalogue: WV 159 (fifth state)

Color drypoint, mezzotint, and wire brush à la poupée

19 9⁄16 x 26 ⅛ in. (49.7 x 66.4 cm) on sheet 25 7⁄16 x 31 7⁄16 in. (64.6 x 79.8 cm)

2005.580

Plate 38

Ceiling: After Kafka's Metamorphosis [Decke (Franz Kafka: Die Verwandlung)], 1979

Cycle: *Rooms*

Edition: 6/40 (100 imp. [e.a. LX + EB 40])

Catalogue: WV 160

Drypoint and wire brush

26 ⅛ x 19 ⅝ in. (66.4 x 49.8 cm) on sheet 31 ⅛ x 25 ¼ in. (79 x 64.1 cm)

2005.581

Plate 51

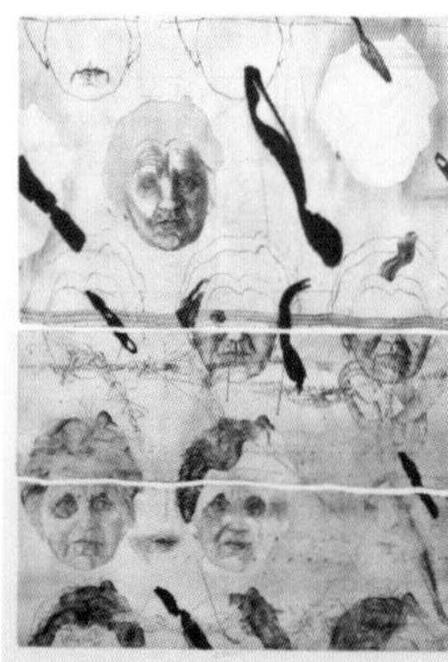

^

My Mother [Meine Mutter], 1979

Cycle: *Portraits in the Passage of Time*

Edition: 10/40 (65 imp. [e.a. XXV + EB 40])

Catalogue: WV 161 (third state)

Drypoint and wire brush

28 ½ x 20 ⅜ in. (72.4 x 51.7 cm) on sheet 31 7⁄16 x 25 ⅛ in. (79.9 x 63.8 cm)

2005.582

Quiet Monologue of Bohumil Hrabal [Stiller Monolog des Bohumil Hrabal], 1979

Edition: 9/50 (100 imp. [e.a. L + EB 50])

Catalogue: WV 162 (second state)

Drypoint, wire brush, wire, and cut plate

19 ⅝ x 25 ¼ in. (49.8 x 64.2 cm) on sheet 25 ¼ x 31 ¾ in. (64.2 x 80.7 cm)

2005.583

Plate 39

Vibrations of Jan Smetana [Vibrationen des Jan Smetana], 1979

Edition: 9/50 (80 imp. [e.a. XXX + EB 50])

Catalogue: WV 163

Drypoint, mezzotint, and wire brush

20 3⁄16 x 26 9⁄16 in. (51.3 x 67.5 cm) on sheet 25 5⁄16 x 31 11⁄16 in. (64.3 x 80.5 cm)

2005.584

Plate 40

Girl Reading Letter III [Brieflesendes Mädchen III], 1979

After Jan Vermeer (Dutch, 1632–1675)

Cycle: *Portraits in the Passage of Time*

Edition: 52/70 (100 imp. [e.a. III + EB 70])

Catalogue: WV 165 (third state)

Color drypoint, mezzotint, and cut plate à la poupée

38 11⁄16 x 25 13⁄16 in. (98.3 x 65.6 cm) on sheet 41 ¾ x 30 13⁄16 in. (106.1 x 78.2 cm)

2005.585

Plate 44

Vox Humana, 1979

After Antonio Pollaiuolo (Italian, ca. 1431/32–1498)

Cycle: *Fragments No. I*

Edition: bon á tirer (85 imp. [e.a. X color + 1/75 – 40/75 black and white World Print Council, San Francisco + EB 41/75 – 75/75 color)

Catalogue: WV 168

Drypoint, mezzotint, and perforated and cut plate

Sheet 38 11⁄16 x 29 ¼ in. (98.2 x 74.3 cm)

2005.586

Plate 52

^

Free Floating Anxiety, 1979

Cycle: *Fragments No. II*

Edition: bon á tirer (Version A 5 unnumbered)

Catalogue: WV 169A (first state); WN 24/79; GR 18/79

Drypoint, mezzotint, and perforated and cut plate

Sheet 38 ⅜ x 29 ⅜ in. (97.5 x 74.6 cm)

2005.587

**Free Floating Anxiety*, 1979

Cycle: *Fragments No. II*

Edition: 4/40 (77 imp. [e.a. XXXVII + EB 40])

Catalogue: WV 169B (second state); WN 24/79; Gr 18/79

Drypoint, mezzotint, and perforated and cut plate

Sheet 38 ¼ x 29 ⅜ in. (97.2 x 74.6 cm)

2005.588

Plate 53

* *The Last Spring of My Grandmother*, 1979

Cycle: *Portraits in the Passage of Time*

Edition: proof (192 imp. [XXX + 70 + 2 + L Baden-Baden + XL San Francisco])

Catalogue: WV 170 proof; WN 25/79; Gr 19/79

Color drypoint and mezzotint à la poupée

Sheet 37 9/16 x 25 in. (95.4 x 63.5 cm)

2005.589

Plate 36

^

The Last Spring of My Grandmother, 1979

Cycle: *Portraits in the Passage of Time*

Edition: 51/70 (192 imp. [XXX + 70 +2 + L Baden-Baden + XL San Francisco])

Catalogue WV 170; WN 25/79; Gr 19/79

Color drypoint and mezzotint à la poupée

Sheet 37 ⅝ x 25 3/16 in. (95.6 x 63.9 cm)

Gift of Judy Weiner, 2005.713

* *Collioni and Isabella d'Este [Collioni und Isabella d'Este]*, 1979

Cycle: *Small Fragments*

Edition: 44/70 (100 imp. [e.a. XXX + EB 70])

Catalogue: WV 171; WN 20/79; Gr 20/79

Color drypoint and mezzotint à la poupée with perforated and cut plate

Sheet 11 11/16 x 18 in. (29.7 x 45.7 cm)

2005.590

Plate 57

* *Revelation [Enthüllung]*, 1980

Cycle: *Fragments No. III*

Edition: 10/50 (96 imp. [e.a. XXXXIII + EB 50 + 3 Biennale])

Catalogue: WV 173; WN 2/80; Gr 2/80

Color drypoint, mezzotint, perforated and cut plate à la poupée

Sheet 37 ⅝ x 23 3/16 in. (95.6 x 64 cm)

2005.591

Plate 54

* *Belle Époque?*, 1980

Cycle: *Fragments No. IV*

Edition: 20/50 (95 imp. [95 imp. [e.a. VL + EB 50]

Catalogue: WV 176; WN 23/80; Gr 5/80

Drypoint, mezzotint, wire brush, perforated and cut plate à la poupée

Sheet 37 ¾ x 25 ⅛ in. (95.8 x 63.8 cm)

Centennial Gift of Anne and Jacques Baruch

1981.233

Plate 55

* *Homage to Victims of Terrorism [Hommage aux Victimes de Terrorisme]*, 1980

Cycle: *Fragments No. V*

Edition: 17/70 (100 imp. [e.a. XXX + EB 70])

Catalogue: WV 178; WN 25/80; Gr 7/80

Color drypoint, mezzotint, cut and perforated plate à la poupée

Sheet 37 ⅝ x 25 1/16 in. (95.5 x 63.7 cm)

2005.592

Plate 56

* *Portrait of Anne B*, 1980

Publisher: Jacques Baruch Gallery, Chicago

Edition: 21/70 (90 imp. [e.a. XX + JBG 70])

Catalogue: WV 180; WN 39/80; Gr 9/80

Color drypoint, mezzotint, perforated and cut plate à la poupée

24 13/16 x 19 ⅝ in. (63 x 49.8 cm) on sheet 31 11/16 x 25 5/16 in. (80.5 x 64.3 cm)

2005.593

Plate 41

* *Soldier [Soldat]*, 1980

Cycle: *Illusion and Reality*

Edition: 56/70 (105 imp. [h.c. 5 + e.a. XXX + EB 70])

Catalogue: WV 183; WN 112/80; Gr 13/80

Drypoint and mezzotint with photocollage

Sheet 37 11/16 x 25 ¼ in. (95.8 x 64.1 cm)

Gift of Anne and Jacques Baruch

1983.251

Plate 59

* *Soldier and Bride [Soldat und Braut]*, 1980

Cycle: *Illusion and Reality*

Edition: 43/50 (104 imp. [h.c. 4 + e.a. L + 50])

Catalogue: WV 184; WN 111/80; Gr 12/80

Drypoint and mezzotint with photocollage

Sheet 37 11/16 x 25 3/16 in. (95.7 x 64 cm)

2005.594

Plate 60

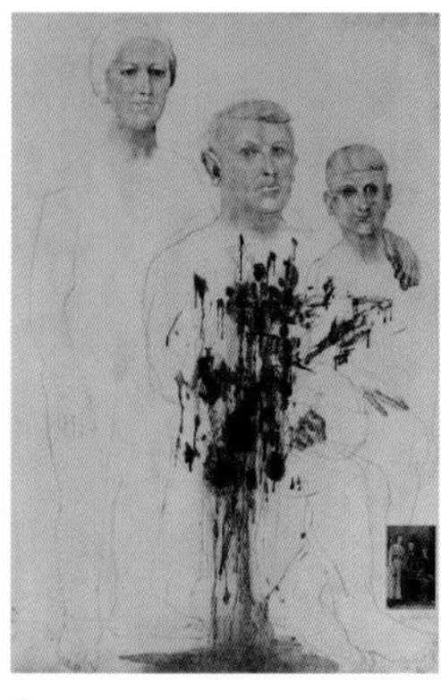

^

Soldier, Son, and Wife [Soldat, Sohn und Frau], 1980

Cycle: *Illusion and Reality*

Edition: 16/35 (89 imp. [h.c. 4 + e.a. L + EB 35])

Catalogue: WV 185; WN 113/80; Gr 14/80

Drypoint and mezzotint with photocollage

Sheet 37 5/8 x 25 1/8 in. (95.6 x 63.8 cm)

2005.595

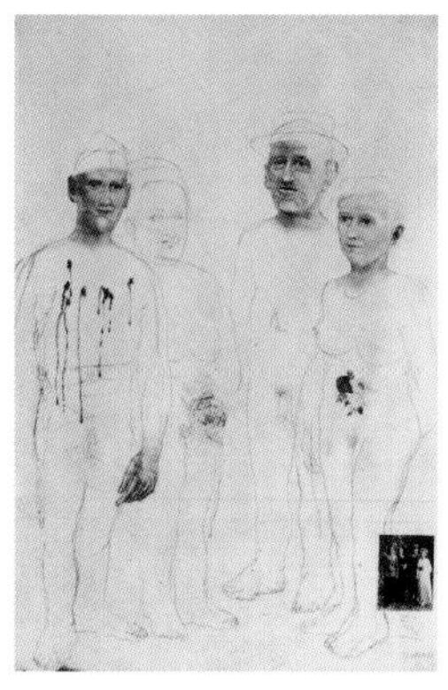

^

Soldier, Girl, and Parents [Soldat, Mädchen und Eltern], 1980

Cycle: *Illusion and Reality*

Edition: 34/35 (89 imp. [h.c. 4 + e.a. L + EB 35])

Catalogue: WV 186; WN 114/80; Gr 15/80

Drypoint and mezzotint with photocollage

Sheet 37 11/16 x 25 3/16 in. (95.7 x 63.9 cm)

2005.596

^

Soldier and Three Women [Soldat und drei Damen], 1980

Cycle: *Illusion and Reality*

Edition: 33/35 (89 imp. [h.c. 4 + e.a. L + EB 35])

Catalogue: WV 187; WN 117/80; Gr 18/80

Drypoint and mezzotint with photocollage

Sheet 37 11/16 x 25 5/16 in. (95.8 x 64.3 cm)

2005.597

* *Madame Favart*, 1980

Cycle: *Portraits in the Passage of Time*

Edition: 24/70 (100 imp. [e.a. XXX + EB 70])

Catalogue: WV 188; WN 115/80; Gr 16/80

Color drypoint, mezzotint, and perforated plate à la poupée

19 5/8 x 26 1/16 in. (49.8 x 66.2 cm) on sheet 25 3/16 x 32 5/16 in. (64 x 82.1 cm)

2005.598

Plate 48

^

Elise Höfer, 1980

Cycle: *Portraits in the Passage of Time*

Edition: 22/70 (100 imp. [e.a. XXX + EB 70])

Catalogue: WV 189; WN 116/80; Gr 17/80

Color drypoint, mezzotint, and perforated plate à la poupée

19 7/16 x 26 3/16 in. (49.4 x 66.5 cm) on sheet 25 3/8 x 32 3/8 in. (64.4 x 82.2 cm)

2005.599

* *Salomé*, 1980

After Pablo Picasso (Spanish, 1881–1973)

Edition: 17/70 (100 imp. [e.a. XXX + EB 70])

Catalogue: WV 191; WN 119/80; Gr 20/80

Color drypoint and mezzotint à la poupée

26 1/8 x 19 1/2 in. (66.4 x 49.5 cm) on sheet 31 3/16 x 25 5/16 in. (79.2 x 64.3 cm)

2005.600

Plate 58

* *Elite (Kaiser and Crown Prince) [Elite (Kaiser und Kronprinz)]*, 1981

Cycle: *Illusion and Reality*

Edition: 47/70 (104 imp. [h.c. 4 + e.a. XXX + EB 70])

Catalogue: WV 192; WN 1/81; Gr 1/81

Drypoint and mezzotint with photocollage

Sheet 11/16 x 25 1/8 in. (95.7 x 63.8 cm)

2005.120

Plate 61

* *Pan, Syrinx, and Old Woman [Pan, Syrinx und alte Frau]*, 1981

Cycle: *Antiquity*

Edition: 20/70 (100 imp. [e.a. XXX + EB 70])

Catalogue: WV 193 (second state); WN 40/81; Gr 2/81

Color drypoint, mezzotint, and cut and perforated plate à la poupée

26 1/8 x 19 7/16 in. (66.3 x 49.4 cm) on sheet 31 5/16 x 25 1/4 in. (79.5 x 64.2 cm)

2005.121

Plate 62

^

Kronos, Rheia, and Two Old Men [Kronos, Rheia und zwei alter Männer], 1981

Cycle: *Antiquity*

Edition: 58/70 (100 imp. [e.a. XXX + EB 70])

Catalogue: WV 194 (second state); WN 41/81; Gr 3/81

Color drypoint, mezzotint, and cut plate à la poupée

12 15/16 x 17 1/16 in. (32.9 x 43.4 cm) on sheet 18 3/4 x 25 3/16 in. 47.7 x 63.9 cm)

2005.122

* *Andromeda and Medusa [Andromeda und Medusa]*, 1981

Cycle: *Antiquity*

Edition: 54/70 (100 imp. [e.a. XXX + EB 70])

Catalogue: WV 195 (second state); WN 42/81; Gr 4/81

Color drypoint, mezzotint, and cut and perforated plate à la poupée

12 15/16 x 17 5/16 in. (32.9 x 43.9 cm) on sheet 12 15/16 x 17 1/4 in. (32.9 x 43.8 cm)

2005.123

Plate 64

* *Perseus and the Graeae [Perseus und die Graien]*, 1981

Cycle: *Antiquity*

Edition: 57/70 (100 imp. [e.a. XXX + EB 70])

Catalogue: WV 196 (second state); WN 43/81; Gr 5/81

Color drypoint, mezzotint and cut plate à la poupée

12 15/16 x 17 1/4 in. (32.9 x 43.8 cm) on sheet 18 13/16 x 25 1/16 in. (47.8 x 63.6 cm)

2005.124

Plate 63

^

Pan and Two Graces [Pan und zwei Grazien], 1981

Cycle: *Antiquity*

Edition: 62/70 (100 imp. [e.a. XXX + EB 70])

Catalogue: WV 197 (second state); WN 44/81; Gr 6/81

Color drypoint, mezzotint, and cut and perforated plate à la poupée

13 x 17 5/16 in. (33 x 44 cm) on sheet 18 7/8 x 25 1/8 in. (47.9 x 63.8 cm)

2005.125

* *Oedipus and Antigone [Oedipus und Antigone]*, 1981

Cycle: *Antiquity*

Edition: 61/70 (100 imp. [e.a. XXX + EB 70])

Catalogue: WV 198 (second state); WN 49/81; Gr 7/81

Color drypoint, mezzotint, and cut and perforated plate à la poupée

11 13/16 x 15 1/2 in. (30 x 39.3 cm) on sheet 18 13/16 x 25 5/16 in. (47.8 x 64.3 cm)

2005.126

Plate 65

^

Beatrice d'Este, 1981

After Leonardo da Vinci (Italian, 1452–1519)

Cycle: *Dialogue with the Great Masters*

Edition: 46/70 (106 imp. [h.c. 6 + e.a. XXX + EB 70])

Catalogue: WV 205; WN 179/81; Gr 15/81

Color drypoint, mezzotint, and cut and perforated plate à la poupée

13 11/16 x 13 5/16 in. (34.8 x 33.8 cm) on sheet 25 1/4 x 18 13/16 in. (64.2 x 47.8 cm)

2005.127

* *Simonetta Vespucci [Donna Simonetta Vespucci]*, 1982

After Piero di Cosimo (Italian, 1462–1521)

Cycle: *Dialogue with the Great Masters*

Edition: 27/70 (106 imp. [h.c. 6 + e.a. XXX + EB 70])

Catalogue: WV 207 (third state); WN 4/82; Gr 2/82

Color drypoint, etching, and mezzotint à la poupée

15 11/16 x 15 7/8 in. (39.9 x 40.3 cm) on sheet 25 3/16 x 18 7/8 in. (64 x 47.9 cm)

2005.128

Plate 70

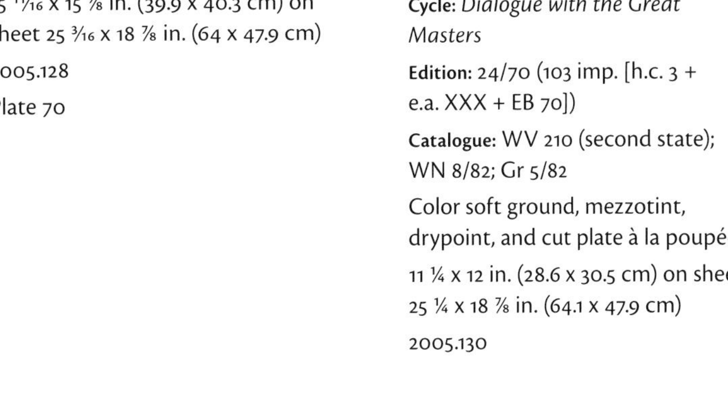

^

Trickster [Gaukler], 1982

After Hieronymus Bosch (Dutch, ca. 1450–1516)

Cycle: *Dialogue with the Great Masters*

Edition: 6/35 (59 imp. [h.c. 4 + e.a. XX + EB 35])

Catalogue: WV 208; WN 5/82; Gr 3/82

Drypoint and etching

26 3/16 x 19 5/8 in. (66.5 x 49.8 cm) on sheet 32 5/16 x 25 5/16 in. (82.1 x 64.3 cm)

2005.129

^

Summer I [Sommer I], 1982

After Giuseppe Arcimboldo (Italian, 1527–1593)

Cycle: *Dialogue with the Great Masters*

Edition: 24/70 (103 imp. [h.c. 3 + e.a. XXX + EB 70])

Catalogue: WV 210 (second state); WN 8/82; Gr 5/82

Color soft ground, mezzotint, drypoint, and cut plate à la poupée

11 1/4 x 12 in. (28.6 x 30.5 cm) on sheet 25 1/4 x 18 7/8 in. (64.1 x 47.9 cm)

2005.130

^

Judith with the Head of Holofernes [Judith mit dem haupt des Holofernes], 1982

After Lucas Cranach the Elder (German, 1472–1553)

Cycle: *Dialogue with the Great Masters*

Edition: 23/70 (106 imp. [h.c. 6 + e.a. XXX + EB 70])

Catalogue: WV 212 (second state); WN 10/82; Gr 7/82

Color etching and drypoint à la poupée

26 1/8 x 19 5/8 in. (66.4 x 49.8 cm) on sheet 32 3/16 x 25 1/4 in. (81.8 x 64.2 cm)

2005.131

^

Toilette I, 1982

After School of Fontainebleau (French, 16th century)

Cycle: *Dialogue with the Great Masters*

Edition: 15/50 (95 imp. [h.c. 5 + e.a. XL + EB 50])

Catalogue: WV 213 (second state); WN 11/82; Gr 8/82

Soft ground etching and drypoint

12 7/16 x 10 9/16 in. (31.6 x 26.8 cm) on sheet 25 1/4 x 18 7/8 in. (64.1 x 47.9 cm)

2005.132

^

Young Woman and Old Man [Junge Frau und alter Mann], 1982

After Lucas Cranach the Elder (German, 1472–1553)

Cycle: *Dialogue with the Great Masters*

Edition: 11/70 (107 imp. [h.c. 7 + e.a. XXX + EB 70])

Catalogue: WV 214; WN 12/82; Gr 9/82

Color soft ground etching and drypoint à la poupée

23 3/8 x 19 7/16 in. (59.3 x 49.4 cm) on sheet 32 5/16 x 25 1/8 in. (82 x 63.8 cm)

2005.133

^

Toilette II, 1982

After School of Fontainebleau (French, 16th century)

Cycle: *Dialogue with the Great Masters*

Edition: 42/70 (106 imp. [h.c. 6 + e.a. XXX + EB 70])

Catalogue: WV 217; WN 15/82; Gr 12/82

Color soft ground etching and drypoint à la poupée

23 9/16 x 19 7/16 in. (59.9 x 49.4 cm) on sheet 31 15/16 x 25 9/16 in. (81.1 x 64.9 cm)

2005.134

^

Christian Charity I [Christliche Liebe I], 1982

After Bernardino Luini (Italian, 1475–1532)

Cycle: *Dialogue with the Great Masters*

Edition: 25/70 (106 imp. [h.c. 6 + e.a. XXX + EB 70])

Catalogue: WV 218; WN 16/82; Gr 13/82

Color soft ground etching and drypoint à la poupée

11 3/4 x 10 13/16 in. (29.8 x 27.4 cm) on sheet 25 1/4 x 18 13/16 in. (64.1 x 47.8 cm)

2005.135

^

Christian Charity II [Christliche Liebe II], 1982

After Bernardino Luini (Italian, 1475–1532)

Cycle: *Dialogue with the Great Masters*

Edition: 11/70 (106 imp. [h.c. 6 + e.a. XXX + EB 70])

Catalogue: WV 219; WN 17/82; Gr 14/82

Color soft ground etching and drypoint à la poupée

26 1/4 x 19 1/2 in. (66.6 x 49.5 cm) on sheet 32 1/4 x 25 3/16 in. (81.9 x 64 cm)

2005.136

^

The Procuress [La procureuse], 1982

After School of Fontainebleau (French, 16th century)

Cycle: *Dialogue with the Great Masters*

Edition: 43/70 (106 imp. [h.c. 6 + e.a. XXX + EB 70])

Catalogue: WV 220; WN 18/82; Gr 15/82

Color soft ground etching and drypoint à la poupée

26 1/4 x 19 5/8 in. (66.6 x 49.8 cm) on sheet 32 3/16 x 25 1/4 in. (81.8 x 64.1 cm)

2005.137

* *Promenade – Lovers and Death [Promenade – Liebespaar und Tod]*, 1982

After Albrecht Dürer (German, 1471–1528)

Cycle: *Dialogue with the Great Masters*

Edition: 15/50 (106 imp. [h.c. 6 + e.a. L + EB 50])

Catalogue: WV 221; WN 19/82; Gr 16/82

Soft ground etching in brown

15 5/8 x 12 15/16 in. (39.7 x 32.8 cm) on sheet 25 1/4 x 18 7/8 in. (64.1 x 47.9 cm)

2005.138

Plate 69

* *Diana of Poitiers [Diana de Poitiers]*, 1982

After François Clouet (French, ca. 1516–1572)

Cycle: *Dialogue with the Great Masters*

Edition: 11/70 (106 imp. [h.c. 6 + e.a. XXX + EB 70])

Catalogue: WV 222; WN 20/82; Gr 17/82

Color soft ground etching and drypoint à la poupée

19 3/8 x 26 1/8 in. (49.2 x 66.4 cm) on sheet 25 1/8 x 32 5/16 in. (63.8 x 82 cm)

2005.139

Plate 71

^

Venus and Two Old Men [Venus und zwei alte Männer], 1982

After Peter Paul Rubens (Flemish, 1577–1640)

Cycle: *Dialogue with the Great Masters*

Edition: 36/50 (107 imp. [h.c. 7 + e.a. L + EB 50])

Catalogue: WV 224; WN 22/82; Gr 19/82

Color soft ground etching and drypoint à la poupée

10 7/8 x 13 1/8 in. (27.6 x 33.3 cm) on sheet 25 1/16 x 18 13/16 in. (63.7 x 47.8 cm)

2005.140

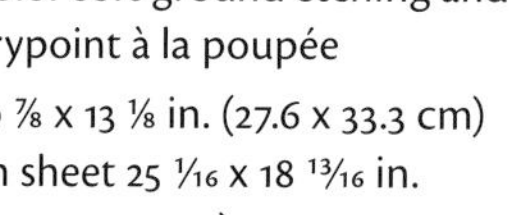

^

Lucrecia [Lucrèce], 1982

After Unidentified Tuscan Master (Italian, 16th century)

Cycle: *Dialogue with the Great Masters*

Edition: 25/70 (106 imp. [h.c. 6 + e.a. XXX + EB 70])

Catalogue: WV 225; WN 23/82; Gr 20/82

Color soft ground etching and drypoint à la poupée

10 x 12 15/16 in. (25.4 x 32.8 cm) on sheet 25 1/8 x 18 13/16 in. (63.8 x 47.8 cm)

2005.141

^

The Bewitched Country Couple [Das verhexte Bauernpaar], 1982

After Albrecht Dürer (German, 1471–1528)

Cycle: *Dialogue with the Great Masters*

Edition: 11/50 (96 imp. [h.c. 6 + e.a. XL + EB 50])

Catalogue: WV 226; WN 24/82; Gr. 21/82

Soft ground etching and drypoint

13 11/16 x 11 7/8 in. (34.7 x 30.2 cm) on sheet 25 1/4 x 18 7/8 in. (64.1 x 48 cm)

2005.142

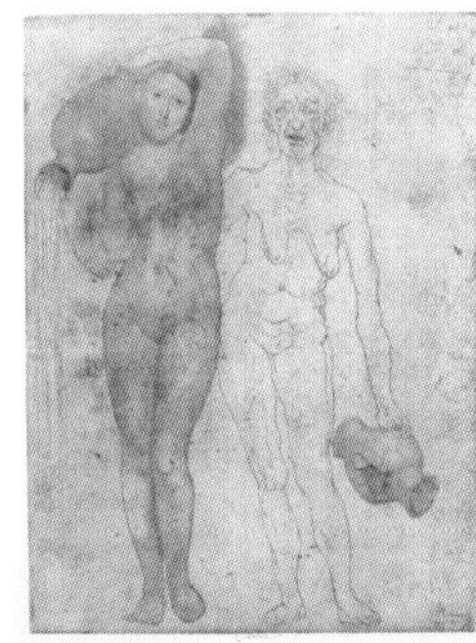

^

The Source [La source], 1982

After Jean Auguste Dominique Ingres (French, 1755–1814)

Cycle: *Dialogue with the Great Masters*

Edition: 23/70 (110 imp. [h.c. 10 + e.a. XXX + EB 70])

Catalogue: WV 227; WN 25/82; Gr 22/82

Soft ground etching

26 3/8 x 19 9/16 in. (67 x 49.7 cm) on sheet 32 3/16 x 25 1/8 in. (81.7 x 63.8 cm)

2005.143

^

Ecce Homo, 1982

After Albrecht Dürer (German, 1471–1528)

Cycle: *Dialogue with the Great Masters*

Edition: 6/20 (40 imp. [5 h.c. + e.a. XV + EB 20])

Catalogue: WV 228; WN 26/82; Gr 23/82

Soft ground etching

26 1/2 x 19 3/8 in. (67.3 x 49.2 cm) on sheet 32 5/16 x 32 5/16 in. (82.1 x 82.1 cm)

2005.144

^

Four Horsemen of the Apocalypse [Vier apokalyptische Reiter], 1982

After Albrecht Dürer (German, 1471–1528)

Cycle: *Dialogue with the Great Masters*

Edition: 13/15 (50 imp. [h.c. 5 + e.a. XXX + EB 15])

Catalogue: WV 229; WN 27/82; Gr 24/82

Soft ground etching and drypoint

26 1/8 x 19 1/2 in. (66.3 x 49.5 cm) on sheet 32 3/16 x 25 3/16 in. (81.7 x 64 cm)

2005.145

* *Bacchus [Bacco]*, 1982

After Michelangelo Caravaggio (Italian, 1573–1610)

Cycle: *Dialogue with the Great Masters*

Edition: 51/70 (107 imp. [h.c. 7 + e.a. XXX + EB 70])

Catalogue: WV 230 (second state); WN 28/82; Gr 25/82

Color soft ground etching and drypoint à la poupée

26 1/8 x 19 1/2 in. (66.3 x 49.5 cm) on sheet 32 1/16 x 25 1/4 in. (81.5 x 64.2 cm)

2005.146

Plate 76

^

Mona Vanna Nuda, 1982

After School of Fontainebleau (French, 16th century)

Cycle: *Dialogue with the Great Masters*

Edition: 11/70 (107 imp. [h.c. 7 + e.a. XXX + EB 70])

Catalogue: WV 232; WN 30/82; Gr 27/82

Color soft ground etching and drypoint à la poupée

24 5/16 x 19 3/4 in. (61.8 x 50.1 cm) on sheet 32 3/8 x 25 3/8 in. (82.2 x 64.4 cm)

2005.147

* *Boy Bitten by a Lizard [Fanciullo morso da un ramarro]*, 1982

After Michelangelo Caravaggio (Italian, 1573–1610)

Cycle: *Dialogue with the Great Masters*

Edition: 39/70 (107 imp. [h.c. 7 + e.a. XXX + EB 70])

Catalogue: WV 233; WN 46/82; Gr 28/82

Color soft ground etching and drypoint à la poupée

26 1/8 x 19 7/16 in. (66.4 x 49.4 cm) on sheet 21 3/16 x 25 1/8 in. (81.8 x 63.8 cm)

2005.148

Plate 77

** Ecce Homo*, 1982
After Albrecht Dürer (German, 1471–1528)
Cycle: *Dialogue with the Great Masters*
Edition: 15/50 (85 imp. [h.c. 5 + e.a. XXX + EB 50])
Catalogue: WV 236; WN 170/82; Gr 31/82
Etching and drypoint
Sheet 37 11/16 x 25 9/16 in. (95.7 x 65 cm)
2005.149
Plate 66

** Riders of the Apocalypse: Death, Hunger, War, and Pestilence [Apokalyptische Reiter, Tod, Hunger, Krieg und Pest über die Welt Bringend]*, 1982
After Albrecht Dürer (German, 1471–1528)
Cycle: *Dialogue with the Great Masters*
Edition: 17/50 (85 imp. [h.c. 5 + e.a. XXX + EB 50])
Catalogue: WV 237; WN 171/82; Gr 32/82
Etching
Sheet 37 11/16 x 25 9/16 in. (95.7 x 65 cm)
2005.150
Plate 67

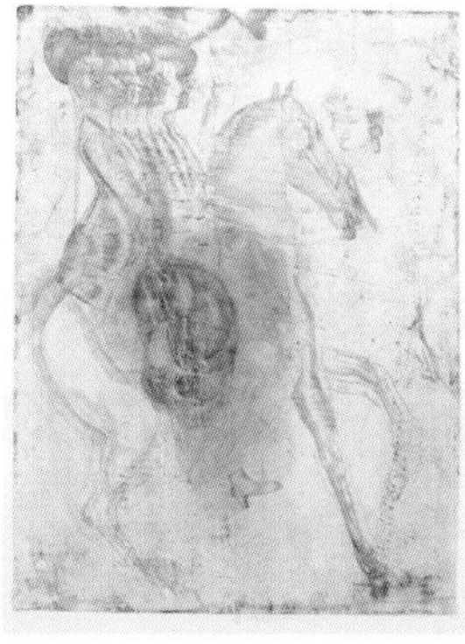

^

Meeting in the Bois de Boulogne [La Rencontre au bois de Boulogne], 1983
Cycle: *Dialogue with the Great Masters*
Edition: 20/70 (106 imp. [h.c. 6 + e.a. XXX + EB 70])
Catalogue: WV 240; WN 26/83; Gr 2/83
Color soft ground etching and drypoint à la poupée
25 7/8 x 19 1/2 in. (65.7 x 49.6 cm) on sheet 32 3/16 x 25 5/16 in. (81.8 x 64.3 cm)
2005.151

** Touch [Gefühl]*, 1983
Jan Saenredam (Dutch, ca. 1565–1607) after Hendrick Goltzius (Dutch, 1558–1617)
Cycle: *Dialogue with the Great Masters*
Edition: 31/70 (106 imp. [h.c. 6 + e.a. XXX + EB 70])
Catalogue: WV 241; WN 42/83; Gr 3/83
Color soft ground etching and drypoint à la poupée
26 1/4 x 19 1/2 in. (66.7 x 49.6 cm) on sheet 32 3/16 x 25 1/4 in. (81.8 x 64.1 cm)
2005.152
Plate 73

** Sight [Gesicht]*, 1983
Jan Saenredam (Dutch, ca. 1565–1607) after Hendrick Goltzius (Dutch, 1558–1616)
Cycle: *Dialogue with the Great Masters*
Edition: 20/70 (106 imp. [h.c. 6 + e.a. XXX + EB 70])
Catalogue: WV 243; WN 44/83; Gr 5/83
Color soft ground etching and drypoint à la poupée
26 x 19 1/2 in. (66 x 49.5 cm)
2005.153
Plate 74

** Sight [Gesicht]*, 1983
Jan Saenredam (Dutch, ca. 1565–1607) after Hendrick Goltzius (Dutch, 1558–1616)
Cycle: *Dialogue with the Great Masters*
Pencil
26 1/8 x 19 5/8 in. (66.4 x 49.8 cm)
2005.209
Plate 75

** Taste [Geschmack]*, 1983
Jan Saenredam (Dutch, ca. 1565–1607) after Hendrick Goltzius (Dutch, 1558–1616)
Cycle: *Dialogue with the Great Masters*
Edition: 27/70 (106 imp. [h.c. 6 + e.a. XXX + EB 70])
Catalogue: WV 245; WN 46/83; Gr 7/83
Color soft ground etching and drypoint à la poupée
26 1/2 x 19 9/16 in. (66.7 x 49.7 cm) on sheet 32 3/16 x 25 5/16 in. (81.7 x 64.3 cm)
2005.154
Plate 72

^

Vanitas I, 1983
Cycle: *Vanitas*
Edition: 26/70 (106 imp. [h.c. 6 + e.a. XXX + EB 70])
Catalogue: WV 247; WN 54/83; Gr 9/83
Color soft ground etching and drypoint à la poupée
12 3/8 x 10 9/16 in. (31.5 x 26.8 cm) on sheet 25 3/16 x 18 13/16 in. (64 x 47.8 cm)
2005.155

^

Vanitas III, 1983
Cycle: *Vanitas*
Edition: 26/70 (106 imp. [h.c. 6 + e.a. XXX + EB 70])
Catalogue: WV 249 (second state); WN 56/83; Gr 11/83
Color soft ground etching and drypoint à la poupée
30 3/16 x 18 1/4 in. (76.6 x 46.3 cm) on sheet 37 11/16 x 25 1/4 in. (95.7 x 64.2 cm)
2005.156

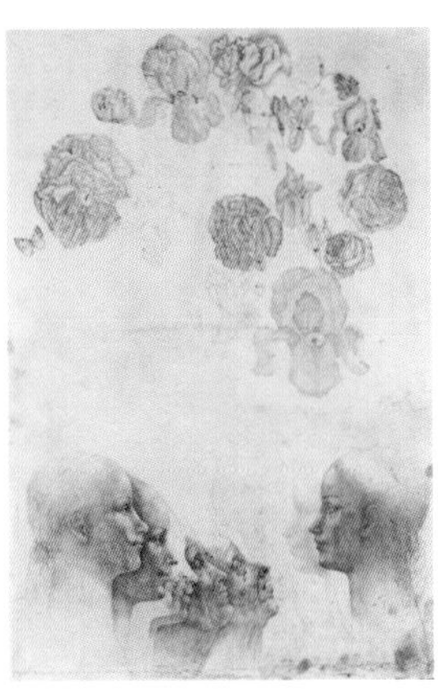

^

Vanitas IV, 1983

Cycle: *Vanitas*

Edition: 24/70 (106 imp. [6. h.c. + e.a. XXX + EB 70])

Catalogue: WV 250 (second state); WN 57/83; Gr 12/83

Color soft ground etching and drypoint à la poupée

Sheet 37 ⅝ x 25 ¼ in. (95.6 x 64.2 cm)

2005.157

^

Vanitas V, 1983

Cycle: *Vanitas*

Edition: 27/70 (115 imp. [h.c. 5 + 10 hand colored + e.a. XXX + EB 70])

Catalogue: WV 252

Color soft ground etching and drypoint à la poupée

27 15/16 x 19 3/16 in. (71 x 48.7 cm) on sheet 33 ¾ x 25 ½ in. (85.8 x 64.8 cm)

2005.158

* *Vanitas VI*, 1983

Cycle: *Vanitas*

Edition: 5/70 (106 imp. [h.c. 6 + e.a. XXX + EB 70])

Catalogue: WV 253 (second state); WN 75/83; Gr 14/83

Color soft ground etching and drypoint à la poupée

Sheet 37 11/16 x 25 9/16 in. (95.7 x 65 cm)

2005.159

Plate 78

* *Beware of Asking What Tomorrow May Bring I [Quid sit futurum cras, fuge quaerere I]*, 1983

Cycle: *Horace: Beware of Asking What Tomorrow May Bring*

Edition: 5/70 (105 imp. [h.c. 5 + e.a. XXX + EB 70])

Catalogue: WV 258; WN 84/83; Gr 20/83

Color drypoint, mezzotint, and soft ground etching à la poupée

36 ¾ x 24 15/16 in. (93.3 x 63.3 cm) on sheet 37 ⅝ x 25 ⅛ in. (95.5 x 63.8 cm)

2005.160

Plate 79

* *Remember That You Are Human! I [Te hominem esse memento! I]*, 1983

Cycle: *Horace: Beware of Asking What Tomorrow May Bring*

Edition: 5/50 (105 imp. [h.c. 5 + e.a. L + EB 50])

Catalogue: WV 261; WN 88/83; Gr 23/83

Soft ground etching, etching, and drypoint

Sheet 37 ⅝ x 25 5/16 in. (95.5 x 64.3 cm)

2005.161

Plate 80

^

Man as Enemy to Men [Homo homini lupus], 1983

Cycle: *Horace: Beware of Asking What Tomorrow May Bring*

Edition: 10/50 (89 imp. [h.c. 4 + e.a. XXXV + EB 50])

Catalogue: WV 262; WN 89/83; Gr 24/83

Soft ground etching

25 ⅞ x 12 ⅞ in. (65.8 x 32.7 cm) on sheet 32 3/16 x 18 3/16 in. (81.8 x 47.8 cm)

2005.162

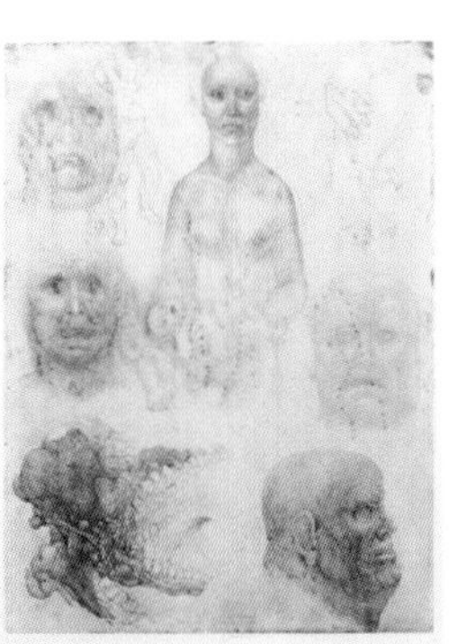

^

I Am Vexed by Anxiety [Coquit me cura], 1983

Cycle: *Horace: Beware of Asking What Tomorrow May Bring*

Edition: 6/50 (94 imp. [h.c. 4 + e.a. XL + EB 50])

Catalogue: WV 263; WN 90/83; Gr 25/83

Soft ground etching and drypoint

27 1/16 x 20 ½ in. (68.7 x 52 cm) on sheet 32 ⅛ x 25 3/16 in. (81.6 x 64 cm)

2005.163

**Girl and Death [Mädchen und Tod]*, 1983

Cycle: *Horace: Beware of Asking What Tomorrow May Bring*

Edition: 48/70 (104 imp. [h.c. 4 + e.a. XXX + EB 70])

Catalogue: WV 264; WN 91/83; Gr 26/83

Color soft ground etching and drypoint à la poupée

26 ¼ x 12 11/16 in. (66.6 x 32.2 cm) on sheet 32 1/16 x 25 ⅛ in. (81.5 x 63.8 cm)

2005.164

Plate 83

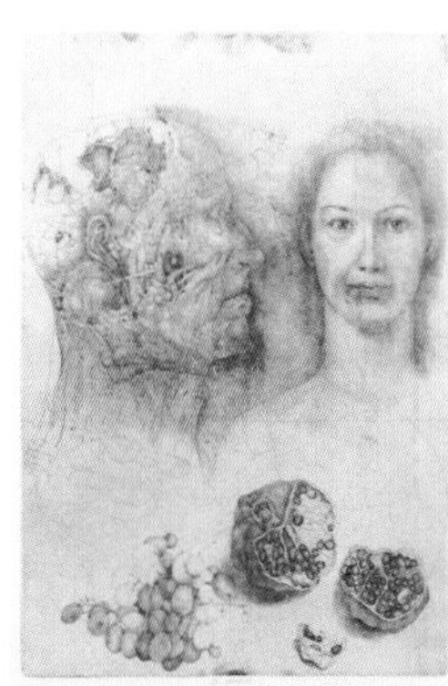

^

Man Is Like a Fruit . . . [Menschen wie Früchte . . .], 1983

Cycle: *Horace: Beware of Asking What Tomorrow May Bring*

Edition: 15/70 (106 imp. [h.c. 6 + e.a. XXX + EB 70])

Catalogue: WV 265; WN 92/83; Gr 27/83

Color soft ground etching and drypoint à la poupée

20 ½ x 14 ⅛ in. (52 x 35.8 cm) on sheet 32 1/16 x 25 ¼ in. (81.5 x 64.1 cm)

2005.165

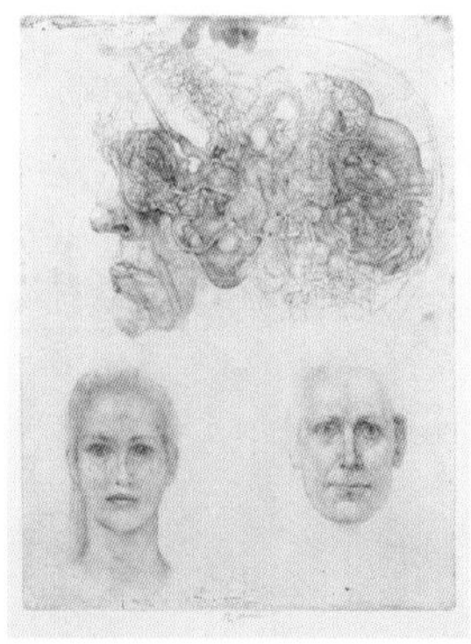

^

What Will We Do? [Quid faciemus?], 1983

Cycle: *Horace: Beware of Asking What Tomorrow May Bring*

Edition: 17/70 (105 imp. [h.c. 5 + e.a. XXX + EB 70])

Catalogue: WV 266; WN 93/83; Gr 28/83

Color soft ground etching and drypoint à la poupée

23 ½ x 17 ⅝ in. (59.7 x 44.8 cm) on sheet 32 ⅛ x 25 ⅞ in. (81.6 x 65.7 cm)

2005.166

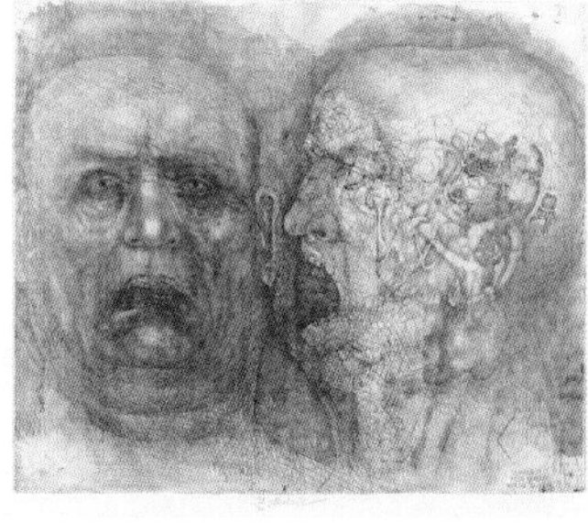

^

Remember That You Are Human! II [Te hominem esse memento! II], 1983

Cycle: *Horace: Beware of Asking What Tomorrow May Bring*

Edition: 10/70 (104 imp. [h.c. 4 + e.a. XXX + EB 70])

Catalogue: WV 267; WN 94/83; Gr 29/83

Soft ground etching

10 11/16 x 12 13/16 in. (27.1 x 32.5 cm) on sheet 25 ⅜ x 18 13/16 in. (64.4 x 47.8 cm)

2005.167

^

Triumphant Beast I [Bestia triumfans I], 1984

Cycle: *Horace: Beware of Asking What Tomorrow May Bring*

Edition: 10/70 (104 imp. [h.c. 4 + e.a. XXX + EB 70])

Catalogue: WV 269; WN 1/84; Gr 1/84

Soft ground etching and drypoint

26 ¼ x 19 ⅜ in. (66.7 x 49.2 cm) on sheet 32 3/16 x 25 5/16 in. (81.8 x 64.3 cm)

2005.168

^

Wars Are Detested by Mothers [Bella matribus detestata], 1984

Cycle: *Horace: Beware of Asking What Tomorrow May Bring*

Edition: 5/70 (105 imp. [h.c. 5 + e.a. XXX + EB 70])

Catalogue: WV 270; WN 2/84; Gr 2/84

Soft ground etching and drypoint

26 ¼ x 19 5/16 in. (66.6 x 49.1 cm) on sheet 32 1/16 x 25 ⅜ in. (81.5 x 64.4 cm)

2005.169

^

If You Do Something Shameful, Your Own Face Will Betray You [Te prodet facies, turpia cum facies], 1984

Cycle: *Horace: Beware of Asking What Tomorrow May Bring*

Edition: 4/35 (69 imp. [h.c. 4 + e.a. XXX + EB 35])

Catalogue: WV 272; WN 4/84; Gr 4/84

Soft ground etching and drypoint

26 ½ x 12 13/16 in. (67.3 x 32.5 cm) on sheet 32 3/16 x 25 ¼ in. (81.7 x 64.1 cm)

2005.170

* *Triumphant Beast III [Bestia triumfans III]*, 1984

Cycle: *Horace: Beware of Asking What Tomorrow May Bring*

Edition: 8/50 (84 imp. [4 h.c. + e.a. XXX + EB 50])

Catalogue: WV 274 (second state); WN 6/84; Gr 6/84

Soft ground etching and drypoint

Sheet 25 5/16 x 37 ⅝ in. (64.3 x 95.5 cm)

2005.171

Plate 81

^

Beware of Asking What Tomorrow May Bring II [Quid si futurum cras, fuge quaerere II], 1983

Cycle: *Horace: Beware of Asking What Tomorrow May Bring*

Edition: 5/70 (105 imp. [h.c. 5 + e.a. XXX + EB 70])

Catalogue: WV 275 (second state); WN 7/84; Gr 7/84

Soft ground etching, drypoint, and etching

Sheet 7 ⅝ x 25 ⅛ in. (95.5 x 63.8 cm).

2005.172

* *And Now Only Tears II – Emperor [Sunt lacrimae rerum II – Imperator]*, 1984

Cycle: *Horace: Beware of Asking What Tomorrow May Bring*

Edition: 6/50 (104 imp. [h.c. 4 + e.a. L + EB 50])

Catalogue: WV 278; WN 10/84; Gr 10/84

Soft ground etching and drypoint

Sheet 37 9/16 x 26 3/16 in. (95.4 x 64 cm)

2005.173

Plate 82

^

Franz Kafka and Death [Franz Kafka und der Tod], 1984

Cycle: *Horace: Beware of Asking What Tomorrow May Bring*

Edition: 33/70 (105 imp. [h.c. 5 + e.a. L + EB 70])

Catalogue: WV 280; WN 23/84; Gr 12/84

Soft ground etching

10 ½ x 12 ½ in. (26.7 x 31.8 cm) on sheet 25 9/16 x 18 7/8 in. (65 x 47.9 cm)

2005.174

^

Franz Kafka and Protokoll, 1985

Printer: Pavel and Milan Dřímal

Edition: unique print outside edition

Catalogue: WV 280 and WV 251 on old letter dated March 5, 1877

Soft ground etching and drypoint on old letter

Sheet 13 9/16 x 16 ½ in. (34.4 x 41.9 cm)

2005.203

* *Carpe diem, carpe noctem I [Seize the day, seize the night I]*, 1984

Cycle: *Carpe diem, carpe noctem I*

Edition: 12/70 (106 imp. [h.c. 6 + e.a. XXX + EB 70])

Catalogue: WV 281; WN 24/84; Gr 13/84

Soft ground etching and etching

Sheet 25 5/16 x 37 5/8 in. (64.3 x 95.5 cm)

2005.175

Plate 84

* *Head of Athena [Kopf der Athena]*, 1984

Cycle: *Carpe diem, carpe noctem II*

Edition: 37/70 (105 imp. [h.c. 5 + e.a. XXX + EB 70])

Catalogue: WV 284; WN 27/84; Gr 16/84

Color soft ground etching and drypoint à la poupée

Sheet 37 5/8 x 25 ¼ in. (95.5 x 64.1 cm)

2005.176

Plate 85

* *Sick Bacchus [Bacchino Malato]*, 1984

Cycle: *Carpe diem, carpe noctem III*

Edition: 5/70 (106 imp. [h.c. 6 + e.a. XXX + EB 70])

Catalogue: WV 285 (second state); WN 28/84; Gr 17/84

Color soft ground etching, etching, and drypoint à la poupée

Sheet 37 11/16 x 25 1/16 in. (95.8 x 63.7 cm)

2005.177

Plate 86

* *Rembrandt and Saskia (Rembrandt und Saskia)*, 1984

Cycle: *Carpe diem, carpe noctem IV*

Edition: 5/70 (106 imp. [h.c. 6 + e.a. XXX + EB 70])

Catalogue: WV 287; WN 38/84; Gr 19/84

Color soft ground etching, etching, and drypoint à la poupée

Sheet 37 5/8 x 25 3/16 in. (95.6 x 64 cm)

2005.178

Plate 87

* *Dürer and Raphael [Dürer und Raffael]*, 1984

Cycle: *Carpe diem, carpe noctem V*

Edition: 5/70 (105 imp. [h.c. 5 + e.a. XXX + EB 70])

Catalogue: WV 289; WN 40/84; Gr 21/84

Color soft ground etching à la poupée

25 7/8 x 19 3/8 in. (65.7 x 49.2 cm) on sheet 31 15/16 x 25 ¾ in. (81.1 x 65.4 cm)

2005.179

Plate 88

^

Horatius: Laetus in praesens, 1984

Cycle: *Carpe diem, carpe noctem VI*

Edition: 6/70 (110 imp. [h.c. 10 + e.a. XXX + EB 70])

Catalogue: WV 290; WN 41/84; Gr 22/84

Color soft ground etching, drypoint, and mezzotint à la poupée

Sheet 37 11/16 x 25 ¼ in. (95.7 x 64.1 cm)

2005.180

^

Amour and Psyche [Amour und Psyche], 1984

After François Gérard (French, 1770–1837)

Cycle: *Dialogue with the Great Masters*

Edition: 8/70 (106 imp. [h.c. 6 + e.a. XXX + EB 70])

Catalogue: WV 292; WN 46/84; Gr 24/84

Color soft ground etching, etching, and drypoint à la poupée

Sheet 37 5/8 x 25 ¼ in. (95.5 x 64.1 cm)

2005.181

* *The Three Duchesses [Die drei Herzoginnen]*, 1985

After Lucas Cranach the Elder (German, 1472–1553)

Cycle: *Dialogue with the Great Masters*

Edition: 6/70 (106 imp. [h.c. 6 + e.a. XXX + EB 70])

Catalogue: WV 293; WN 47/84; Gr 25/84

Color soft ground etching and etching à la poupée

Sheet 37 5/8 x 29 11/16 in. (95.6 x 75.4 cm)

2005.182

Plate 89

Fortuna, 1984
After Albrecht Dürer (German, 1471–1528)
Cycle: *Dialogue with the Great Masters*
Edition: h.c. (106 imp. [h.c. 6 + e.a. XXX + EB 70])
Catalogue: WV 294; WN 49/84; Gr 26/84
Color soft ground etching à la poupée
26 1/16 x 19 3/8 in. (66.2 x 49.2 cm) on sheet 32 1/16 x 25 5/8 in. (81.5 x 65.1 cm)
2005.183
Plate 68

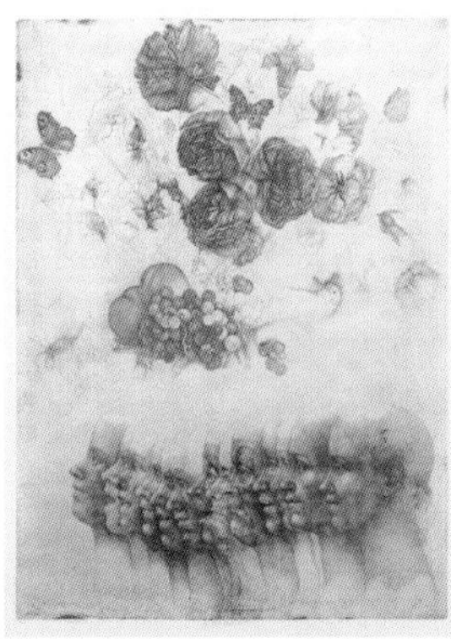

^
Vanitas IX, 1984
Cycle: *Vanitas*
Publisher: Galerie Platýs, Prague
Edition: XXXII/L (253 imp. [h.c. 3 + e.a. L + GP 200])
Catalogue: WV 295; WN 47/84; Gr 25/84
Color soft ground etching and drypoint à la poupée
26 1/8 x 19 3/8 in. (66.3 x 49.2 cm) on sheet 31 15/16 x 25 5/16 in. (81.1 x 64.3 cm)
2005.184

^
Triumphant Beast IV [Bestia triumfans IV], 1984
Cycle: *Horace: Beware of Asking What Tomorrow May Bring*
Edition: 13/50 (95 imp. [h.c. 5 + e.a. XL + EB 50])
Catalogue: WV 296; WN 51/84; Gr 28/84
Soft ground etching, etching, and drypoint
Sheet 25 3/16 x 37 11/16 in. (64 x 95.7 cm)
2005.185

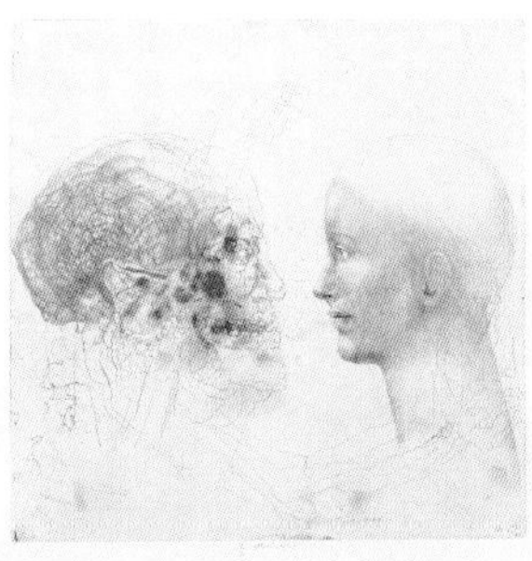

^
Dialogue [Dialog], 1985
Edition: 6/70 (100 imp. [e.a. XXX + EG 70])
Catalogue: WV 305; WN 3/85; Gr 3/85
Color soft ground etching and etching à la poupée
12 11/16 x 13 1/16 in. (32.2 x 33.2 cm) on sheet 25 1/4 x 18 5/8 in. (64.1 x 47.3 cm)
2005.186

^
Instability [L'inconstance], 1985
Edition: 8/70 (100 imp. [e.a. XXX + EG 70])
Catalogue: WV 306; WN 5/85; Gr 4/85
Color soft ground etching and etching à la poupée
19 5/16 x 12 15/16 in. (49 x 32.8 cm) on sheet 25 1/4 x 18 11/16 in. (64.1 x 47.5 cm)
2005.187

Goodbye [Les Adieux], 1985
After Jean Michel Moreau, called Moreau le Jeune (French, 1741–1814)
Cycle: *Gallant Scenes*
Edition: 5/70 (100 imp. [e.a. XXX + EG 70])
Catalogue: WV 309; WN 8/85; Gr 7/85
Color soft ground etching and etching à la poupée
19 5/16 x 13 1/16 in. (49.1 x 33.2 cm) on sheet 25 3/16 x 18 5/8 in. (64 x 47.3 cm)
2005.188
Plate 90

^
Yes or No [Oui ou Non], 1985
After Jean Michel Moreau, called Moreau le Jeune (French, 1741–1814)
Cycle: *Gallant Scenes*
Edition: 11/70 (100 imp. [e.a. XXX + EG 70])
Catalogue: WV 311; WN 10/85; Gr 9/85
Color soft ground etching and etching à la poupée
19 5/16 x 13 3/16 in. (49 x 33.5 cm) on sheet 25 1/4 x 18 11/16 in. (64.1 x 47.4 cm)
2005.189

^
Madame Henriette and Protokoll, 1987
Printer: Pavel and Milan Dřímal
Edition: unique print outside edition
Catalogue: WV 312
Soft ground etching and etching on old letter
Sheet 13 9/16 x 17 1/16 in. (34.5 x 43.3 cm)
2005.204

** Jester's Head I – Full Face [Kopf des Narren I – en face], 1985*

Cycle: *Commedia dell'arte*

Edition: 6/40 (57 imp. [e.a. XV + 2 + EG 40])

Catalogue: WV 321; WN 59/85; Gr 19/85

Crayon resist, etching, aquatint, and drypoint in brown

12 15/16 x 9 13/16 in. (32.9 x 25 cm) on sheet 25 1/2 x 18 13/16 in. (64.7 x 47.8 cm)

2005.190

Plate 92

** Jester's Head II – Profile [Kopf des Narren II– im Profil], 1985*

Cycle: *Commedia dell'arte*

Edition: 6/40 (56 imp. [e.a. XV + 1 + EG 40])

Catalogue: WV 322; WN 60/85; Gr 20/85

Crayon resist, etching, aquatint, and drypoint in brown

12 15/16 x 9 13/16 in. (32.8 x 25 cm) on sheet 25 1/2 x 18 13/16 in. (64.7 x 47.8 cm)

2005.191

Plate 93

** The King Kicks the Jester [Der König tritt den Narren], 1985*

Cycle: *Commedia dell'arte*

Edition: XXXV/XLV (85 imp. [e.a. XLV + EG 40])

Catalogue: WV 335; WN 73/85; Gr 33/85

Crayon resist, etching, and drypoint in brown

Sheet 37 5/8 x 25 3/4 in. (95.6 x 65.4 cm)

Gift of the artist in memory of Anne and Jacques Baruch

2008.19

Plate 95

** The King and Jester with Beautiful Mask [König und Narr mit schöner Maske], 1985*

Cycle: *Commedia dell'arte*

Edition: 10/40 (85 imp. [e.a. XLV + EG 40])

Catalogue: WV 337; WN 75/85; Gr 33/85

Color crayon resist, and etching à la poupée

Sheet 37 5/8 x 25 5/16 in. (95.5 x 64.3 cm)

2005.192

Plate 94

** The King Kills the Jesters [Der König bringt den narren um], 1985–86*

Cycle: *Commedia dell'arte*

Edition: XXX/XLV (95 imp. [e.a. XLV + EG 50])

Catalogue: WV 339; WN 78/85; Gr 37/85

Crayon resist, etching, and drypoint in brown

Sheet 37 5/8 x 25 11/16 in. (95.6 x 65.3 cm)

Gift of the artist in memory of Anne and Jacques Baruch

2008.20

Plate 96

** Non omnium dierum sol occidit [The sun of all the days has not yet set], 1985*

Cycle: *Livius*

Edition: 6/50 (100 imp. [e.a. L + EG 50])

Catalogue: WV 341; WN 79/85; Gr 38/85

Soft ground etching and etching à la poupée

25 13/16 x 19 1/8 in. (65.5 x 48.5 cm) on sheet 32 7/16 x 25 1/4 in. (82.4 x 64.1 cm)

2005.193

Plate 91

^

Akcie Nr. 14739, 1987

Printer: Pavel and Milan Dřímal

Edition: unique print outside edition

Catalogue: WV 356

Sheet 17 3/8 x 13 in. (44.1 x 33 cm)

2005.205

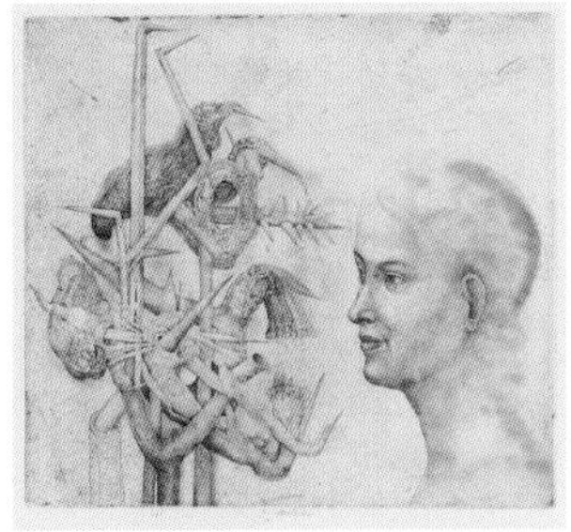

^

Dialogue [Dialog], 1987

Edition: 9/50 (75 imp. [e.a. XV + 10 + EG 50])

Catalogue: WV 365; WN 95/87; Gr 6/87

Color soft ground etching and etching à la poupée

12 15/16 x 14 7/16 in. (32.8 x 36.6 cm) on sheet 25 3/16 x 18 13/16 in. (64 x 47.8 cm)

2005.194

^

Prosba – Bitte!, 1987

Printer: Tomáš Svoboda, Prague

Edition: 48/60

Catalogue: WV 370; WN 317/87; Gr 11/87

Color offset lithograph

23 5/16 x 19 1/16 in. (59.2 x 48.4 cm) on sheet 29 7/16 x 24 3/4 in. (74.7 x 62.8 cm)

2005.195

** Figure on Dark Ground I [Figur auf dunklem Grund I], 1990*

Cycle: *Commedia dell'arte*

Edition: e.a. (95 imp. [e.a. XV + EG 80])

Catalogue: WV 400; WN 248/90; Gr 2/90

Crayon resist, aquatint, and drypoint

19 7/16 x 13 1/16 in. (29.3 x 33.1 cm) on sheet 25 1/2 x 18 7/8 in. (64.8 x 47.9 cm)

2005.196

Plate 97

** Figure on Dark Ground II [Figur auf dunklem Grund II], 1990*

Cycle: *Commedia dell'arte*

Edition: e.a. (55 imp. [e.a. XV + EG 40])

Catalogue: WV 401; WN 249/90; Gr 3/90

Crayon resist, scraping, aquatint, and drypoint

19 11/16 x 13 1/16 in. (50 x 33.1 cm) on sheet 25 1/2 x 18 7/8 in. (64.7 x 47.9 cm)

2005.197

Plate 98

* *The Festival Eater [Festesser]*, 1992
Cycle: *Appassionata Humana*
Edition: e.a. hand colored (115 imp. [e.a. XV + EG 100])
Catalogue: WV 409; WN 257/90; Gr 11/90
Etching, drypoint, and aquatint with colored pencil
9 ⅝ x 17 ¹¹⁄₁₆ in. (24.5 x 45 cm) on sheet 18 ¾ x 25 ³⁄₁₆ in. (47.6 x 64 cm)
2005.198
Plate 99

^
Children's Games, 1992
Edition: unique print
Catalogue: WV 473
Etching in brown with colored pencil and origami collage
16 3/8 x 11 ¹³⁄₁₆ in. (41.6 x 30 cm) on sheet 27 ¾ x 19 ¹¹⁄₁₆ in. (70.5 x 50 cm)
2005.199

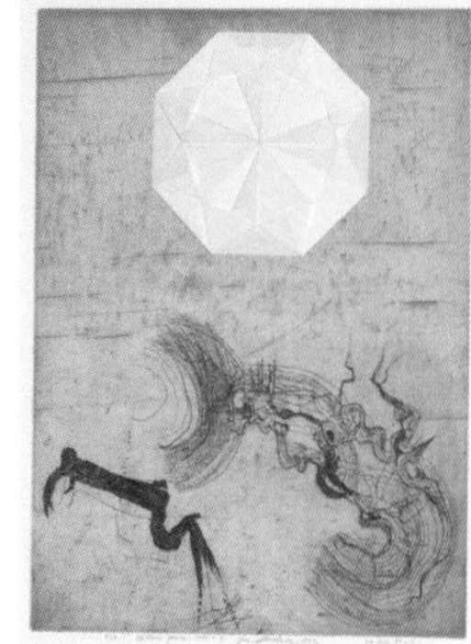

^
Children's Games, 1992
Edition: unique print
Catalogue: WV 474
Etching in brown with colored pencil and origami collage
16 ⁵⁄₁₆ x 11 ¹¹⁄₁₆ in. (41.4 x 29.7 cm) on sheet 27 ¹¹⁄₁₆ x 19 ½ in. (70.4 x 49.5 cm)
2005.200

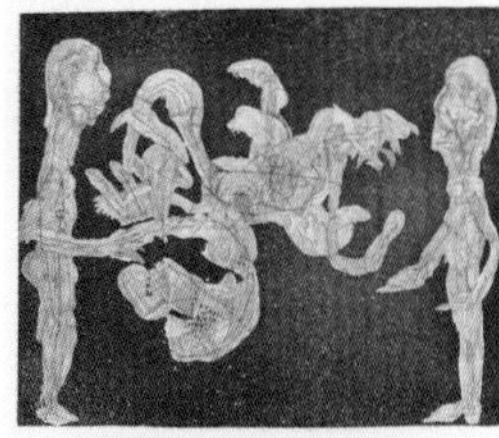

^
Untitled, 1992
Edition: unique print
Catalogue: WV 477/478
Etching, drypoint, and aquatint with colored pencil
17 ½ x 12 ¼ in. (44.5 x 31.1 cm) on sheet 27 ¹³⁄₁₆ x 19 ⅝ in. (70.6 x 49.8 cm)
2005.201

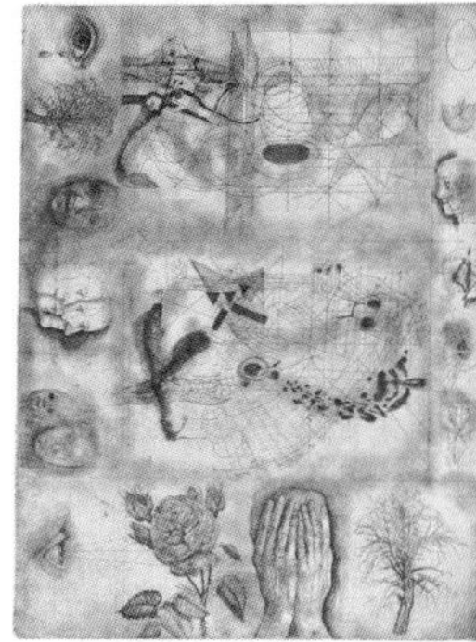

^
Stories I, 1992
Publisher: the artist
Edition: 5/50
Catalogue: WV 480
Soft ground etching and etching in brown
12 ¹⁵⁄₁₆ x 9 ⅞ in. (32.8 x 25.1 cm) on sheet 27 ⅝ x 19 ½ in. (70.1 x 49.5 cm)
2005.202

* *Banquet*, 1991–93
Cycle: *Appassionata Humana*
Edition: e.a. (unknown)
Catalogue: WV 496
Color etching and drypoint à la poupée
Sheet 37 ½ x 25 ⁵⁄₁₆ in. (95.2 x 64.3 cm)
Gift of the artist in memory of Anne and Jacques Baruch
2008.21
Plate 100

DRAWINGS

^
Hunger der Irene Saxinger am Donnerstag, 1975
Pencil
Sheet 11 ¾ x 16 ⁹⁄₁₆ in. (29.8 x 42 cm)
2005.207

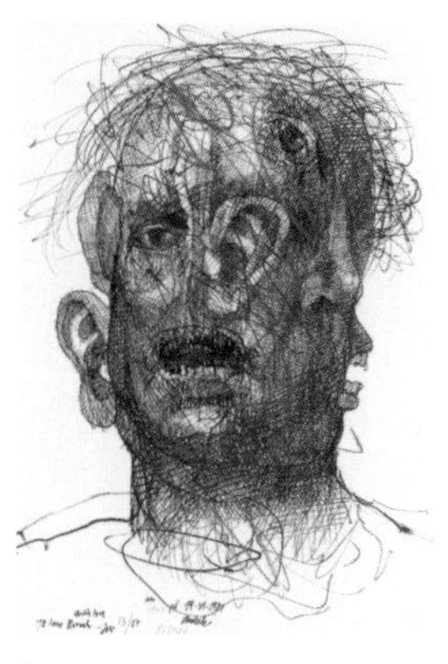

^
Untitled, 1981
Pen and black ink, crayon
Sheet 11 ¾ x 8 ⁵⁄₁₆ in. (29.8 x 21.1 cm)
2005.208

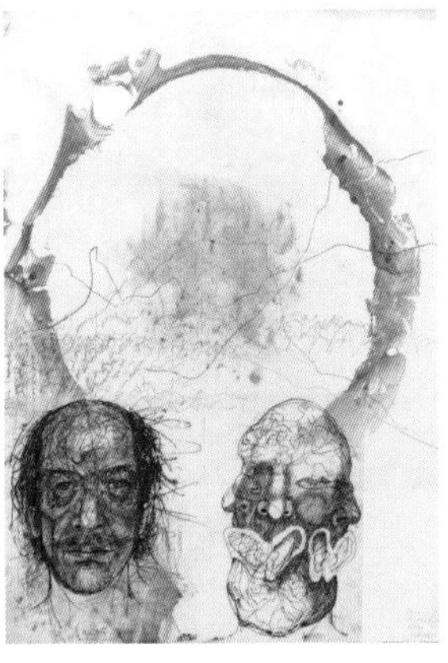

^

Jacques Baruch, 1982

Cycle: *Apocalyptic Genetics*

Printer: Vladimír Lutterer

Edition: unique

Pencil, colored pencil and gray wash on lithographic offset print with collaged pen and black ink drawing on tracing paper.

Sheet 34 ½ x 25 ⅝ in. (87.7 x 66.5 cm)

2005.206

^

Untitled, 1987

Black chalk and brush and gray wash

Sheet 23 x 16 3/16 in. (58.4 x 41.1 cm)

2005.210

^

Remembering the Most Beautiful, 1997

Colored pencil

Sheet 9 ½ x 13 ⅜ in. (24.1 x 34 cm)

2005.211

^

Remembering Jacques, 1997

Colored pencil

Sheet 9 ½ x 13 ⅜ in. (24.1 x 34 cm)

2005.212